D0765397

# Hugo Grotius
## The Miracle
## of Holland

*A Study in Political
and Legal Thought*

Grotius in 1631

*It is rare that any man born of woman has a title to continued remembrance; it is still rarer that he has more than one title; and certainly there can be few in the annals of history who have more varied and more permanent claims to remembrance than Grotius; who in his youth was called the "Miracle of Holland," and who has justified that title before posterity.*

—James Brown Scott

# Hugo Grotius
## The Miracle of Holland

*A Study in Political and Legal Thought*

## Charles S. Edwards

*With Introduction by*
Richard A. Falk

# Nelson-Hall nh Chicago

**Library of Congress Cataloging in Publication Data**


Edwards, Charles S., 1928–
 Hugo Grotius, the miracle of Holland.

 Bibliography: p.
 Includes index.
 1. Grotius, Hugo, 1583–1645.   2. International law.
3. Natural law.   I. Title.   JX2099.E38   341.'092'4   81-4592
ISBN 0-88229-624-8                                      AACR2

Copyright © 1981 by Charles S. Edwards

Manufactured in the United States of America

10   9   8   7   6   5   4   3   2   1

*Lucy—who else?*

# Contents

# Preface

MY INTEREST IN THE importance of Hugo Grotius for the history of Western thought dates back to a period of graduate study at Harvard University in the 1950s. In relation to some of my courses on government, I began to do research on the origins of international law. I wrote several papers on the subject, one in particular for Professor Inis Claude, who suggested that I engage in deeper reflection on some aspects of my inquiry. My interest in Grotius was revived when, after pursuing other endeavors, I matriculated at the Department of Politics at Princeton University in the 1960s to complete the requirements for the doctor of philosophy degree. I chose to devote my dissertation to a study of late medieval and early modern political and legal theory with a major focus on Grotius.

In September 1966 I became a staff member in the Department of Political Science at Baylor University. A colleague at Baylor read my dissertation and suggested that I prepare a manuscript for publication, since there was a need for updated scholarship on Grotius. The suggestion appealed to me, and I set myself to the task, first testing the possibility of a book by preparing two journal articles. They were published in 1970, but the writing of them made me aware that, if I wanted to deal adequately with my subject, I would have to have access to materials not available in the

United States. I applied for and received financial assistance from the Faculty Enrichment Program at Baylor. I spent the summer of 1971 in the Netherlands at the international law library at the Hague, at the university library in Leiden, and at the Juridische Studiecentr of the University of Leiden located, appropriately enough, at 27 Hugo de Grootstraat. The people at Leiden University are quite proud of their famous son, Hugo Grotius; his original manuscripts and the works about him in their library comprise one of the finest collections to be found anywhere. The library at The Hague is, of course, a rich storehouse of information on international law, but it also has some materials on Grotius not available at Leiden. I am extremely grateful to the administrators at Baylor for having made that summer possible.

I was able to finish three chapters of my manuscript by the end of 1972, but progress thereafter proved to be slow because of my teaching responsibilities and other professional obligations. In fact, the manuscript was laid aside because there were some "tag ends" of research that had to be finalized before my project could be concluded. For the summer of 1976 I was most fortunate in obtaining a grant under the auspices of the National Endowment for the Humanities to return again to the Netherlands to resume my research. Obtaining the information I needed, I moved forward with the manuscript and finished it in January 1977. I am grateful to Baylor University and to the National Endowment for the Humanities for making it possible for me to do that necessary research.

I also feel a particular regard for all those who, over the years, have been helpful and instructive in my own intellectual development. I think, for example, of Carl Friedrich and Inis Claude at Harvard in the 1950s, and of Paul Sigmund, Richard Falk, and Michael Walzer at Princeton in the 1960s. For Harold Sprout, formerly professor at Princeton, now deceased, I have a special debt of gratitude. He was mentor and friend to me, and certainly he had been an inspiration as man and teacher to many, many students over a long period of time.

I want to express thanks to Mrs. Dorothy Hitt for supervising the preparation of the typescript and to Miss Lisa Stonestreet for assisting in the typing.

Finally, I accept full accountability for any errors in fact or in interpretation.

C.S.E.

# Introduction:
# *The Grotian Quest*

IN DARK TIMES LIKE OURS, decent men and women are often drawn toward the light, only to perish like so many moths. Rousseau perceives his utopian contemporary, Abbé Saint-Pierre, as such a victim: "This rare man, an ornament to his age and to his kind—the only man, perhaps, in all the history of the human race whose only passion was the passion for reason—nevertheless only advanced from error to error in all his systems, because he wished to make all men like himself instead of taking them as they are and as they will continue to be." (*The Confessions*, IX, 393, Penguin ed.)

While he opposed endowing illusions with solemn pretensions, Rousseau celebrated the enlivening effects of fantasy: "I created for myself societies of perfect creatures celestial in their virtue and their beauty, and of reliable, tender, and fruitful friends such as I had never found here below." (same, IX, 398.)

If, however, the purpose of our endeavors is to create a better world, then fantasy, whether self-deceived or self-aware, is of little help. We require instead a special sort of creativity that blends thought and imagination without neglecting obstacles to change. We require, in effect, an understanding of those elements of structure that resist change, as well as a feel for the possibilities of innovation that lie within the shadowland cast backward by emergent potential structures of power. Only within this shadowland, if at all, is it possible to discern "openings" that contain significant potential for reform, including the possibility of exerting an impact on the character of the emergent system.

This shadowland lies necessarily at the outer edge of the realm of politics, although its special emphasis is upon those political possibilities not yet evident to politicians. As such, it is dangerous intellectual work that often engenders rejection and may even stimulate repression. Power-wielders tend to be scornful of the apparent challenge to their competence—while purists are likely to be alienated by the failure to extend the conception of reform to include structural changes. The more impressive the discernment of possibilities for change in the shadowland, the more likely it will be that those with vested interests will either co-opt the vision to conform to their wishes and interests or reject those who explore the shadowland of structural reform through some form of distortion. The relevance of the shadowland is especially great when an emergent new structure has not yet fully superseded an old structure in times of transition when the need for bridges between the past and future is the greatest.

In many respects Hugo Grotius was an exemplary visionary of the shadowland, whose life coincided with the time of transition in Europe from the old feudal order to the new order of sovereign states. It is probably not accidental, then, that he led such a difficult life, despite the triumphs of his precocious early years. Grotius became a political prisoner in his own country, escaped from jail with a daring plot, lived his remaining years in exile, became a diplomat on behalf of foreign royal leaders, produced his greatest work abroad, and was honored in death by burial close to the very Dutch princes who tormented him while alive. In essence, Grotius was a person of deep conscience who was neither radical nor acquiescent and who yet was deeply committed to leaving the world a better place than he found it. It is also not accidental that Grotius' thought has been misconstrued by detractors and admirers alike over the years, which is one of the fates of those who construe the shadowland.

Grotius came to maturity at a time of religious and political strife, of emergent claims of absolute state sovereignty by the leading monarchs of Europe, and of steadily declining prestige and capacity of the Church of Rome to assert even symbolic authority over the whole of Christendom. It was the time also when feudal traditions were being displaced by statist tendencies that emphasized territoriality and the domestic centralization of both legitimate authority and military power. Accompanying this process, as with any profound transition in the way collective life is organized, were bloody struggles between those who represented the new order and those who held fast to the old.

Grotius approved of this historical process, yet was appalled by its apparent tendency to generate brutality and unrestrained behavior, an apparent relapse in the moral quality of relations among separate societies. What Grotius attempted, whether wittingly or not, was to provide the foundation for a new normative order in international society that acknowledged the realities of an emergent state system while remaining faithful to the shared heritage of spiritual, moral, and legal ideas that any Christian society could still be presumed to affirm as valid. Out of this heritage Grotius fashioned a grand intellectual synthesis that culminated in the publication of *De Jure Belli ac Pacis* in 1625, that is, over twenty years before the rulers of Europe assembled at the end of the Thirty Years' War to produce the Peace of Westphalia, the occasion most often selected to mark the beginning of the modern states system.

The shadowland that Grotius explored rested on the idea that restraint and decency could be grounded in law despite the realities of the new age of statist diplomacy. Grotius' system of mutual legal restraint was premised on the reality of an overarching Christian conscience which it seemed reasonable to believe continued to matter for the rulers of the day, whose Christianity persisted, despite the increase in their secular autonomy and sovereign stature. In effect, Grotius believed that by activating the Christian conscience of rulers, peaceful methods short of war could be promoted to resolve disputes between royal sovereigns, and that where in exceptional circumstances war did occur, its character could be sufficiently regulated to moderate its cruel character and effects. In retrospect, what Grotius proposed seemed like the only way to acknowledge sovereign prerogatives without endorsing their most nihilistic implications. By drawing on rationality and natural law, Grotius encouraged European rulers of his day to reconcile their practical pursuits as statesmen with their spiritual and intellectual heritage and thereby fill in an acceptable form the moral vacuum created by the collapse of the Roman Church as a source of international unity and authority.

In what respects, if any, the Grotian approach did in fact moderate interstate diplomacy is a matter of controversial interpretation, although it has assuredly shaped subsequent efforts to introduce normative elements into the practice of statecraft. The sufficiency of the Grotian approach also needs to be considered in light of the evolving technology of war; whereas *moderation* might have been a sufficient seventeenth-century solution, *abolition* or at least substantial abridgement of the war system might alone suffice in the era of nuclear weaponry. That is, from our perspective in history a shadowland approach only promises sufficiency of result if we correctly discern emergent structures of a new system of world order. It is a question of great current historical moment whether those who discern emergent structures are wishful thinkers like Abbé Saint-Pierre or are shadowland explorers like Grotius. Given the dangers that confront us, it seems prudent to suspend critical judgment and to remain as receptive as possible to approaches that advance shadowland claims.

Perhaps Grotius is vulnerable to the charge of accommodating statism to an excessive and unnecessary degree. Perhaps the degree of his acknowledgment of statist legitimacy, as against the claims of popular sovereignty, did contribute to the neglect of human rights for so long in international legal theory and practice. Until recently, only states were subjects of international law, whereas individuals were objects whose rights were derivative from the state and dependent upon the government for protection. Even now, despite an upsurge of interest in human rights, practical and formal realities make individuals almost totally dependent upon the benevolence of their national government. Grotius, so attentive to the shadowland, may also have been motivated, as Rousseau carps, by the logic of his personal situation to solicit royal patronage at the expense of individual or personal rights. In effect, Grotius' peculiar sensitivity to the implications of state sovereignty as the new ordering principle of world affairs seems to have been coupled with some insensitivity, from a normative standpoint, to the fate of individuals and groups confronted by repressive patterns of governance.

Charles Edwards has produced a magnificent new interpretation of Grotius' achievement that clarifies its peculiar relevance to our contemporary torments. Edwards is scrupulous and precise in his appreciation of Grotius, neither exaggerating nor underestimating his contributions. We are gently guided by Edwards through complex thickets of academic controversy and thereby permitted a more accurate apprehension of Grotian thought. In particular, Edwards clarifies the extent to which Grotius combined religious with secular concerns, the degree to which he adapted the natural law tradition to new international circumstances, and the sense in which it seems appropriate to regard him as "the father of international law." Edwards provides a persuasive well-evidenced account of these controversies. He also gives us an appreciation of the heroic scale of the Grotian quest to mold disparate moral, legal, and political perspectives into a coherent conception of world order, challenging the secular imagination without abandoning it for either backward-looking religious or forward-looking secularist utopian solutions.

What is more, Edwards speculates about what Grotius might do if confronted by the current international situation. This exercise sharpens the distinction between the substance of the Grotian solution to the pre-Westphalian puzzle with its limited relevance for our situation and the timelessness of the Grotian quest for openings to the future through shadowland exploration. The particular applicability of the Grotian quest at this moment of history depends on whether the prevailing structure of world order can be sufficiently synthesized with that of the future to provide help in this period of transition—whether, in effect, the future order is sufficiently crystalized to cast its shadow backwards into the present.

Grotius makes clear that the sort of normative identity he attributed to human society did not imply any belief in the necessity or desirability of institutionalization beyond the state, much less world government; on the contrary, any insistence on supranationalism would have run against the current of territorial sovereignty emergent in the seventeenth century. As such, it would have been a species of forward-looking utopianism, allowing wishes rather than observation of possibilities to supply the identity of the emergent structure. In our period, in contrast, it is the state system that is being challenged by a variety of emergent forms of supranationalism (regional, functional, global in scope and orientation), although in an ambiguous and perhaps preliminary fashion.

Another important development in the 350 years since Grotius did his main work is the changed character of the sovereign state. The government of such a state can no longer be associated with the administration of power by a series of European Christian princes. In the contemporary world the state is more typically dominated by a faceless bureaucracy whose leaders are selected and rejected at short intervals or are kept in power for longer periods by sheer brute force and whose religious and cultural background embraces the diversities of the main global traditions. The Grotian solution presupposed the personal character of royal rulership in Europe and is not fully transferable to the global bureaucratization and secularization of power that has evolved into the modern post-seventeenth-century state and that has steadily diffused the responsibility and eroded the spirituality of political leadership. It is a mistake to suppose, as do such recent commentators on Grotius as Hersh Lauterpacht and Hedley Bull, that the Grotian solution suggests substantive answers that can be directly applied to the transitional twentieth-century torments of the state system. Such a mistake flows, it seems to me, from confusing the Grotian solution with the Grotian quest.

Given the peculiar burdens posed by nuclear weaponry, ecological decay, population pressures, and expectations of equity, Edwards suggests, I think persuasively, that the renewal of the Grotian quest in our time could not credibly rely on a shared heritage of normative tradition or the conscience of contemporary leaders. What makes our situation seem so desperate is the vagueness, and even dubiousness, of the normative heritage (especially for non-Western societies) and the uncertainty of the emergent structure. We seem caught in a historical movement where the burdens on the old order are too great to bear and yet the new alternative order that may lie beyond the presently perceived horizon of attainability casts backwards from the future no shadow that can be reliably discerned. As a consequence, advocacy of global normative approaches is often perceived as neo-Machiavellian by governments of large states that harbor imperial ambitions—in recent decades, mainly the United States and secondly the Soviet Union.

Perhaps, we should regard the faddish prominence

accorded human rights diplomacy as a pathetic reenactment of the Grotian quest. The normative claim embodied in human rights is, quite simply, that leaders of governments can continue to pursue nationalistic economic, social, and political goals, if only they will abide by the most minimal decencies required by international law in governing peoples within their territory. No further accusation is mounted by most human rights advocates against the state system as such. Admittedly, the humanizing potential of adhering to human rights is considerable, and should not be belittled. Whether contemporary global and national structures of power actually allow this potential to be tapped is doubtful. Repression seems integral to the structure, rather than an aspect of the shadowland, although it may partake of both. It is as revealing as it is disquieting to note that the international concern of governments for human rights, realized after it became a goal of American foreign policy at the outset of the Carter presidency, has receded as quickly as it was stimulated.

Compared to the ferment of the seventeenth century, with the new logic of the state system taking over from the feudal logic, our transition challenge is more dangerous and bewildering. The statist logic has not yet been seriously challenged by an alternate logic that conceives the *whole* as necessarily prior to the *part* in matters of ecological stability and military security. The shadowland cast backward onto the present situation of world order does not seem yet to exist. Perhaps we await a Grotius who can teach us to "see" the shadowland, according sufficient status to international developments that depart from the premises of the state system without losing persuasiveness.

Grotius came from an independent state in the Protestant north of Europe that was the setting for revolt against holistic domination of Europe by the Catholic south. One would similarly expect that our Grotius, if he or she emerges, will come from the Third World rather than from the Trilateral group of advanced industrial countries. The shadowland is more accessible to those who are victims of the old order, apostles of the new order, but who yet see that the hopes for a benign transition depend on the success of an ideological synthesis.

Our prospects as a civilization, even as a species, continue to seem poor. We cannot manage the technology at our disposal and at the same time sustain present patterns of life. Our social and political relations are distorted by pervasive inequalities that make both the powerful and weak seem dependent on violence, even terror. To submit to such a reality is tantamount to renouncing hope for the future. To project mere images of a viable future is to fiddle while Rome burns. To embark upon a revolutionary voyage, given all we know about the tendency of revolutions to devour their children, is probably to opt for a violent course of terror that doesn't even contain much promise of genuine transformation.

Without indulging illusions, I believe that the Grotian quest remains our best hope. It offers no easy solace or spectacular outcomes. Yet the Grotian quest, because it is both normatively grounded and future-oriented, synthesizes old and new while it cherishes continuities and legitimizes discontinuities. Our political life is now so bureaucratized that it is doubtful that anyone listens to the voice of conscience, or if he or she hears and heeds, could long remain influential. The Grotian quest should probably concentrate more on mobilizing the consciences of the people than on activating the consciences of their rulers.

Whatever else, no venture into the future will succeed without anchors in our past. Charles Edwards deserves our gratitude for providing this strong, tested, and reliable Grotian anchor.

Richard A. Falk
Princeton University
Summer, 1978

# 1.

# Grotius
# the Man

IN 1598 HUGO GROTIUS, a mere lad of fifteen, was chosen to accompany a diplomatic mission from the "Kingdom of the Netherlands" to the court of Henry IV of France.[1] The Dutch were already engaged in a protracted struggle for independence from Spain, and the purpose of the mission was to establish a helpful alliance with the French.[2] At a royal reception the young Grotius was presented to the French monarch, who reportedly exclaimed to the assembled dignitaries, "Behold the miracle of Holland! Look you upon the miracle of Holland!" To commemorate the occasion, King Henry gave the youth a gold chain with a pendant bearing the royal visage.

How had so tender a youth acquired such prominence as to evoke an expression of superlative praise from a reigning monarch? By age fifteen Grotius had already revealed an intellect and a scholarly capability which were to make him one of the most distinguished men of his time.[3] Grotius was born in Delft, Holland on April 10, 1583. He was the firstborn son of a fairly well-to-do and cultured man, Jan de Groot, who served as a burgomaster of Delft and as a trustee of the University of Leiden. Quite early the father undertook the education of the boy, stimulating his mind in the sciences and in the humanities. It is said that by age eight the young Grotius was an avid reader, and having mastered

1

Latin and Greek, he began composing verses in those languages. With such rapid mental development, Grotius matriculated at Leiden University in 1594 at age eleven, there to become the protégé of the leading Dutch intellectuals of his day. The records show that he did not devote himself to any one discipline; rather, he saturated his mind with a broad choice of courses representative of the scholarly offerings of the university. In addition to his curriculum work, Grotius continued to write verse, took part in philosophical debates, and delivered public discourses on mathematics, philosophy, and law. He was soon touted as "a youth without equal," and even before he had completed his undergraduate program, he was invited to accompany the Dutch diplomatic mission to Paris. That ended his formal association with Leiden University, but it did not mark the end of his formal education. During the year that he remained in France, Grotius, almost in confirmation of the French monarch's characterization of him, obtained the degree of doctor of laws from the University of Orléans.

Upon returning from France in 1599 Grotius decided to pursue a career in the law. He began practicing at The Hague and was quickly pleading cases before the highest courts in the province of Holland. In 1607 he was appointed advocate general (attorney general) of Holland and gave up his private practice of law to devote himself to the duties of that office. In this period of his life he also began to publish his first scholarly works.[4] As a recognized author, Grotius was subsequently selected by the States-General of the United Provinces to write a history of the Netherlands.[5]

The following years were fairly tranquil, and Grotius might well have continued to pursue a successful legal career and to cultivate further his scholarly interests, but a controversy occurred which was to change his life markedly. Jacobus Arminius, a professor of theology at Leiden, had been called upon to defend what is now termed the "supralapsarian" posture on divine purpose. The controversy centered on a theological refinement, for the pressing question was: Had God decreed "election" to salvation for some and then allowed the "fall" of man to justify the decree (*supra lapsum*), or had God foreseen and allowed man to fall and then decreed divine election, after the fact, as a means for saving some? The question was of no little consequence in the Netherlands where the teachings of John Calvin on predestination had firmed into orthodoxy amongst the Protestants. The issue was of concern, not just to theologians, but to the general body of the faithful as well. As Arminius pondered the question, along with other related matters, he came to doubt the rigid doctrine of unconditional predestination, and to ascribe to man a moral freedom which was contradictory to conservative Calvinism. Bitter opposition developed between Arminius and a colleague at the university, one Franz Gomarus, and it was not long before the Protestants of the Netherlands were divided into "Arminian" and "Gomarist" factions. The views of the Arminians were refined to the point where, under the instigation of Johan van Oldenbarneveldt, they were drawn up into a position paper entitled the "Remonstrance."[6] The Gomarists responded with a "Counter Remonstrance," which fed the fires of the controversy all of the more.

What had begun as a theological dispute soon began to assume ominous political overtones. The people of the provinces of Holland and Utrecht came to identify with the Remonstrants or Arminians, whereas the people of the five other provinces identified primarily with the Gomarists. The Remonstrants advocated religious toleration, a decentralization of national power in favor of provincial sovereignty, and efforts for promoting peace with the Spanish. The Counter Remonstrants, on the other hand, wanted the "pure" Calvinist church as a state church, favored a greater degree of centralized power for the united republic, and advocated a resumption of hostilities against Spain under the leadership of the House of Orange. Prince Maurice, whose ambitions had grown to where he sought a pretext for obtaining control of the central government and for getting rid of Oldenbarneveldt as a political opponent, happily accepted the role as the standard-bearer for the Counter Remonstrant causes. Maurice had evidently concluded that his own ambitions would be best served by becoming a staunch partisan rather than by playing mediator in an attempt to reconcile the contending groups.

In the initial years of growing civil foment, Grotius tried not to take sides. He firmly believed that internal religious dissension would be disruptive to civil order, as, indeed, it proved to be. On one occasion he was called upon to try to restore peace by drawing up a conciliatory statement for both groups, but his attempt was looked upon by Prince Maurice and the Gomarists as too much inclined to the Arminian views. Unable to maintain his neutralist stance, Grotius became politicized and cast his lot with the Arminians—and with Oldenbarneveldt. As a consequence, both he and the elder statesman fell into greater disfavor with Maurice. In another effort to restore civil order, Grotius submitted a proposal to Maurice in which he suggested that the Arminian posture be examined by a synod held in the province of Holland, with any decision subject to review by a national synod made up of delegates from all the provinces. Maurice reacted negatively, indicating his sole preference for a national synod representative of all the provinces and by expressing his determination to utilize military force if necessary to restore order.

Remonstrant partisans, including Grotius, met at Utrecht to plan their course of action. Learning of this, Maurice marched on the city with troops and seized it, compelling Grotius and his companions to flee to The Hague. Convinced that civil order could be achieved only by destroying the Remonstrant leadership, Maurice persisted against his enemies until both Grotius and Oldenbarneveldt were apprehended and imprisoned. Exulting in success, Maurice tried to consolidate his gains by calling a national synod for November 1618. When the delegates assembled, they quickly branded all Remonstrants as outlaws and as guilty of corrupting religion, and they also declared that Remonstrant clergy were to be banished and their properties confiscated. Grotius and Oldenbarneveldt were held over for trial, with intimations that they were guilty of seditious, even treasonous, behavior.[7]

On the urging of Maurice, the States-General set up a court at The Hague on November 19, 1618, to hear charges. Grotius was brought forward and promptly convicted of treason in a trial which has ever since been considered as a travesty on justice. Grotius was then reconfined to await sentence. Oldenbarneveldt was not tried until March of the following year. His trial, too, left much to be desired in terms of due process of law, and, as expected, he was convicted. Oldenbarneveldt was then beheaded in accordance with pronounced sentence. It appeared that Grotius might meet the same fate, but, when he was called before the court for sentencing, he was given life imprisonment with forfeiture of all property. In June 1619 he was transported to the fortress at Loevenstein near Gorcum. Grotius was then thirty-six years of age.

Confinement for Grotius was at first stringent, but then his wife was given permission for cohabitation. She was provided two rooms in the prison for herself and her children.[8] Thereafter Grotius himself was not subjected to any disciplined regimen as punishment; in fact, his imprisonment provided him with ample leisure for intensive reading and writing. He was allowed to have books brought in, and many hours were devoted to law, history, literature, and philosophy.[9] The books were carried to and from the prison in a large chest or trunk, with the house of a friend, three miles distant, being used as a clearing station. At first the trunk was carefully inspected, but, before too long the prison personnel grew lax and allowed it to pass relatively unexamined. With this lapse in security, Grotius' wife worked out a plan of escape for her husband. What transpired was a daring feat rivaling any to be found in creative literature. Under his wife's supervision, Grotius practiced fitting himself into the trunk, and, when he had become quite adept at it, a day was chosen for the attempted escape.

On March 22, 1621, Grotius climbed into the trunk, clad only in linen underwear and silk stockings and using a New Testament as a headrest. The trunk was then locked and the key given to a maidservant. Grotius' wife withdrew behind the drawn curtains of their bed, leaving her husband's outer clothing lying on a chair to give the impression that he, too, was in bed. With everything in readiness, the maidservant summoned the guards. When they appeared, Grotius' wife called out from behind the curtains that she was not feeling well and that the maidservant would accompany the trunk in her stead to the clearing house. Suspecting nothing, the guards lifted the burden, with one complaining that it seemed overly heavy. Hearing that, the wife of Grotius, somewhat alarmed, quickly reassured the guards that the trunk was filled to capacity with Arminian books. Apparently satisfied, the guards half lifted, half carried the chest from the room, with another of their number grumbling that the Arminian himself must be inside! Without further ado, the trunk was transported to the clearing station where, after the guards had departed and all seemed safe, Grotius was released. He was outfitted in the clothes of a common worker so that he might journey to Antwerp and then to Paris. He arrived in the latter city on March 23, 1621. His wife joined him in September of that same year.[10]

Grotius was most welcome in France. He rented a house and once again devoted himself to intense intellectual activity. Pressed for money, however, he entreated Louis XIII, the reigning monarch, for assistance, and Louis responded by granting him an audience and a modest pension.[11] In 1622 Grotius published his *Justification on the Lawful Government of Holland and West Friesland* and had begun compiling material for what would become his masterpiece, *De Jure Belli ac Pacis* or *The Law of War and Peace*. He began writing this major treatise in 1623, and, astonishingly, completed it in about one year.[12] The work was published in Paris in June 1625 and dedicated to Louis XIII, a "Most Christian King."

About this time, back in the Netherlands, Maurice had died, and Grotius entertained thoughts of returning to his native soil. Dutch officials remained hostile toward Arminians, however, and Grotius had to live the rest of his life as an exile. Ever restless and increasingly in need of income, Grotius began to show interest in practical diplomatic service. In 1624 he had already received offers from the princes of Holstein and Denmark to serve them but, being engrossed in his writing, he refused.[13] Grotius remained in Paris for several years after the appearance of his *De Jure Belli ac Pacis* in 1625, but mounting financial difficulties plagued him and inclined him to be more receptive to new offers. A chance meeting with one Salvius, vice-chancellor of Sweden, led to the appointment of Grotius as ambassador from Sweden to France. Grotius then made the difficult decision to renounce his Dutch allegiance, and on July 13, 1634, he sent two letters to the prince of Orange declaring his new allegiance to the queen of Sweden.[14]

During his tenure as a practicing statesman, Grotius was by no means intellectually idle. His mind ranged widely and he wrote new works and revised old ones in the disciplines of classical studies, history, theology, and literature. He continued with his busy life until time began to take its toll. In 1641 Grotius wrote a letter to his brother in which he stated, "I am tired of honors; old age approaches and will soon require rest."[15] With a growing desire to return to private life, Grotius eventually wrote to Queen Christina of Sweden that she recall him. The request was granted, with the queen expressing her appreciation to the famous Dutchman for services rendered, but she was reluctant to lose him entirely. In the summer of 1645 Grotius was back in

Stockholm where he had several audiences with the monarch. The queen tried to prevail upon him to accept the position of counselor of state. Grotius had resolved to retire, however, and, without a passport, he attempted to depart from Sweden. He had gone but a few miles when he was summoned to return. In a final surprise audience Queen Christina gave him a large sum of money, a gift of silver plate, and his passport!

Grotius left Stockholm by ship, destination unknown to history. A violent North Sea storm arose, lasting for three days, exhausting both crew and passengers, and damaging the ship whereby it was forced ashore on the coast of Pomerania. Physically spent, Grotius journeyed by cart a distance of sixty miles to Rostock. The elements and added fatigue contributed to his physical decline, and when he arrived at his destination on August 26 he was gravely ill. His condition rapidly grew worse, and the great man himself sensed that the end was near. A clergyman was called to administer the act of penance, and the last words of Grotius to the churchman were, "I hear your voice well, but I understand with difficulty what you say." Near midnight on August 28, 1645, Grotius died at the age of sixty-two.

The vital organs were removed from Grotius' body, sealed in a copper container, and buried in the cathedral at Rostock. His mortal remains were sent to Delft, Holland, where they were entombed in the Nieuwe Kerk, or New Church, situated on the public square.[16] Ironically, Grotius was laid to rest amidst the tombs of the princes of Orange, one of whom had compelled him to live for so many years as a fugitive from justice. In time, an epitaph proposed by Grotius himself some years earlier in a letter to his brother was engraved on his tomb. The epitaph revealed his pride in diplomatic service but also expressed an uncharacteristic note of bitterness toward the people of the land he loved so much. The epitaph read:

*Grotius hic Hugo est, Batavum captivus*
*et exul, Legatus Regni, Suecia magna, tui.*[17]

# 2.

# A Case of Dual Paternity

OVER THE YEARS Grotius has been given recognition by numerous interpreters and commentators for a dual paternity regarding natural law and a law among nations. He has been loosely characterized as both "the father of modern natural law" and "the father of international law." The range of opinion concerning this dual paternity has been wide and diverse. Some writers give emphasis to the contribution Grotius made to natural law theory and support a claim for his fatherhood of a modern "secularized" version, while giving only passing attention to the claim for his fatherhood of international law. Other writers attempt to refute the first claim but seem to agree that his reputation in reference to the second is fairly secure. Still others try to deny him credit on both counts, but proceed to grant him recognition for an important role in the evolution of both natural law and international legal theory. Finally, there are those who grant Grotius a place in scholarly legal history but tend to relegate him to an inferior position and to bring to the fore theorists of their own choosing. As a consequence of all of these clashing views, one might be thrust into a state of confusion and be compelled to ask the question: Is there any validity to the assertions for a dual "fatherhood?" Grotius is unquestionably associated with the development of natural law theory and international legal theory, but the whole

9

controversy as to his specific role raises issues as to the originality and extent of his contributions. Therefore, a serious analysis of his thinking is in order to try to bring clarification to areas of theory and law which have suffered the damaging effects of inadequate study and loose generalization.

The claim for Grotius as being the father of modern natural law has been largely attributed to Samuel Pufendorf. A. P. D'Entreves says, for example:

> Hugo Grotius, a Dutchman (1583-1645), has long been considered the father of the modern theory of natural law. This judgment goes back to Pufendorf (1632-1694). . . . Pufendorf praised Grotius as the *vir incomparabilis* who dared to go beyond what had been taught in the schools, and to draw the theory out of the darkness in which it had lain for centuries. This judgment is still repeated in many handbooks. Along with Bacon and Descartes in the field of philosophy, with Galileo and Newton in the field of experimental science, Grotius has a special place reserved in the field of jurisprudence as one of the prophets of the brave new world.[1]

Though opposed to acknowledging Grotius as the father of modern natural law, Anton-Hermann Chroust, in the same manner as D'Entreves, attributes that judgment to Pufendorf. He writes:

> Since Pufendorf it has become a totally unwarranted academic tradition to consider Hugo Grotius the true and unique "Father of Natural Law." As to the reason for this rather rash statement, Pufendorf asserts that it was Grotius who divorced Natural Law from theology (and religion) by grounding it solely in the "social nature" and natural reason of man.[2]

Chroust goes on to say that Pufendorf considered Stoic philosophy and "Stoic Natural Law" to be superior to Platonic and Aristotelian philosophy and natural law, with the implication that Stoic thought did not relate natural law to transcendent realities but rather to psychological propositions derived exclusively from a commanding social impulse in man, and that Stoic thought therefore comprised a basis for a modern law of nature. In his oft repeated attacks upon medieval thinkers, says Chroust, Pufendorf always came to the conclusion that Scholastic philosophy was entirely dependent upon Aristotle. Thus:

> Thanks to Pufendorf's efforts and influence, it has become an academic dogma that there is no such thing as Natural Law during the Middle Ages; that the Schoolmen have done nothing but spread complete darkness over Natural Law and morals by following Aristotle instead of the Stoics and by confounding thus law and politics, natural and positive law. To Grotius, and to him alone, supposedly goes the credit of having brought Natural Law out of the night of this utter confusion.[3]

Taken at face value, these assertions would seem convincing enough to mark Pufendorf as having made out a case for Grotius as the father of a modern secularized natural law. Over the years, however, much more may have been read into Pufendorf than was actually there. In 1729 there appeared an English translation of Jean Barbeyrac's preface to Pufendorf's *De Jure Naturae et Gentium* which had been published in 1660. Barbeyrac, a Swiss, wanted to popularize the writings of Pufendorf and ultimately became the best-known editor and translator of Pufendorf of the eighteenth century. In the preface, Barbeyrac paid tribute to Francis Bacon who, he said, had discovered the "imperfections" of the prevailing state of philosophy and had "laid down most excellent plans for its reformation."[4] Barbeyrac also paid tribute to Philip Melancthon, humanistic scholar and professor of Greek at Wittenberg, and to George Winckler, a churchman at Halle, for having attempted to depart from "the Method of the Schoolmen." But, asserted Barbeyrac:

> . . . neither the one, nor the other has afforded any more than a small Gleam of Light; not sufficient to dissipate those thick Clouds of Darkness, in which the world has been so

long invelop'd. Besides, Melancthon was too much prepossess'd in favour of the Peripatetick [Aristotelian] Philosophy, ever to make any great Progress in the Knowledge of the true fundamental Principles of the Law of Nature, and the right Method of explaining that Science. Grotius therefore ought to be regarded, as the first who broke the Ice; and most certain it is, that no Man could be better qualify'd, for such an Enterprise.[5]

After the publication of Grotius' treatise, *De Jure Belli ac Pacis*, continued Barbeyrac, numerous disputes arose over the "sense of his Words" and over "the barbarous terms and ridiculous Subleties of the Schoolmen, of which Grotius had purg'd his Work." As a consequence, a German summoned the courage to "shake off the tyrannical and pernicious Yoke of Custom; and bravely follow the Footsteps of that great Man:"

I mean the illustrious Samuel Pufendorf; who has thereby acquir'd an immortal reputation: a Reputation, whose Lustre not all the Efforts of his envious Competitours [*sic*] will ever be able to efface. He pursu'd the Genius and Method of Grotius: He examin'd and weigh'd Things in their Originals; and making the best Use he could, of the Discoveries of those who had gone before him, he then added his own; which soon gave very great Hopes of his accomplishing that Work, which as yet was but in Embryo. The Principles of the new Philosophy, which he exceedingly relish'd, but without blindly adopting all the Opinions of the Cartesians; together with the Mathematicks, which he study'd under a celebrated Professour in the University of Jena; did not a little contribute towards the perfecting his natural Qualifications; and rendering him more capable of so vast a Work.[6]

Barbeyrac then explained the circumstances under which Pufendorf produced his first writing,[7] *Elements of Universal Jurisprudence*, and added this interesting observation:

He owns in his Preface, that, besides Grotius and Hobbes, the Professour [*sic*] of Mathematicks mentioned before, had afforded him some Light. His Method is, in some measure, that of the Geometricians: For he first lays down his Definitions and Axioms; afterwards he explains 'em; and then draws out the Consequences they contain.[8]

Accordingly, Barbeyrac offered his opinion that Grotius had made a significant accomplishment and was worthy of praise, but "had Mr. Pufendorf been in the place of Grotius, and Grotius in the place of Mr. Pufendorf," the latter would have been proclaimed the greater of the two.[9]

Such judgment constitutes high praise for Pufendorf, and, indirectly, for Grotius, but the fact of the matter is that Barbeyrac, in attempting to confirm natural law conclusions of his own, had proceeded to misinterpret and to misrepresent both Grotius and Pufendorf for succeeding generations. This is the contention made and documented by Leonard Krieger, professor of history at the University of Chicago, who in a study of Pufendorf states:

> Barbeyrac . . . worked out the cardinal points of his own natural law doctrine in the form of a running commentary upon his translation of Pufendorf. . . . The Pufendorf who was read by many of the Western Europeans was not the original but Barbeyrac's version of it, which manifested its internal problems into perceptible inconsistencies and correspondingly strained the bases of the system.[10]

The misinterpretation had far-reaching consequences, as Krieger points out. In Barbeyrac's translation, he says, Pufendorf's works were not confined to the geographical limits of the European community, but also "crossed the Atlantic and entered early into the early growth of American political literature."[11] What Barbeyrac had done, in effect, was to present both Grotius and Pufendorf as being representative of a growing seventeenth-century secularism. This was erroneous as far as Krieger is concerned, because throughout his book he demonstrates that, even though Grotius and Pufendorf comprised a reaction to medieval thought, their reaction was of a late medieval character rather than one of "modern" secularism.

Krieger maintains that both Grotius and Pufendorf reacted against traditional medievalism, and that this rejection was epistomological and metaphysical. Krieger's conclusion is that Grotius and Pufendorf fully represented the fruits of the revival of Aristotelianism, and it was others (Hobbes, Descartes, et al.) who attempted to substitute intuited ideas and mathematically grounded axioms for the disputed authority of Aristotle and the theological schools as a source of first principles. These latter men were to be the "modern" secularists, and Grotius and Pufendorf were decidedly not of their company.[12]

What might be derived from all this? Apparently, succeeding interpreters and commentators have taken Barbeyrac's words and drawn generalizations from them for over two hundred years. An exhaustive examination of Pufendorf's political writings shows that in none of them does he state directly that Grotius was the "Father of Natural Law," as Chroust has written and as D'Entreves and others have repeated, and in no way did he indicate that Grotius was the proponent of a secularistic theory of natural law in the sense that it was totally devoid of theological connotations.[13] Barbeyrac himself, as we have learned, did not employ that title in reference to Grotius, even though he claimed that the Dutch scholar was the first "to break the ice" in departing from Scholastic philosophy. It is true enough that Pufendorf expressed an indebtedness to Grotius and, further, that he made numerous references to Grotius in the texts of his works, but it cannot be said that Pufendorf had coined the phrase or promoted the secularistic theory which have been so long associated with the name of Grotius.

Refutation of Grotius' fatherhood in regard to natural law coupled with efforts to affirm his fatherhood of inter-national law can be found in the specific views of some twentieth-century commentators, most notably Sir Freder-ick Pollock, Hersh Lauterpacht, and Arthur Nussbaum.[14] These representative writers generally acknowledge that

Grotius utilized historical natural law theory by reworking it and making it serve as the basis for a new system of international law.

> The task of Grotius and his precursors and followers [says Pollock] was to define and specialize a branch of the law of nature to which all men professed to bow, not to invent that which was ready to their hands.[15]

The term "Law of Nature" or natural law, he points out, had a long history of development.[16] All political and moral discussions had been dominated for centuries by an elaborate theory of a law of nature which could be traced to three distinct sources. Pollock states again:

> It was constructed, and quite openly constructed, in part on the Aristotelian texts which speak of natural justice, in part on the expositions of later Greek philosophical views, mostly Stoic, found in Cicero and other writers down to the Fathers of the Church, and in part on the technical development of those same views by Roman jurists in search of a theoretical basis for a law which, from being national or tribal, had become cosmopolitan.[17]

Since the time of the late Roman republic, Pollock goes on, natural law had undergone various applications which tended to obscure its main idea. Nurtured by its classical sources, it emerged in the late middle ages as a rule of conduct independent of positive enactment and even of special divine revelation and was binding always and everywhere by virtue of its intricate reasoning. Pollock then contends that the classical tradition of natural law suffered neglect as a result of the upheavals of the Renaissance and the Reformation, and this neglect served to obscure the fact that it had

> . . . a perfectly continuous history down to the date of its greatest and most beneficient achievement—one might almost say its apotheosis—in the foundation of the modern Law of Nations by Grotius. Much that has been written on this subject, even by eminent authors, assumes or suggests

that Grotius revived for his own purposes an almost dormant conception of the Roman lawyers. In fact, the Law of Nature, as Grotius found it, was no mere speculative survival or rhetorical ornament. It was a quite living doctrine, with a definite and highly important place in the medieval theory of society. What is more, it never ceased to be essentially rationalist and progressive. Modern aberrations have led to a widespread belief that the Law of Nature is only a cloak for arbitrary dogmas or fancies. The element of truth in this belief is that, when the authority of natural law was universally allowed, every disputant strove to make out that it was on his side.[18]

Pollock's overall conclusion is that Grotius founded his modern law of nations on a "revised scheme" of natural law.[19] Since the Protestant writers did not accept the authority of the Roman Church, of the Canon Law, or of Aristotle, and since the Roman Catholic defenders of natural law in the Counter Reformation period felt impelled to dispute with the Protestants on their own ground, the tendency was to bring the texts of classical Roman law into prominence. "Thus a more definitely secular and legal cast was given to the whole treatment of the Law of Nature and the way was prepared for the great construction of Grotius."[20]

If Pollock suggested that Grotius "revised" the law of nature, Hersh Lauterpacht went far beyond this evaluation by implying that the revision was of a radical nature—so much so that Lauterpacht might have been on common ground if he had aligned himself with those who postulated Grotius as the father of a modernized natural law. Lauterpacht puts himself on record as stating that the development of international law was made possible through the modernization and secularization of natural law by Grotius, and in this context Lauterpacht easily labels Grotius as the "father of international law." Grotius, he says, "called in" the law of nature and gave it fresh vitality and authority in order to found the modern system of international law.

. . . much of the new dignity which he imparted to the law of nature came from the fact that it was made the basis for that so much needed law governing the relations of sovereign states. . . . International Law, by thus endowing the law of nature with a great historic function, gave it a new lease on life and a new significance.[21]

Lauterpacht was critical of Grotius for vagueness and arbitrariness in his treatment of natural law. He felt there was a justification for this, however. At a period of history when newly emergent states were finding the laws of sovereign authority in the persons of the monarchs, an authority of reason, no matter how vague, had to approximate a direct source of law so as to forestall political anarchy in the developing system of states. This authority of reason—the law of nature—would supplement the voluntary laws of nations and provide a standard by which the latter could be measured for its adequacy. Despite vagueness, then, says Lauterpacht:

. . . the uncertainty of the "higher law" is preferable to the arbitrariness and insolence of naked force. These considerations explain the significance of this aspect of the Grotian tradition in the history of the law of nations. He secularized the law of nature. He gave it added authority and dignity by making it an integral part of the exposition of a system of law which became essential to civilized life. By doing this he laid, more truly than any writer before him, the foundations of international law.[22]

With a directness that allows no latitude for misunderstanding, Arthur Nussbaum dismisses the opinions of those who readily and willingly set Grotius up as the father of natural law. He states:

No doubt Grotius's merits have been exaggerated at times, especially during the nineteenth century, when it was frequently said that he was the originator of the doctrine of natural law. This, of course, was a gross mistake.[23]

Nussbaum then criticizes the *De Jure Belli ac Pacis* on numerous counts, but he concludes with a strong opinion of his own:

> However this may be, *On the Law of War and Peace* made an epoch in the history of international law. In fact it initiated the doctrine of modern international law, which we have seen is bound to be secular and indiscriminate. Rightly, therefore, Grotius has been considered the "founder" or "father" of international law. He presented the new doctrine with a tremendous force of conviction. From the pages of his work the picture emerges of a man absorbed in his ideals, of a devout and profound seeker after truth and right, and of a passionate and unswerving advocate of humaneness and conciliation—a picture borne out by his life. The personal and spiritual factors explain the success of his undertaking.[24]

Two scholars of renown, T. A. Walker and L. F. Oppenheim, and a more recent interpreter of Grotius, P. P. Remec, may be singled out from those who are reluctant to give full credence to generalized titles but who, at the same time, are quite willing to acknowledge Grotius as the foremost figure in the long historical evolution of a law of nations. Walker traces the development of international law over the centuries, beginning with the ancient Israelites and carrying the study up to the time of Grotius. He lauds the predecessors of Grotius, particularly the Spanish theologians, for having represented Christendom as a society of independent princes and free commonwealths with rights *inter se* defined by *jus naturale et gentium*. Of the great Dutchman himself, Walker says, "If there was little novel in the legal system of Grotius, there was equally but little original in either the arrangement or the matter of his work."[25] He "ransacked" all history for precedents and dicta, says Walker; every precedent of value was "drawn into his net," and he helped himself freely wherever information was to be obtained.

Victoria, Covarruvius, Vasquez, Ayala, Gentili, Bodin and others amongst his immediate forerunners are laid under contribution equally with classical authors, medieval Fathers, Schoolmen, Canonists and Civilians. Again and again the reader of the pages of Grotius, who shall have made the acquaintance of the lights of moral and legal learning of the sixteenth century, will catch the echo of their opinions and their very phrases. And, as he advances, he will gradually understand that the work of Grotius is in fact a species of digest, and he may even be at times tempted to think of the famous Dutchman, as Dumont thought of Mirabeau, that if each who had contributed to the *De Jure Belli ac Pacis* were to claim his own but little would remain as the author's share.[26]

Under such a judgment, how can Grotius be given a prominent place in the history of international law? Walker immediately comes to his rescue by asserting that it would be unjust to regard his work as that of a mere compiler. Grotius put his stamp of originality on international law in method and comprehensiveness; he went far beyond his predecessors in the detailed elaboration of principles, and his use of old materials was a main cause of his success. In the final test, says Walker:

The best justification of any method of teaching is, however, its success. The prompt and universal applause which hailed the appearance of *De Jure Belli ac Pacis*, coupled with its obvious and permanent influence in the field of practice, constitutes the fullest and highest proof of the correctness of its author's diagnosis at once of the needs of his day, and of the moral qualities of men. Modern International Law may date its beginnings as a distinct branch of scientific study from the labours of Hugo Grotius.[27]

International law, says L. F. Oppenheim, "is of comparatively modern origin," and "science dutifully traces it back to Hugo Grotius as its father."[28] The law of nature, he states further, provided a theoretical basis for the erection of a system of international law, and "this likewise is dutifully

traced back by science to Grotius."[29] Oppenheim does not
accept the judgments of "science" uncritically, though, for
he asserts that in regard to both natural law and international law, Grotius "stood on the shoulders of his
predecessors."[30] Whatever the debt of Grotius to such
predecessors, however, Oppenheim does give credit to him
for an important role in the evolution of international law.
The time was ripe for a creative work, he says, and it was
Grotius who rose to the occasion.

> The idea of an international community of law could not
> have obtained acceptance before a time when there existed
> a number of completely independent states, internally akin
> in virtue of a community of intensive civilization and inter-
> course. It was in this way that an international community of
> law was begotten at the end of the middle ages out of
> Christian civilization and mutual intercourse. Grotius and
> his forerunners would not have been able to create
> international law, had not the conception of a community
> of law between Christian states enjoyed a general recog-
> nition, and had not international intercourse before their day
> evolved already a large number of rules of intercourse,
> which were based on custom and in part on very ancient
> usages.[31]

P. P. Remec parallels the opinions of Walker and
Oppenheim. Too frequently Grotius has been proclaimed
the father of international law, he maintains, and, as a
result, the contributions of his predecessors have been
neglected.

> Nevertheless, Grotius' claim to be the first who success-
> fully presented in a "comprehensive and systematic manner"
> the "body of law concerned with mutual relations among
> states or rulers of states" cannot be denied.[32]

Unfortunately, Remec says, not all the detailed rules which
Grotius proposed were adopted in practice, and the main
tenet of his work—the concept of a just war—did not find
full acceptance. Still:

> . . . it is true, too, that Grotius' doctrine was evaluated, quoted and commented upon by almost every writer in international law until today. Even if his ideas were not accepted, they nevertheless formed a standing body of reference which influenced the growth of international law at least indirectly. Furthermore, his attempt to combine the legal principles derived in theoretical reasoning from the fundamentals of the law of nature with the practical rules created by the positive, customary practice, showed the way for all future commentators on international law.[33]

Finally, there are those who refuse to entertain any suggestion that Grotius might have been the father of natural law or the father of international law. It is not the intention of these writers to strip Grotius of any credit whatever in matters of theory and substantive law, but they do attempt to deny any generalized titles in association with the name of Grotius and they take pains to qualify his role in the evolutionary growth of international law. James Brown Scott, Coleman Phillipson, and G. H. J. van Der Molen are prominent among this group. Scott, for example, praises Grotius as a great scholar. He admits that the Dutchman was not a mere compiler of other people's ideas and gives him place as "the first systematic expounder of international law," but Scott wanted to make clear that Grotius, for all his achievements, built upon the theoretical and legal foundations which had been laid by others. As early as 1906 Scott had written:

> Grotius is universally considered as the founder of International Law. . . . He was not the founder nor was he the father of the science any more than Adam Smith was the founder or father of Political Economy as a science. . . . We look beyond Grotius and see that the international law of today is rooted in a more remote past.[34]

Scott firmly insists that the Spanish jurists and theologians, especially Suarez and Victoria, were the real founders of international law. In the sixteenth century, he says, international law was in need of theoretical foundation, and this was supplied by Suarez, who analyzed natural law, civil law, and the law of nations as separate and distinct branches of jurisprudence.[35] Scott also calls attention to Grotius' early work *Mare Liberum*, or *Freedom of the Seas*, in which he feels that Grotius had revealed his dependence upon Victoria for substantive matter and in which he had paid tribute to Victoria by mentioning the latter as the author of "the specific and unimpeachable axioms of the Law of Nations."[36] All this points to one conclusion for Scott:

> It may well be that the *Freedom of the Seas* is Grotius' masterpiece; but if it is to be regarded as having founded international law, there is something to be said in behalf of Francisco de Victoria, *prima* professor of theology in the University of Salamanca. . . . He may be considered as the founder of the modern law of nations, for he was assuredly its unconscious founder as Grotius was its conscious expositor.[37]

Coleman Phillipson, like Scott, insists that Grotius must be evaluated against a background of the contributions of many who preceded him:

> It has been too long the custom to speak of Grotius as though he were the "sole begetter" of modern international law, or to regard him as a resplendent luminary in a dark juristic age, and accompanied at a great distance by a few minor satellites barely worthy of consideration. The influence of Grotius has undoubtedly been immense; the modern law of nations owes him an enormous debt. This fact is universally recognized and unceasingly reiterated. But we have been too apt to forget that his great work is considerably indebted to numerous precursors. . . .[38]

The precursors who deserve proper acknowledgment, says Phillipson, include the moral theologians of the Reformation and post-Reformation period and also several jurists, foremost among whom was Alberico Gentili.[39]

> Thanks to the inspiration of Gentili, writers came to look at the whole subject [of a law of nations] from a broader

point of view, to observe the relation of its component
elements, to deal with them more precisely and appositively,
to systematize them more logically, to emphasize their
relationships to actual practice and practical fitness, and to
liberate them from the inveterate burdens of theology,
casuistry, and scholasticism.[40]

Phillipson then goes on to maintain that Grotius was heavily
influenced by Gentili.

Grotius himself, with his learning, width, force of
intellect, and passion for mankind, is indebted to Gentili.
Indeed, the signal achievement of the great Dutch jurist
could not have been what it was, in the absence of the
forcible, reasoned, and comparatively pioneer work of the
Italian lawyer. Grotius admits, though inadequately,
Gentili's service to him. . . .[41]

G. H. J. van Der Molen leaves no room for ambiguity
in taking a position. For a long time, says Van Der Molen,
Grotius was not only looked upon as the father of
international law but also as the father of natural law.
However:

The fairy tale of this double paternity can now be
disposed of, in spite of all the appreciation for the ingenious
way in which Grotius approached these two problems.[42]

In contrast to James Brown Scott and in harmony with
Coleman Phillipson, van Der Molen comes forth as a
champion of Alberico Gentili, arguing that Grotius owed
much more to the Italian jurist than was stated in the
wording of the Prolegomena to the *De Jure Belli ac Pacis*.[43]
In fact, van Der Molen contends, when Grotius wrote his
earlier work, *De Jure Praedae*, he was familiar with Gentili's
principal work and quoted from him several times. During
his imprisonment in Holland from 1619 to 1621, Grotius
read Gentili and also turned to him when he fled to France
and began preparation for writing his masterpiece. All that
Grotius produced showed Gentili's influence and agreement

with his opinions. In sum, van Der Molen concludes that Grotius was very much a compiler rather than a creator and refutes any claims for a dual fatherhood on the part of Grotius.

> Natural law no more dropped from the skies in the seventeenth century than did international law, neither did it spring from the ingenious brain of a single human being. It is true that from this period both developed into a more independent conception, though the close relationship between natural law and international law cannot be denied even now. The intimate tie between the two is so prominent that there is not only frequent confusion in the terminology, but identification of the two has even often occurred.[44]

If, as van Der Molen suggests, neither natural law nor international law "dropped from the skies" in the seventeenth century, and, moreover, if neither sprang from the "ingenious brain" of any one person, then an in-depth investigation of both is warranted in order to ascertain what status they had assumed when Grotius decided to write the treatise which has given him a prominent place in the history of political and legal thought. Such an investigation is all the more imperative because of the generalities and contradictions that attend the opinions expressed over the years about his theoretical endeavors—opinions that have placed him on a scale ranging from that of a creator to a revisionist, to an equal, and to a mere compiler or recorder of other people's ideas. If it be true, as van Der Molen again suggests, that the tie between natural law and international law since Grotius has become so accepted as to lead to confusion or identification of the concepts, then it is necessary further to examine the thought of Grotius to see whether he is deserving of censure or praise for the part he played in the whole process.

It must be recognized at the outset that any attempt to deal with the history of natural law theory apart from the history of international legal theory will be problematical, but for the purposes of this inquiry the analytical separation will be made as much as possible. The following chapter, then, will be devoted to a summary historical examination of natural law theory and then to a detailed analysis of the way in which Grotius conceived it and incorporated it into the totality of his thought. Successive chapters will deal in like manner with the subjects of the law of nations and the law of war. Chapter 6 will be given to some evaluations and reflections on the place of Grotius in the whole spectrum of western political and legal thought, and the final chapter will be devoted to some speculation on the significance of Grotian thought for our own time.

# 3.

# Grotius
# and the
# Law of Nature*

THE IDEA OF A LAW of nature perhaps had its inception in man's earliest speculations about himself and his place in the universe. Extended theoretical development of the concept, however, had to await the intellectual formulations of the thinkers of classic Greece. In the sixth century B.C. the pre-Socratics rejected prevailing supernatural interpretations of nature in favor of attempted rational explanations. These efforts were initially concerned with physical phenomena, but in time thought became more abstract. A transition was made from things "seen" to the "unseen"; that is to say, there was a shift in attention from mere physics to metaphysics. Penetrating questions began to be asked about the origin of being and the meaning of existence, whether creation was accidental or purposive, and whether universal principles, if discoverable, could be applicable to individual moral behavior and to collective social experience. Those who inclined to the view that nature had something eternal and unchangeable to tell about ethical values were countered by those who felt that nature was ethically unfathomable, and that human beings would have to go it

---

* A large portion of this chapter, with some changes and additions, first appeared as a published article. See Charles S. Edwards, "The Law of Nature in the Thought of Hugo Grotius," *Journal of Politics* (November 1970), vol. 32, no. 4, pp. 784-807.

alone within their own existential circumstance in their
search for norms for living.[1]

Some fifth century B.C. Sophists heightened intellectual
disputation by embracing an ethical relativism which
challenged any claim to universal principles in nature.
According to their view, the locus of goodness or badness
was merely in human nature.[2] Anything "good" or "bad"
could not be measured against an "ideal good" presumably
perceived by human reason in the ultimate scheme of things.
Protagoras, for example, was one who took this stance.[3] He
maintained, "Man is the measure of all things." Laws and
political institutions were man-made and did not have to
square with any principles of nature. Callicles was another.
He was an exponent of a theory that might makes right. If
observation of human behavior revealed anything, it was
that the strong should rule over the weak.[4] Thrasymachus
and Glaucon, two Sophists featured in Plato's *Republic,*
gave assent to this power thesis—the one amplifying it and
the other giving a variation on the theme. Thrasymachus
asserted that any established political society was simply an
expression of the rule of the strong, so ". . . the conclusion
of right reasoning is that . . . the interest of the stronger is
everywhere just."[5] What was, was. Law was the creation of,
belonged to, and served the interests of the powerful.
Glaucon, no less cynical than Callicles and Thrasymachus,
and no less exhorting an argument for convention,
contended that law comprised restraints imposed upon the
strong by the weak to forestall the possibility of injury and
exploitation.[6] This kind of law flew in the face of a human
inclination to dominate.

The fifth century B.C. intellectual giants—Socrates, Plato,
and Aristotle—spoke out in reaction to the Sophists.
Socrates was firm in positing the rationality of creation. The
life quest of the wise man, he taught, should be directed
toward an understanding of the real order that existed.
Virtue—harmony with the highest good of nature—was a
concomitant of knowledge; lack of virtue was simply the

result of ignorance. Socrates formulated the rudiments of the doctrine of Forms or "Ideas" (*eidos*) and Plato, student of Socrates, built upon the foundation. According to this doctrine, the mind of man could rise from an observation of the phenomenal world to a contemplation of noumena through "pure" reasoning (without aid of senses) and thereby grasp an understanding of that which was real and true. Concepts, whether relating to things tangible or intangible, had an existence outside the mind, "in the heaven above the heavens." The Forms were eternal and unchanging, having a separate and independent existence from particulars in the world and from any thoughts about them. The culminating principle of all essences was the Ultimate Good, the archetypal Idea in which all other Forms found their meaning. Human beings could find harmony—justice—in their earthly lives if they placed themselves in conformity with the truths of nature.[7]

Plato, not unlike the Sophists, made place for a conception of human nature in his thought, but, in contrast to the Sophists, he projected it against a larger backdrop. Plato was holistic in that he saw human nature as a part of a naturalistic totality. Reason, thus, had to rise above a narrow focus on human psychology within an earthly experience and relate human nature to an eternal referent. Glenn R. Morrow says that Plato identified the order of nature and the order of true being, and that he sought and found the ultimate principles of the visible world, the changeless beyond the changing, namely, the realm of immutable ideas.[8] Morrow goes on to suggest that Plato's great accomplishment was to provide a philosophical foundation for "a transformation of *physis*, so as to permit the incorporation of the peculiarly human conception of a law, as an intelligent ordering of an end, into the very structure of the cosmos."

Aristotle basically agreed with Plato on univerals, but he took a different approach as to how one could gain an understanding of what was true in nature. Here Aristotle's preference for teleology showed through. Empirical observation, with a comprehension of the evolutionary dynamic development of anything, would indicate the end or purpose (*telos*) for which that thing was intended by nature. Purpose or design was detectable in the thing; form and function provided the clues. Universals did not exist in a transcendental realm, and, therefore, could not be grasped by abstraction; rather, by means of an inductive-deductive process in relation to what was, one could proceed logically from observed particulars to an understanding of the universals. Aristotle then applied the same logic to human relations. Values detectable in perceived regularities of human behavior, confirmed in custom and law, were indicative of fundamental ethical principles grounded in human nature and reflective of all of nature. Happiness, for Aristotle, meant a yielding to the individual and social purposes which nature intended for everyone; happiness was fulfillment of all natural inclinations.[9]

Even though they gave credence to the notion of universals in nature, neither Socrates nor Plato nor Aristotle ever used the term "natural law." Aristotle, however, in his juristic reflections, came close to articulating it. In his *Nichomachean Ethics* he made a distinction between justice that was natural and that which was conventional. Moreover, in his *Art of Rhetoric* he made reference to law that was particular and law that was general.[10] The former were those laws, written and unwritten, established by the people of a political society for their own specific needs, but the latter, on the other hand, were—as best his words can be translated from the original Greek—those rules which were "common among men according to nature." These laws were unwritten, finding their validity in custom or usage. This was teleologically consistent, for it would seem that rules evidenced in custom were an unconscious manifestation of universal principles which were confirmed by reason after the fact of practical expression. As such these rules had an indirect relation to nature and in no way were in conflict with nature. If this were the case, then Aristotle's concept of general (common) law could be analytically separable from a concept of principles deduced directly from nature by reason and then consciously applied to human social life. The truth is, Aristotle did not clarify this conceptual duality, but his discussion of general law was to have great significance for subsequent theorists who would attempt to make the distinction.

The early Stoics of Greece appropriated the ideas of natural justice and general law and exalted them as guiding principles immanent in the universe, but an elitist element in their teachings gave them limited appeal. Zeno of Citium (336-264 B.C.), founder of the Stoic school, specifically followed a Cynic, Diogenes, in the belief that humanity could be divided between the wise and the unwise. All wise men everywhere were members of a distinctive society; each was a cosmopolitan, a citizen of the *cosmopolis* or city of the world. Zeno had a pantheistic outlook with an emphasis upon the oneness and perfection of nature. The natural order was governed throughout, he believed, by a universal law to which all things, including human beings, must conform. But, applying Cynic dualism, he asserted that the universal law was identical to reason and only rational men (the wise) had a true affinity to nature. The comprehensiveness of the universal law drew all reasonable beings together into a common bond. The wise man's duty in life was to develop his reason and to tune himself to the law; in this way he could live a moral life. Early Stoicism thus moved intellectually forward in the direction of a concept of natural law, but its elitism prevented it from embracing a meaningful universal humanism.

When Rome emerged as the supreme power in the ancient world at the conclusion of the Punic Wars in 146 B.C., Stoicism was incorporated with some alteration into Roman thought. Panaetius of Rhodes (185-110 B.C.) rejected the attribution of reason only to the wise and stressed the intrinsic worth of every human personality, with the necessary implications of equality and a common humanity. It was this broader version of Stoicism which found acceptance among Roman intellectuals after the conquest of Greece. All men, Panaetius said, were possessors of reason and had a relationship to divine reason. By reason all principles came into being, subjecting all men to universal norms of rightness and justice. These norms comprised ideal law, and this law constituted the moral basis for a universal society. Consequently, any human laws that were not in accordance with this superseding law were disharmonious with nature. In the turn to empire, and with the decline of the significance of the city-state as the optimum form of political association for human happiness, a cosmopolitan sense of human unity was fostered. The new orientation to a spiritual world community was of enormous import for the history of natural law theory.

It was in the writings of Cicero (106-43 B.C.) that a doctrine of natural law received logically consistent treatment. His natural law theory cannot be underestimated by any means, because he gave a coherent exposition of it and placed his own creative imprint upon it. Cicero had read widely and borrowed from predecessors, but he applied his learning uniquely to the Roman setting. The influence of Stoicism on Cicero shows through quite clearly in his *De Republica* (*The Commonwealth*) which was designed as a dialogue among the members of the Scipionic Circle, an intellectual group composed of the friends of the Roman general Scipio Africanus the younger. Through one spokesman, Carneades, Cicero first elaborated on the traditional Sophistic view that justice and law were only conventional and that all political life was motivated by self-interest and expediency, but then through another spokesman, Laelius, he set forth his own Stoic-like response. Laelius countered Carneades by stating that justice was a true and eternal principle behind all law. Justice, said he, emanated from universal reason. Nature was ruled by reason which God had in perfection and in which man shared.[11] Human reason could be right reason, a moral faculty which could enable men to determine right conduct. True justice must be manifested in law, and all of human society should be subject to universal law.

It was in *The Commonwealth* (book 3, chapter 22) that Cicero set forth his concise but inclusive summation of natural law:

> There is in fact a true law—namely right reason—which is in accordance with nature, applies to all men, and is unchangeable and eternal. By its commands this law summons men to the performance of their duties; by its prohibitions it restrains them from doing wrong. Its commands and prohibitions always influence good men, but are without effect upon the bad. To invalidate this law by human legislation is never morally right, nor is it permissible ever to restrict its operation, and to annul it wholly is impossible. Neither the Senate nor the people can absolve us from our obligation to obey this law, and it requires no Sextus Aelius to expound it and interpret it. It will not lay down one rule at Rome and another at Athens, nor will it be one rule today and another tomorrow. But there will be one law, eternal and unchangeable, binding at all times upon all peoples; and there will be, as it were, one common master and ruler of men, namely God, who is the author of this law, its interpreter, and its sponsor. The man who will not obey it will abandon his better self, and, in denying the true nature of a man, will thereby suffer the severest of penalties, though he has escaped all the other consequences which men call punishment.[12]

Cicero made no attempt to spell out any substantive rules of natural law. He rested content merely to assert broad outlines for natural law theory and to base such theory—as later would Grotius—on a natural religion proposition, namely, that first principles in creation must be attributed to ultimate mind and purpose, the reason of God. These principles could not be altered nor could their implications be suspended. Natural law was unchangeable, and, consistent with the Stoic doctrine of invalidation, Cicero made clear that any human laws not in conformity with natural law were no laws at all.

Stoic natural law conceptualism intruded into Roman legalism as evidenced through the writings of some Roman jurists, but, since these men were more concerned with the practical rather than the theoretical aspect of the law, they had some confusions and contradictions in their presentations which went unresolved for quite some time. The most significant period in the development of Roman law occurred in the second and third centuries A.D., and the juristic writings of that time were later incorporated into the *Corpus Juris Civilis* (*Corpus of Civil Law*) prepared by legal commissions created by the Eastern emperor Justinian in the sixth century A.D. The *Corpus* actually consisted of three separate parts: A *Digest*, which was a compendium of legal writings, statutes enacted during the years of the Roman republic, and decrees of the early empire; a *Code*, which comprised the decrees of the later empire; and the *Institutes*, which had been designed as an elementary law manual or "handbook" for legal students, lawyers, and judges. All law in the *Corpus* was theoretically divided into a trilogy of *ius naturale* (law of nature), *ius gentium* (law of nations) and *ius civile* (civil law or the law of the state). The opening words of the *Institutes* (book 1, title 2) seemingly subscribed to a theory of universal human rationality and to a theory of natural equality: ". . . by the law of nature all men from the beginning were born free." Gaius, a jurist of the second century A.D., addressing himself to the topic of natural law, evinced the Stoic influence by stating that it could be known by human reason. One Ulpian, however, writing in the third century A.D., said natural law was "that which animals had been taught by nature. . . . From it comes the union of man and woman called by us matrimony, and therewith the procreation and rearing of children; we find in fact that animals in general, the very wild beasts, are marked by acquaintance with this law."[13] Ulpian, apparently, was equating natural law with biological instinct more than with reason. Still a third jurist, Paulus, writing also in the third century A.D., said that natural law was always "that which was equitable and good," suggesting that it may not have been directly deduced from nature but was, instead, manifested in custom and usage, which was a confirmation of reason. Despite these unresolved confusions, the *Corpus* was a valuable repository of Roman Law, and it proved to be influential in late medieval disputation when theorists of that era began to examine traditional medieval formulations and to move in the direction of a renewed emphasis on rationalism.[14]

The advent of Christian thought into Western civilization brought new factors to bear on the whole concept of a law of nature. Christian apologists, who accepted the Hebraic "fall" of man as a fundamental tenet in their evolving theology, came to consider nature as having been corrupted by "sin," that is, human pride in opposition to the will of God. These apologists were compelled to struggle with the theoretical conflict of man as a rational creature, as most of the classicists had proposed, and man as a creature whose reason had been wounded or impaired by a turning away from God's plan for creation. The result was an ambivalence in early Christian thought in relation to the law of nature with an eventual transition by some theorists in the medieval period toward an identification of such law with God's *revealed* will. Stoic natural law ideas were partially present in the teachings of St. Paul. In Romans 2:14-15, for example, we find this passage:

> For when the Gentiles, which have not the law, do by nature the things contained in the law, these having not the law, are a law unto themselves: which shew the work of the laws written in their hearts, their conscience also bearing witness and their thoughts the meanwhile accusing or else excusing one another.

The emphasis in that statement was upon the moral law as known through the promptings of conscience, through intuition more or less, instead of through rational deductions from nature, but this did not become orthodox Christian doctrine. The fact is that developing Christian thought on balance came to be weighted on the side of the corruption of human nature. The tendency was to downgrade "unaided" human reason, with a corresponding need for "grace," which was recontact with God through God's own initiative (revelation). Only in that way could fallen human beings achieve a restored relationship with divine will. In the writings of the church fathers this shift in thought became increasingly apparent. Tertullian, a second century cleric, asserted forthrightly that the revealed truths of Christianity need not be proved by reason. His belief was aptly summed up in the statement, *"Certum est, quia impossible est"*—"it is certain, because it is impossible."[15]

Augustine, a fifth-century figure and the most renowned exponent of patristic doctrine, clearly showed the problem of ambivalence by not entirely rejecting human reason as a source for moral law but by opting for the weakness of man and the need for man's throwing himself on God's mercy. Augustine drew the distinction between nature and grace. Prior to the fall, human nature was unimpaired and reason could readily have served to provide ideal standards for social living, but after the fall, sinful human nature was such as to make it impossible for man to avail himself of the principles which reason might have recognized. Man, through weakness, had incapacitated himself for actualizing universal truths. Reason, therefore, could most effectively be utilized by applying it to knowledge obtained through revelation. By the inspiration of faith, and by the insights into reality superadded by faith, human beings could be restored to a oneness with true nature.[16] Augustine's theologizing in turn conditioned his political views. Those who embraced the true faith and who committed themselves to the one God, as that God had revealed himself, were the only ones who could achieve ordered living. Sinful human beings were not naturally social creatures who could find total fulfillment according to nature. Government was ordained by God after the fall, therefore, to keep corrupt people in order. It was not intended by nature to actualize human happiness, but it was, instead, a necessary divine coercive instrument for civil order. Justice was not possible in a pagan state not committed to God's will; true justice could be realized only through an acceptance of God's revelation. Only a Christian political community could be a genuine commonwealth. *Res publica* was not applicable to a non-Christian state. In sum, man was not sufficient unto himself for happiness. Unaided human reason was inadequate. The revelation of God through Christ and through the divine "word" brought a new dawn of history whereby the means had been provided for man's reunion with his creator. Hence, even though Augustine gave credence to a natural order and to natural law, his stress upon divine law as comprising the predominant and instrumental principles for humanity prepared the way all the more for others to move in the direction of equating natural law with divine will, or at least in the direction of obfuscating a distinction between the two, as was done subsequently by later clerics and by some of the canon lawyers of the Rome-centered Christian church.[17]

The trend toward an equation of natural law with divine law found its boldest expression in the writings of Isodore of Seville, a seventh-century churchman. In many passages of his works he openly made the identification and at the same time contrasted the universality and permanence of this natural law with the provinciality and temporality of man-made law. Isodore's view was then incorporated into the introduction of a twelfth-century work entitled *Concordantia Discordantium Canonum* (*Concordance of Discordant Canons*). This was attempted as a study in depth of accumulative church law by a canonist of Bologna named Gratian. It was a collection, with commentary, of the decisions of church councils, extracts from the church fathers and other ecclesiastical apologists, decrees of popes, and citations from the *Corpus Juris Civilis* of Justinian and other sources. It was well titled in that it contained conflicting ideas with Gratian made little effort to reconcile.[18] In his commentary of natural law, Gratian wrote,

> The human race is ruled in two ways: by natural law and custom. Natural law is what is contained in the Old and New Testaments, which commands every man to do unto another what he would have done unto himself. . . .[19]

Here was an effort, not just at the general association of natural law with Scripture, both the Old and New Testaments, but also a curious attempt to equate natural law with the so-called "Golden Rule." Gratian seemed most representative of the clerics of the high medieval period who tended to fuse both natural law and divine law. His formulation, however, was a high-water mark for that kind of thinking because Gratian, ironically, lived at a time when the West was beginning to undergo a renaissance in culture that would see another vast change in intellectual direction.

It has been said that theorizing in the middle ages amounted to little more than political and legal theologizing, as though the West had become a monolithic, religious-political society totally conditioned by dogma, that is, by deductions from faith tenets. There is no question that political and legal thought were influenced by the medieval Christian world view and that there was a dearth of church-free theoretical writings up to the twelfth century, but to suggest that there were no intellectual tensions or conflicts is to distort history. Christian apologists themselves were not always of a common mind on issues, and undercurrents of classical thought persisted to haunt and challenge even the most determined ecclesiastical traditionalists. The classical continuities would, in fact, find a resurgence in a restored confidence in unaided reason which would characterize the period that loomed ahead. Old concepts and issues would resurface for intensive examination, and new interpretations and conclusions to be drawn therefrom were to have vast implications for the future.

Creative thought was greatly stimulated in the twelfth century by the growth of universities. These institutions became catalysts for the new learning by providing opportunities for research and by prompting increased logical inquiry into theoretical and practical problems. The most important accomplishments of the scholars who gathered at the universities were a reacquaintance with classical writings and a revival of interest in ancient Roman law. Much of the knowledge that burst upon the West in the twelfth century, undergirding the veritable intellectual revolution, was derived from the Islamic civilization with which Christians had come into contact in North Africa, Sicily, and Spain. The Muslims had preserved the texts of classical literature, translating them from Greek into Arabic and adding some refinements of their own. The Christian scholars of the West in the high medieval period began to translate these works into Latin. Above all, they translated Aristotle. Writes R. R. Palmer,

> The Europeans barely emerging from barbarism, were overwhelmed by this sudden disclosure of an undreamed universe of knowledge. Aristotle became The Philosopher, the unparalleled authority on all branches of knowledge other than religious.[20]

At first there was resistance to the return of Aristotle to Western consciousness. Traditional medieval minds were not immediately receptive to the notion that unaided reason was adequate for human happiness. Furthermore, Averroes, a twelfth-century philosopher of Spain, had attempted to harmonize Aristotle with the Muslim faith. His thought was heavily pantheistic, stressing the unity of human intellect and hence negating the reality of a human soul. Obviously, this did not set well with Christian doctrine. The opposition was short-lived, however, because once Aristotelian thought caught on in intellectual circles, there was no stopping it. It became a matter, not of resistance, but of accommodation, and this process was to proceed concurrently with significant added developments regarding the theory and practice of law.

The university at Bologna, Italy, became the foremost center for a revived study of the ancient collections of Roman Law. Texts of Justinian's *Corpus Juris Civilis* had survived over the centuries in the West, but they had been pretty well ignored because of the political, economic, and social institutions peculiar to feudalism. Feudalistic law had incorporated the values and practices of the tribalistic customs of the "dark ages," but when feudalism began to crumble as a result of vast social changes in the wake of the twelfth-century renaissance, there arose a felt need all across the West for a more viable legal system to meet the changing time's necessities. As a consequence, the *Corpus Juris Civilis* of Justinian was seized upon and dissected. At Bologna, a scholar by the name of Irnerius studied the ancient law in an endeavor to resolve confusions and to reinterpret the old formulations for new circumstances. With his "glosses" he developed an innovative, systematic method of research which eventually affected the whole late medieval approach to legal speculation and legal teaching.

Faculties of law sprang up in many of the universities, and the members of these faculties were soon distinguished from the canon lawyers of the church. Increasingly, this new group of jurists turned to ancient Roman, rather than to traditional medieval, concepts of law, and with their glosses, and later with their separate commentaries on the old texts, they contributed significantly to the trend of questioning and then altering medieval legal meanings for a rapidly transforming West. Of the greatest significance was their reassertion of Stoic natural law conceptualism.

They were evidently impressed with the stoic idea of a common humanity characterized by a universal reason. The opening words of Justinian's *Institutes* appealed to them, and they, in their glosses and comments, singled out natural law as being essentially deduced by human reason, even referring to it as *ratio scripta* or "written reason." They avoided associating it with animal instinct, as Ulpian had done, and they also avoided an equation of it with divine will, as so many of the Christian canonists had done. Thus, the natural law theory of old received new vitality through the resurrection and study of classical legal texts. Rationally derived natural law was looked upon once more as a possible standard by which all other human laws could be measured. Persons other than emperors, kings, or popes could assert the validity of a "higher law," so these scholars asserted, and they went on to suggest, in good Stoic fashion, that any human laws that were not in harmony with natural law could be considered as invalid. Certainly, this kind of thinking had great import for legal theory, but it also had great import for issues of political legitimacy, political authority, and the obligation or lack of obligation on the part of subjects for obedience.

A whole new class of practicing lawyers came into being which also affected the further growth and interpretation of law. This class—the "civilians" or Roman civil lawyers—were engaged in the realistic task of applying law to contemporary situations. They came to emphasize Roman legal prescriptions, grounded in the *ratio scripta*, and in litigation they recommended that conflicts be resolved by utilizing natural law principles or by resorting to equity procedures, which had their roots in Aristotle. This development in practical legalism gave added strength to classical natural law theory and customary law, and served to move the West all the more away from traditional medieval thought forms and in the direction of "modernism."

The evolution of civil law was paralleled by an equally

meaningful development in canon law. Through the twelfth century, as has been observed, church canons had been collected in random fashion and were frequently inconsistent. Gratian's *Concordantia Discordantium Canonum* of A.D. 1140 was a ready example of this. Subsequent efforts at systematization were undertaken to try to impose some order and uniformity. These efforts brought a shift in theoretical emphasis on natural law, in much the same way as had occurred in studies of Roman law. Staff members on canon law, intermixed with those of the Roman law, appeared in the universities, and some of these lawyers showed an inclination to reassert the classical notion of natural law as rational and human and as a category separate from divine law. These glossators and commentators on canon law, whether intentionally or unintentionally, began to undermine the influence of the medieval church apologists who had identified natural law with divine law and, as a result, signified another move in the direction of strengthening the claims of rationalism.

Needless to say, those committed to traditional medieval views were somewhat alarmed at all of the developments attendant upon the new learning. The new opinions, especially the indications of a growing confidence in unaided reason, challenged the entire framework of medieval Christian imagery. Dogma was under attack, and church authority was being questioned. Intimations were abroad that earthly life and secular community could have value in themselves, separate and apart from church interpretations. There were warning signs that twelfth-century scholarship, heavily bolstered by Aristotelianism, would win its autonomy from theology. This was a crisis of no small dimension for Christian apologists. The new learning would not go away, and the pressing question now was: how could it be reconciled with Christian views, or, put another way, how could reason be melded with faith? If the church was to remain an influential force in western civilization, and if divine law was to have a role for human happiness, then the attempt would have to be made. The task, in short, was to rescue Christianity from the blows of a resurgent humanism, and this task was taken up by the most eminent thinker of all in the thirteenth century, namely, Thomas Aquinas. Aquinas was a Dominican monk and teacher, and he made his contribution to Western thought, not as a statesman nor even primarily as a churchman, but rather as a Scholastic. Through his "Great Synthesis" he would make rationalism credible to church apologists and make faith tenable for those who read and accepted Aristotle.

At the outset Aquinas realized he would have to clarify the vague and imprecise treatment given to natural law and divine law by his medieval predecessors and to weave those two concepts into a complete legal system reflective of the divine plan for creation as he, Aquinas, envisioned it. Committed Christian that he was, Aquinas felt a need to preserve the necessity of divine law for human fulfillment, but he also wanted, in Aristotelian fashion, to make place for human reason as a source of guidance for rightful human conduct. Aquinas wrote no separate treatise on law, but his ruminations on the subject can be found in a portion of his monumental *Summa Theologica*.[21] Applying scholastic method to his purpose, Aquinas first contended that a function of the mind was to provide an understanding of reality—of God, of creation, and of the origin and destiny of man. Knowledge, however, could come from two sources: from nature and from supernature, from rational human discernment of the truth that was and from direct revelation by God, the Author of all things. On the fundamentals of faith—purposeful creation, the fall, sin, the need for grace, and the need for a sacramental system administered by an institutionalized church—Aquinas was in basic agreement with Augustine, but he obviously parted company with him on the issue of human reason. Whereas Augustine had de-emphasized reason and had given priority to faith, Aquinas opted for a synthesis of the two. God himself was rational and had created an ordered universe. Though man's reason had been somewhat wounded by the fall, man could still utilize reason to understand *and to fulfill* natural social goals. Natural fulfillment, though, was not enough; it was, in fact, only half the story. Man also needed supernatural fulfillment, and for this faith was essential. Faith and reason were not incompatible; rather, faith completed reason. Faith was a supplement, and a necessary one, for lifting man to the level of perfect happiness. "Nature is not destroyed by grace," wrote Aquinas, "but perfected by it." Man had natural powers which enabled him to achieve happiness on earth but, in addition, he had the superadded gift of revelation to help him attain supernatural fulfillment. The ultimate end for man was absorption in God, the contemplation of God through eternal life in a heavenly realm. Christians, therefore, did not have to suffer in trepidation before the onslaught of Aristotelian rationalism. Along with faith, Christians could embrace the new learning and use it to good purpose.

In dealing pointedly with law, Aquinas rationalized and integrated virtually everything that had gone before. He defined law as "any enactment of reason directed toward the common good" and then went on to delineate his analytical scheme, carefully distinguishing, and at the same time relating, both the natural and the divine. First and foremost in his scheme was eternal law, "the rational guidance of created things on the part of God." Eternal law embraced the vision or purposeful plan which God had set for himself and for all creation. Only God comprehended the wholeness of it. Eternal law was archetypal for all other deduced law; therefore, it followed in the logic of Aquinas that natural law was derived from it. All other laws, said Aquinas, "insofar as they partake of right reason, are derived from eternal law." Natural law was that part of eternal law which man could grasp through his own reason—"participation in the eternal law by rational creatures," as Aquinas put it. Not being able to know all of eternal law (for this would have put man on an equal plane with God), man could nevertheless share in God's reason and could aspire to a high degree of conformity to God's plan. Aquinas made reference to several precepts which he thought clearly exemplified natural law, but he did not elaborate on the content of such law in any great detail. He stated generally that natural law comprised "first principles" for rightful human behavior, but the number of these principles was not fixed at any point in time. Even though natural law was immutable, new precepts could be added. An understanding of natural law could be altered in the sense that man's rational grasp of the composite of eternal law through deduced principles could be expanded by an increased human awareness. These "additions," in effect, became part of the growing stock of natural law.

Evidently, for Aquinas, natural law was not looked upon as human law, because it partook directly of eternal law. It was essentially from God, since it was God's reason shared with man. If human reason had been able to participate completely in divine reason, Aquinas continued, then human or "positive" law would have been unnecessary.[22] Since this was not the case, further refinements or deductions had to be made from the first principles of natural law to apply to specific human circumstances. Known first principles had to be reinterpreted, and these secondary principles constituted "subtractions" from the natural law, and they were the laws which a political community legislated for itself. They were the precepts which made up the body of civil law essential to public order and happiness. This *ius civile*, not unlike any other law, was "the rational ordering of things for the common good." Valid civil laws could not be in opposition to the natural law, but invalid laws were disharmonious and could be resisted so long as resistance did not bring about a greater evil of social disintegration.

Finally, Aquinas set forth divine law as a separate, independent source of law. Divine law was God's direct revelation to man through Christ and the Scriptures; it was supplemental to natural law and specifically appropriate to the quest for supernatural fulfillment. It was indeed directive law, because it was willed by command of him who created it. Said Aquinas, "Since man is ordained to an end of eternal happiness [he] should be directed to his end by a law given by God." Human law was not capable of judging interior motives, whereas divine law could be judge of that which was hidden. Divine law, in sum, confirmed the natural law, but it also added principles which could not be known by reason alone. Though not contrary to reason, it was not discoverable by reason. Any conflict between natural law and revelation was only the result of faulty reasoning. Divine law could not err, insisted Aquinas, but it was possible for men to err. If divine law and rationally deduced law disagreed, it was human beings who had failed in their interpretations of natural and divine precepts.

All four categories of Aquinas' law taken together made up God's inclusive principles for governing the universe and for ordering man's social life on earth. The analytical scheme of Aquinas indicated his conviction that the Christian requisite for a supernatural end for man could be combined with Aristotelian naturalism so as to bring about the possibility of perfect happiness.[23] In the thought of Aquinas, classical and medieval conceptions of natural law obviously underwent a synthesis, and it can well be said that the Thomistic analysis of law certainly represented a new level in late medieval theorizing. Subsequent theologians and jurists would continue with disputation on law, but, in the main, their reflections would be cast within the Thomistic framework and would focus on mere refinements or on minor exceptions in content. Aquinas opened the way to modernism, if we conceive of modernism as the effort to bring to the fore in western thought elements of classical rationalism which, in turn, significantly influenced a departure from traditional medievalism. It would be an error to assume that Aquinas represented a radical departure from natural law theorizing in western history or to try in any way to associate him with views expressed later by Thomas Hobbes and other empiricists of the seventeenth and eighteenth centuries. Much the same is true of Hugo Grotius, on whom we must now center our attention. A strong case can be made for Grotius as having expounded ideas that were fully in keeping with late medieval developments. Assuredly, an extensive examination of his views would now be appropriate in order to confirm this.

Over the years, as has already been observed, numerous commentators have persisted in describing Hugo Grotius as a "modernist," characterizing him as a rationalist and a secularist who exemplified a drastic departure from medieval concepts of man and morality. Some have seen Grotius as one who attempted to postulate a theory of natural law disassociated from its traditional medieval tie with divine revelation, and yet they have labeled him as a secularist even though they recognized his conceptualism as falling within the context of natural religion. Others have indicated that his rationalism and secularism could be attributed to the fact that he sought to ground natural law in the rationality of man apart from any theological presuppositions.[24] A secularist—in the sense in which the word will be used here—is one who views life or any particular matter on the premise that theological considerations, whether revealed or natural, should be excluded. The thesis of this study will be that, even though Grotius was a late medievalist who freed natural law theory from its traditional medieval tie, he was not a secularist in terms of the above definition because he retained theological presuppositions in his thought and, like Aquinas, stressed the dependence of man on the divine order.

Before analyzing Grotius himself it will be useful to note that many commentators have failed to perceive the importance of another philosophical posture, nominalism, and its derivative, the rationalist-nominalist controversy, for Grotius' theory on natural law. Traditional realists, both Platonists and Aristotelians, persisted in arguing for the existence of universals in nature. The medieval nominalists—men like Duns Scotus and William of Occam—took an opposite stance, asserting that there were no universals beyond or in anything and that words, names, or terms denoted only particular things and did not imply the existence of general things designated by them. Genera and species were merely subjective combinations of similar elements.[25] The rationalist-voluntarist controversy followed upon the tension generated between the realists and the nominalists and centered upon the dualism of the intellect and the will. The question was whether reason should be exalted over will or will over reason? The rationalists contended that God's reason was superior to his will because it involved knowledge and perception and was directly related to reality. An act of will was determined by a recognition of what was good and true. The will merely responded in a necessary way to the divine nature or absolute goodness. In conformity with his nature, then, God could not give to real beings or things essences other than those he had already ascribed to them. All reality, including the laws of nature and the laws of morality, was characterized by immutability. The voluntarists, for their part, challenged this conception and asserted the primacy of will over reason. The divine will was determined by nothing beyond itself; it was free of all necessity. All reality was absolute only in the sense that it was willed by God. If God so desired, he could at any time give to real beings and things different essences or natures than those they possessed. An entirely different natural and moral order would be quite conceivable. If God chose to do this, then the laws of nature could be altered by his choice. Natural law could be other than what it was because it had no intrinsic relation to God's essence.

Quite obviously, voluntarism struck at the vital center of the natural law doctrine based on the primacy of reason. If, as the voluntarists held, natural law was solely divine positive law, and if the basis of the rightness of certain actions was not found in their conformity with nature but in the absolute will of God, then God was free to prescribe arbitrarily an opposite course of action. The rationalists, of course, believed that such a posture threatened the entire foundation of rational natural law theory, for it gave no credence to the constancy of law as primarily rooted in reason.

Four of the scholars to whom we have alluded— Cassirer, Gierke, D'Entreves, and Friedrich—acknowledge that some of the late scholastics had initiated a departure from medieval thought by suggesting that natural law might be valid even if there were no God, but three of them—D'Entreves excluded—failed to see any connection between the rationalist-voluntarist controversy and these theorists and, in turn, between this controversy and Grotius. D'Entreves was the only one who came close to seeing the relation, but he missed the essential point. He actually credited both the late medievalists and Grotius with having rejected a voluntarist approach, but he then concluded that the rejection was equivalent to an espousal of the purely rationalistic and secularistic philosophy of the seventeenth century. His own words convey this clearly:

> One point, at any rate is certain, that the revival of natural law which takes place toward the turn of the sixteenth and seventeenth centuries is essentially a rejection of the "Nominalist" or "voluntarist" theory of law. This is apparent in Hooker. It was equally apparent, and historically far more important in Grotius. For Hooker was mainly restating the old Thomist arguments against his Puritan opponents. But Grotius was the founder of the modern theory of natural law. . . . Thus Grotius' proposition that law could retain its

validity even if God did not exist, once again appears as a
turning point in the history of thought. It was the answer to
the challenge of voluntaristic ethics. It meant the assertion
that command is not the essence of law.[26]

Thus, D'Entreves was at the very threshold of a critical
insight into the theory of Grotius, but the insight eluded
him, and he assessed the statement of the great Dutchman
as meaning that command simply was not the essence of
law. "He secured a new lease on life for the doctrine of
natural law," said D'Entreves, "and for the notion that
law is not merely an expression of will."[27] That is not to be
questioned, but what D'Entreves failed to see was that the
new lease was largely a restatement of ideas that had
already been expressed by others. Above all, he failed to
see that Grotius' assertion that natural law was valid even
if there were no God was not only a hypothetical argument
designed as a rejection of "pure" voluntarism, but, as we
shall see, that it was also a rejection of what we might call
"extreme" and "moderate" rationalism in favor of a
"median" position elaborated by Thomas Aquinas and,
later in the sixteenth century, by Francisco Suarez.[28]

In order to determine whether Grotius was a medievalist
who emphasized the primacy of divine law and divine will,
or a late medievalist who incorporated classic elements into
his thought, or a kind of modernist, particularly one who
sought a new philosophic foundation for his ideas, it may
be best to take his natural law theory as a focal point and,
through it, examine his ideas on God, man, society, law, and
obligation. Caution must be exercised, however, for to
delve into his philosophy bit by bit is a course fraught with
danger. His natural law theory is not a unified presentation.
His references to natural law are scattered throughout the
theoretical portions of his *De Jure Belli ac Pacis*, and the
analyst is compelled to indulge in hard and careful reading
in order to put the pieces together. Indeed, much cross-
referencing and matching are required before the reader
can wring full significance out of some of his sentences.

Grotius' masterpiece is an extensive treatise, but in many places he leaves much unsaid.[29] In certain instances he only hints at concepts, and, in consequence, the analyst has to "read between the lines" or examine his ideas within the larger framework of the thinking of his predecessors— Suarez, particularly, for this inquiry—with whom he shows a close parallel. One might suggest that the proclivity of many interpreters towards labeling Grotius as a rational secularist arises in large measure from yielding to the temptation of seeking easy answers or from endeavoring to oversimplify a highly complex subject. Grotius himself provided the lure for shallow conclusions, not deliberately, of course, but through the literary style he utilized and through the format he developed for elaborating his entire scheme of law. If an analyst does misinterpret the natural law theory, he might write off whatever unresolved questions remain with the charge that Grotius was confused, inconsistent, thoroughly unsystematic, or simply an inadequate philosopher. If the conclusion is reached that Grotius was a rational secularist, any reference to God or to theological concepts might be dismissed as totally irrelevant to the argument. From such a perspective, Grotius can easily be considered as the pioneering modernist who opened the way for others to follow.

For a full grasp of his natural law theory, one has to start from the bottom, with fundamental concepts, and work upward to the subtleties of his thought. A good departure point for launching into the inquiry is his concept of man and of the state. Referring to Cicero and the Stoics, he draws a clear distinction between instincts, which come first in the natural order, and principles which come later and which take precedence over the instincts.[30] Only a creature who was able to apply general principles, who was able to differentiate them from instincts, was capable of law. Revealing an Aristotelian bent, Grotius said man was distinguished from the animals. Man stood apart in that he was the possessor of reason and of a unique instrument, speech. "He has been endowed with the faculty of knowing, and of acting in accordance with general principles. Whatever accords with that faculty is not common to all animals, but peculiar to the nature of man."[31] Grotius obviously felt the necessity for setting forth a foundation for a system of morality. Like Aristotle, he was convinced that law had to be based on a firm theory of ethics. Man, therefore, as the possessor of reason, was capable of knowing what ought to be right, and that oughtness could be imparted to law.

Regarding human association, Grotius wrote that there was no time in human experience when men were not in a condition of sociability. Even prior to the establishment of formal civil institutions, men lived as cooperative social creatures. All of mankind comprised one universal, natural human society. This was so, not because their instincts drove them to it, but because they could recognize the rational principle that society was indeed in conformity with human nature. Men had automatically responded to their reason, and society had always been an existent fact.

> But among the traits characteristic of man [he said] is an impelling desire for society, that is, for the social life—not of any and every sort, but peaceful, and organized according to the measure of his intelligence, with those who are of his own kind; this social trend the Stoics called "sociableness."[32]

Grotius made allowance for the fact that men were weak and that this weakness "constrained" them toward self-preservation through social living, but this was not all-compelling, for the very nature of men led them into the mutual relations of society even if they did not lack anything.[33] Man's weakness merely reinforced his rational recognition of the naturalness of society. In all of this, Grotius was obviously of the classic tradition—both Aristotelian and Stoic. His conviction that sociableness was in keeping with human nature, then, formed the proper basis for civil society. Though he held that states came into existence by the express or implied consent of men, this did not constitute a crucial departure that negated his basic belief in the naturalness of sociability. He did not look upon civil society as an artificial creation. It was not a negation of nor an exit from nature; it was, rather, an extension or an improvement made in order to render natural society more serviceable to men's needs.[34] Heavily reminiscent of Stoic thought, Grotius clearly imparted his added conviction that civil society was built upon the universal human society that had existed in nature. It was a microcosm of the larger reality. The purpose of civil society was to enable men better to fulfill natural aims.

Law was derived from society, natural and civil. In Prolegomena 8 Grotius stated, "This maintenance of the social order, which we have roughly sketched, and which is consonant with human intelligence, is the source of law properly so-called." In book 1, chapter 1, he called attention to three definitions of law and accepted the third as the object of his work:

> There is a third meaning of the word law, which has the same force as statute whenever this word is taken in the broadest sense as a rule of moral actions imposing obligations as to what is right. We have need of an obligation; for counsels and instructions of every sort, which enjoin what is knowable indeed but do not impose an obligation, do not come under the term statute or law.[35]

This definition included all rules and statutes that indicated what was just and that qualified the actions of human beings as lawful or unlawful. The sense of obligation was necessary, for only by fulfilling the obligation could a person feel that he was acting justly. Having expressed this definition of law, Grotius, presumably following Aristotle, then distinguished between natural and volitional law.[36] Natural law, he argued, consisted of the dictates of right reason. Rational beings in natural society recognized binding natural obligations. Since the universal human society never ceased to exist, even after the evolution of civil societies,

the natural obligations carried over into civil society, and
rational men retained the capability for discerning additional natural obligations common to all. Grotius singled
out Carneades, the Sceptic of the second century B.C., in
order to reject the argument that all law was mere convention and proceeded to argue for the universality of law, as in
Prolegomena 9, by equating the law of nature with the
nature of man. Again, in Prolegomena 16, he stated "For
the very nature of man . . . is the mother of the law of
nature." Thus, the general principles known to man through
reason constituted the basic laws governing human behavior
in all its aspects. Volitional law he divided into divine and
human law, with the latter grounded in the law of nature.
Divine law he defined as that having its origin in the divine
will,[37] whereas human law was that emanating from the civil
or sovereign powers.[38]

Thus far there seems to be every justification for calling
Grotius a rational secularist on natural law, especially when
one's attention is directed to Prolegomena 11 where he
asserted, "What we have been saying would have a degree of
validity even if we should concede . . . that there is no God,
or that the affairs of men are of no concern to Him." How
can a case possibly be made for him as representing a
continuation of classical and late medieval ideas, and as
including theological presuppositions in his thought on
natural law? To make such a case one must probe into the
subtleties of his thinking and read between the lines where
he left so much unsaid. The gaps of his thought can be filled
in most readily by examining the thought of Francisco
Suarez, with whom, as we shall learn, Grotius obviously
agreed in his own theory on the law of nature. In his *De
Legibus ac Deo Legislatore*, Suarez raised the question
whether natural law was preceptive divine law, that is, an
act of willing on the part of him who issues the command, or
whether it was demonstrative law, that is, an indication of
the will of him who issued the command.[39] This question
comprised a philosophic subtlety that had a direct bearing

on the rationalist-voluntarist controversy and that bore great import for a proper interpretation of Grotius. The whole issue for Suarez, in simplified terms, was: Can law be divine even if it is not given directly by the command of God as a lawmaker? Suarez revealed his preference for natural law in its demonstrative sense, but, by means of a refined argument, he also defended it as preceptive or true law. He began by asserting that God could be looked upon as lawmaker even though God may not have issued direct commands to men, and he maintained that the natural reason of man and its dictates could be considered as a divine gift descending from God. An extended quotation from him is necessary in order to obtain an understanding of the fundamentals of his position:

> It is one thing, however, to say that this natural law is from God, as from an efficient primary cause; and it is quite another to say that the same law is derived from him as a lawgiver who commands and imposes obligations. For the former statement is most certain, and a matter of faith, both because God is the primary cause of all good things in the natural order, among which is the use of right reason and the illumination which it affords constitutes a great good; and also because, in this sense, every manifestation of truth is from God. . . . Therefore, without doubt, God is the efficient cause and teacher (as it were) of the natural law; but it does not follow from this that He is its legislator, for the natural law does not reveal God issuing commands, but (simply) indicates what is in itself good or evil, just as the sight of a certain object reveals it as being black or white, and just as an effect produced by God reveals Him as its author, but not as lawgiver. It is in this way, then that we must think of (God in relation to) the natural law.[40]

Suarez then discussed the "extreme" and "moderate" rationalistic approaches to natural law, as exemplified in the writings of some late medieval theorists, and the voluntaristic position, as exemplified by the Scotists and the Occamites. These two approaches were immediately used by Suarez as a background against which he could develop his own "median" or middle approach. The "extreme" rationalists, he wrote, argued that the dictates of natural reason were intrinsically necessary and independent of every will, even the divine will. The Occamites, in contrast, argued that natural law consisted entirely of a divine command or prohibition proceeding from the will of God as Author and Ruler of nature. They assumed, further, that the natural laws, which consisted of divine precepts laid down by God, were susceptible of abrogation and alteration by him. "These authorities," said Suarez, "also add that the whole basis of good and evil in matters pertaining to the law of nature is in God's will, and not in a judgement of reason even on the part of God Himself, nor in the very things which are prescribed or forbidden by that law."[41] Thus, actions were not good or evil save as they were ordered or prohibited by God. God did not will to command or forbid an action because the action was good or evil. Whatever God willed was just.

It could be argued, Suarez went on to explain, that a pure demonstrative law might be sufficient for man, and this was the position maintained by such men as Gregory of Rimini, Hugh of St. Victor, and others. These men contended that natural law was not preceptive; it was, rather, a law indicating merely what should be done, and what should be avoided, what was intrinsically good and necessary, and what was intrinsically evil. This law was not derived from God as a lawgiver, that is, from will. This being so, Suarez then stated the extent to which these men took their thinking:

Indeed, on the contrary Gregory, whom the others follow, says that even if God did not exist or if He did not judge of things correctly, nevertheless, if the same dictates of right reason dwelt within man, constantly assuring him, for example, that lying is evil, those dictates would still have the same legal character which they actually possess,

because they would constitute a law pointing out the evil that
exists intrinsically in the object condemned.[42]

Suarez rejected this position as untenable. Placing the
obligation for the performance or the nonperformance of an
act in the nature of a principle itself—even though the
principle were an indication of the will of God—was, for
him, only half the story, for absolute obligation could still be
found in God. Neither rationalism, in either of its two forms,
nor voluntarism was adequate as a single explanation. He
endeavored, therefore, to develop a "middle course," a
course he attributed to Thomas Aquinas and other
theologians. In support of his position, Suarez advanced
three propositions. First, he cited Thomas Aquinas (*Summa
Theologica*, qu. 100, art. 2) to the effect that God could not
deny himself, and, therefore, could not abolish the order of
his own justice. That is to say, God could not really be
separate from his creation in any way and, hence, could not
fail ultimately to prohibit those things that were evil and
contrary to natural reason. Natural law was bound by an
absolute precept, even though the law may be only an
indication of the divine will. He wrote:

> God has complete providence over men; therefore, it
> becomes Him, as the supreme Governor of nature, to
> prohibit evil and prescribe what is good; hence, although the
> natural reason reveals what is good and what is bad to
> rational nature, nevertheless God, as the Author and
> Governor of that nature, commands that certain actions
> should be performed or avoided, in accordance with the
> dictates of reason.[43]

The natural reason, which indicated what was in itself evil or
good for mankind, indicated accordingly that it was fully in
conformity with the divine will that the good should be
chosen and the evil avoided. Furthermore, God willed
absolutely that an act should be done or not be done, insofar
as anything related to his role as a just governor; that the
nature of volition was such that, through it, God desired to

oblige his subjects to perform a given action or to leave it unperformed.

> . . . the natural law, as it exists in us, is an indication of some divine volition; hence, it is pre-eminently an indication of that volition whereby He wills to oblige us to the keeping of that law; and thus it follows that the natural law includes the will of God.[44]

In the second proposition Suarez emphasized that divine will was not the sole reason for obligation. Natural law presupposed the existence of a certain righteousness or turpitude in actions, and thereby attached to them a special obligation. A natural law was the dictate of right reason showing the moral turpitude or the moral necessity of an act. By "moral necessity" nothing more was meant than that the laws of nature must always be binding. The natural law prohibited those things that were intrinsically bad, and this law was a true divine law. As such it provided an additional obligation to perform a good or to avoid an evil that were already good or evil by their very nature.

> Therefore, the law of nature, as it is true divine law, may also superimpose its own moral obligation, derived from a precept over and above what may be called the natural evil or virtue inherent in the subject matter in regard to which a precept is imposed.[45]

In his third proposition Suarez postulated the interdependence—indeed, the identity—of natural law in both man and God. Natural law was truly and properly divine law, of which God was the author:

> . . . as existing in God, it implies, to be sure, according to the order of thought, an exercise of judgment on the part of God Himself, with respect to the fitness or unfitness of the actions concerned, and annexes to that judgment the will to bind men to observe the dictates of right reason.[46]

The exercise of judgment resulting in the will to bind men created preceptive obligation for men. This being so, then:

. . . one concludes, finally, that the natural law, as it exists in man, does not merely indicate what is evil, but actually obliges us to avoid the same; and that it consequently does not merely point out the natural disharmony of a particular act or object, with rational nature, but is also a manifestation of the divine will prohibiting that act or object.[47]

The result of all this was: *Since an obligation in natural law was dualistic—both preceptive and demonstrative—the ultimate measure was theological, not human.* Whatever appeared self-evident to man was obligated in the ultimate sense.

Suarez supplied one additional insight that was specifically related to the rationalist-voluntarist controversy. Nothing in creation, he said, could be contrary to nature. To imply that something would be true if God did not exist was only a hypothetical way of saying that what God himself had willed he would not change. God would not will something that was self-contradictory. God would not forsake the order of his justice, just as he would not deny himself or be unfaithful to his promises. Suarez anticipated an objection by asking, Wasn't God's will free so that he could will that two plus two might equal something other than four? His answer was that, even though God's will was free in the external sense, it did not go back on itself and it did not conflict with its reason. He wrote:

In like manner, if it is the divine will to create the world and to preserve the same in such a way as to fulfill a certain end, then there cannot fail to exist a providential care over that world; and assuming the existence of the will to exercise such providential care, there cannot be but a perfect providence in harmony with the goodness and wisdom of the divine will. . . . For just as God cannot lie neither can He govern unwisely or unjustly; and it would be a form of providence in the highest degree foreign to the divine wisdom and goodness, to refrain from forbidding or prescribing to those who were subject to that providence, such things as are, respectively, intrinsically evil, or necessary and righteous.[48]

Where, then, can one find evidence of Suarez's influence
on the thought of Grotius in order to argue that the latter
was not the secularistic modernist that many interpreters
claim him to be? It must be recognized that a theorist could
well be a rationalist without being a secularist, so careful
examination must be made of Grotius' thinking to determine
whether this was true of him. If it be determined that he was
not a secularist, then further analysis is necessary to specify
the character of his rationalism. We have seen that Suarez
rejected the approach of Vasquez and also that of Gregory
of Rimini and Hugh of St. Victor, and it will now be
contended that Grotius did the same. Initially, one fact
must constantly be kept in mind for a full comprehension of
Grotius' natural law theory and for an evaluation of his
rationalism, namely, that he was a dedicated Christian with
a profound belief in God.[49] Grotius, a theist, saw God as
external to creation and as the supreme source and value
of all finite existence. Grotius did not view God with the
rationalism of a deist or a pantheist, in the same vein as a
Voltaire or a Spinoza, for example, nor did he thrust God
far into the background and seize upon the mechanistic
scientism of a Hobbes, a Hume, or a Descartes. Throughout
his treatise Grotius made numerous statements extolling
God as the "Author" of nature. In book 2 he cited four
ideas of God that he believed had been most generally
accepted through the ages: first, that God is, and God is
One; second, that God is more exalted than all things seen;
third, that God has a concern for human affairs and judges
with righteousness; and fourth, that God is the Creator of all
things besides Himself.[50] As a creator, God was the efficient
cause of the nature of man and of the natural laws by which
men regulated their behavior. Completely in harmony with
Suarez, Grotius looked upon God as a lawmaker even
though God did not issue commands directly to men apart
from the special laws of revelation. The natural reason of
man and its dictates, society, and the laws derived from
social existence were of divine origin in the absolute sense.
After he had equated the law of nature with the nature of

man in Prolegomena 9, Grotius went on to explain in Prolegomena 12:

> . . . the law of nature of which we have spoken, comprising alike that which relates to the social life of man and that which is so called in a larger sense, proceeding as it does from the essential traits implanted in man, can nevertheless be rightly attributed to God, because of His having willed that such traits exist in us.[51]

God, having willed all traits in man, had instituted society by an absolute preceptive act and was, thus, the efficient cause of social organization. In Prolegomena 6, as previously quoted, Grotius wrote that "an impelling desire for society" was one of the characteristic traits of man, and in Prolegomena 16 he stated ". . . for the Author of nature willed that as individuals we should be weak, and should lack many things needed in order to live properly, to the end that we might be the more constrained to cultivate the social life."[52] From the cultivation of social life came law—natural and volitional. By the dictates of reason—reason being implanted by God—man discerned the natural laws, for, as Grotius wrote in Prolegomena 7, man "has been endowed with the faculty of knowing and of acting in accordance with general principles." Here, emphasis must be laid upon the distinction Grotius made between revealed religion and natural religion, much in the manner of Thomas Aquinas. According to Aquinas, reason could discover and establish a great body of truth, including natural religion and ethics, but the truths that were distinctive of faith were revealed to, not discovered by, the human mind.[53] St. Thomas never intended to assert a separate absolute source for each, much less an opposition, between the two, and neither, it must be said, did Grotius.

Grotius gave his definition of divinely revealed truth by stating, "What volitional divine law is we may well understand from the meaning of the words. It is, of course, that law which has its origin in the divine will. . . ." He then proceeded to assert that by such an origin it was distinguished from the law of nature "which, also, as we have said, *may be called divine.*"[54] At that point Grotius gave a cross-reference to Prolegomena 12 where he had stated that the law of nature could be attributed to God because of his having willed the trait of reason in man. As though that were not sufficient, Grotius footnoted that statement with a quotation from St. Chrysostom, a fourth-century church father, who wrote, "When I say nature, I mean God, for He is the author of nature."[55] These statements can be overlooked only at the peril of misinterpreting the whole theory of Grotius. Ernest Barker, in writing of Aquinas, noted that the great Schoolman found room for several kinds of law in his philosophy and that "all hung by golden chains to God."[56] Barker, along with the other commentators, classed Grotius as a seventeenth-century rational secularist, but if he had analyzed the theory of Grotius in greater depth, he might have concluded that the types of laws that the Hollander delineated might also have been hung by golden chains to God. All of the commentators, it appears, were too easily mesmerized by his compartmentalization of divine volitional law along with his other forms of law; they failed, however, to perceive the connecting doors between the compartments. Furthermore, having discerned his distinction between revealed truth and natural truth, the commentators were misled and were prone to utilize his assertion in Prolegomena 11 about the validity of natural law even if there were no God to make a case for him as a rationalistic secularist. Failing to see the significance of the rationalist-voluntarist controversy and ignoring the fact that his natural law could have had theological presuppositions based in natural religion, they were inclined to reject whatever traditionalism may have been in his thought and to see him wholly as a secularistic modernist.

The concept of obligation was a vital factor in the thinking of Suarez, and Grotius' statements revealed that this concept was as significant for him as it was for his predecessor. Like Suarez, Grotius dealt with it in a two-fold manner, making it an intrinsic aspect of every law of nature, and, since God was the efficient cause of all reality and the ultimate will in the universe, obligation also became an absolute precept enjoining what was in accord with reason and prohibiting what was contrary to reason. These aspects could be separated analytically, but in relation to any law of nature they comprised a unified concept. Suarez, we learned, wrote that the law of nature "superimposed" its own moral obligation which was derived from a precept "over and above" the natural evil or virtue inherent in the subject matter. Grotius followed suit, indicating that one aspect without the other would provide only partial validity for any natural law. Partial validity would be possible only if God did not exist, he suggested, but such an idea could not be entertained, for God could not be nonexistent.[57] This view of obligation was quite apparent in his full definition of natural law in book 1, and he elaborated on it quite explicitly in the section immediately following the definition:

> The law of nature is a dictate of right reason which points out that an act, according as it is or is not in conformity with rational nature, has in it a quality of moral baseness or moral necessity; and that in consequence, such an act is either forbidden or enjoined by the author of nature, God.[58]

Measured against the thinking of Suarez, the meaning of this statement cannot be misconstrued. Grotius' use of the phrase "moral necessity" demonstrated his agreement with Suarez on the belief that there must be an obligation for the performance or the nonperformance of a law of nature, and, further, that this obligation had a dual character. Any law of nature that of itself indicated what was evil or good and that contained its own principle of obligation also contained an absolute precept of obligation to obey or not to obey grounded in the command or will of God. Then came the added force for this conviction:

The acts in regard to which such a dictate exists are, in themselves, either obligatory or not permissible, and so it is understood that necessarily they are enjoined or forbidden by God. In this characteristic the law of nature differs not only from human law, but also from volitional divine law; for volitional divine law does not enjoin or forbid those things which in themselves and by their own nature are obligatory or not permissible, but by forbidding things it makes them unlawful, and by commanding things it makes them obligatory.[59]

In pointing out that volitional divine law had no demonstrative principle of obligation, for whatever God willed in this regard was good or evil apart from any act of man, and in stressing the dual character of obligation for natural law, Grotius made very obvious the comparison between his view and that of both the extreme and moderate rationalists and the voluntarists.[60]

Other passages from Grotius relating to natural law are fully consonant with the contention that he accepted the "middle course" of Suarez. Indeed, all of Grotius' statements fall into a pattern of logical consistency that cannot be maintained if one labels him as a modern rationalistic secularist. His dual view of obligation provided clarification for the controversial passage of Prolegomena 11 which so many interpreters utilized for their own purposes and, in the process, left numerous puzzling questions unanswered, and it also provided enlightenment for the passage in subsection 5, of section 10, book 1, chapter 1, where he argued for the unchangeability of natural law. In making the hypothetical argument in Prolegomena 11 that natural law would have a degree of validity even if God did not exist, Grotius was almost making his dualism on obligation stand out in relief. The word "degree" was of critical import. What Grotius was saying, in effect, was this: if half of the concept of obligation were stripped away (that is, the absolute precept of God that an act should be performed or not performed), the natural obligation that formed an intrinsic part of the law might still be looked upon as theoretically valid. However, since the two aspects of obligation were only analytically distinguishable but not operationally separable (the absolute precept being superimposed), Grotius hastened to say within the very first sentence that it was impossible for God not to exist. The remainder of the passage was an encomium expressive of God's creativity and never-failing providence —hardly the sentiment of one who would want to write God off as having no concern with "the affairs of men."[61] Thus, Grotius turned away from the position of the voluntarists who insisted that all law had to emanate directly from the will of God and from the position of the moderate rationalists who held that a natural, inherent obligation was wholly adequate for the validity of law.

The passage relating to the unchangeability of natural law was another masterful denial of the voluntarists. He wrote:

> The law of nature, again, is unchangeable—even in the sense that it cannot be changed by God. Measureless as is the power of God, nevertheless it can be said that there are certain things over which that power does not extend; for things of which this is said are spoken only, having no sense corresponding with reality and being mutually contradictory. Just as even God, then, cannot cause that two times two should not make four, so He cannot cause that which is intrinsically evil be not evil.[62]

The voluntarists, we must remember, contended that all law emanated directly from the will of God and that it had to correspond with reality. If God, exercising free will, wanted to give real beings and things essences or natures other than those they already possessed, he could do so, but natural law would have to undergo a corresponding change. Grotius, however, maintained that natural law comprised moral principles—they were "spoken only"—and did not have to correspond with reality. Hence, even if God wanted to alter reality and did so, the laws of nature would remain unalterable, for they would have to be consistent with the rational, moral nature of God, which could not change. The laws of nature, as discerned by the reason of men, indicated the absolute will of God, and this will, though externally free, was not arbitrary in moral matters. God was self-limited or committed to his own moral nature. "Measureless as is the power of God," wrote Grotius, "nevertheless it can be said that there are certain things over which that power does not extend. . . . Just as even God, then, cannot cause that two times two should not make four, so He cannot cause that which is intrinsically evil be not evil." In the final portion of that passage Grotius declared specifically that God himself deemed that he should be judged by his own moral standards, and Grotius listed many Old Testament citations (volitional divine law) as attempted proof of this.[63]

Two final passages that are deserving of consideration for this study are Prolegomena 39 and Prolegomena 58, passages which have also been used by some commentators to characterize Grotius as a rationalistic secularist, even to the extent of crediting him with the creation of a mathematics of law. In Prolegomena 39 Grotius said:

> First of all, I have made it my concern to refer the proofs of things touching the law of nature to certain fundamental conceptions which are beyond question, so that no one can deny them without doing violence to himself. For the principles of that law, if only you pay strict heed to them, are in themselves manifest and clear, almost as evident as are those things which we perceive by the external senses.[64]

This cannot be taken to mean, as some assume, that Grotius was arguing exclusively for the derivation of natural laws by pure secularistic reasoning, much as one would derive geometric theorems. By a close analysis of the passage, and by weighing it in the light of all the preceding material, one is led to the conclusion that Grotius was making reference to the basic philosophic conceptions in which he himself grounded natural law. He was merely referring to the proofs of things "touching the law of nature," to "fundamental conceptions" that, he believed, should be obvious to reasonable men. These concepts have already been discussed at length above: his concepts of man, of society and of law; his concept of God as author of nature and as efficient cause of all reality, including man, his reason, and the norms by which he lives; his concept of dual obligation as intrinsic in a natural law and as residing in the absolute precept of God; and his concept of the immutability of natural law as conforming to the faithfulness and righteousness of God. These were the things, he believed, that should be beyond question, if only reasonable men would ponder them. Once the philosophic conceptions had been comprehended and accepted, then the "principles" of natural law—moral rules or standards—should be manifest and clear, "almost" as clear as the things men perceived by their external senses. Grotius later confirmed all this in another passage where he made it apparent that his methodology for deriving the principles of natural law bore only a loose analogy to scientific method:

> . . . we should carefully distinguish between general principles, as, for example, that one must live honourably, that is according to reason, and certain principles akin to these, but so evident that they do not admit of doubt, as that one must not seize what belongs to another, and inferences; such inferences in some cases easily gain recognition, as that, for example, accepting marriage, we cannot commit adultery, but in other cases are not so easily accepted, as the inference that vengeance which is satisfied with the pain of others is wicked. Here we have almost the same thing as in mathematics, where there are certain primary notions, or notions akin to those that are primary, certain proofs which are at once recognized and admitted, and certain others which are true indeed but not evident at all.[65]

The portion of Prolegomena 58 frequently quoted by commentators is a prime example of the way in which a misinterpretation can arise from the practice of taking sentences out of context. It was claimed that Grotius revealed his pure secularistic rationalism in no uncertain terms when he wrote, "With all truthfulness I aver that, just as mathematicians treat their figures as abstracted from bodies, so in treating law I have withdrawn my mind from every particular fact." Here was proof indisputable, some argued, that Grotius exalted secularized reason for the study of law. Again, however, his analogy from mathematical methodology amounted to nothing more than a loose generalization on the procedure he followed, as can be seen by an examination of the passages that precede the oft-quoted sentence. In Prolegomena 56 Grotius stated that in his work "as a whole" he was attempting to make as lucid a presentation of law as possible. In Prolegomena 57 he elaborated on how he tried to do this:

> I have refrained from discussing topics which belong to another subject, such as those that teach what may be advantageous in practice. For such topics have their own special field, which Aristotle rightly treats of itself without introducing extraneous matters into it. Bodin, on the contrary, mixed up politics with the body of law with which we are concerned. In some places nevertheless I have made mention of that which is expedient, but only in passing, and in order to distinguish it more clearly from what is lawful.[66]

He was saying here that he wanted to treat the subject of law as objectively as he could. In developing a theoretical study of the whole field, he did not want to bias his conclusions by considerations of expediency. With the objective of creating a universal system of law applicable to all persons and nations, he did not want his judgments influenced by parochial or national interests, as did some of his predecessors and contemporaries who produced works on the laws of nations. In short, Grotius did not want to mix politics and law. He lauded Aristotle for treating politics as a study in itself, and he criticized Bodin because the latter "mixed up politics with the body of the law with which we are concerned." He particularly wanted to avoid any accusations of having written under the pressures of the political controversies of his day, either actual or potential, for he said in Prolegomena 58:

> If any one thinks that I have had in view any controversies of our own times, either those that have arisen or those which can be foreseen as likely to arise, he will do me an injustice. With all truthfulness I aver that just as mathematicians treat their figures as abstracted from bodies, so in treating law I have withdrawn my mind from every particular fact.[67]

Viewed in that context, his last sentence takes on a vastly different meaning than that attributed to him by advocates of a rational secularist posture. The practice of proof-texting can indeed be full of hazards, especially where one seeks corroboration for predisposed, but questionable, assumptions, or when one attempts an analysis on the basis of unrefined definitions. The thought of Grotius, when examined in proper historical intellectual perspective, takes on a markedly different cast than that attributed to him through shallow and hasty judgment.

# 4.

# Grotius and the Law of Nations

SEMANTIC PRECISION REQUIRES that the term "modern international law" be used only in relation to the modern states system.[1] The historical evolution of what was to become international law, however, began far back in antiquity, because viable rules affecting the interactions of self-conscious political societies were functional even then. The Greeks of the city-states, for example, engaged in such activities as conquering and possessing other territories, establishing colonies, entering into alliances and confederations, trading across political boundaries, and in concluding political compacts such as peace treaties. There is some scholarly dispute, however, on the practical Greek contribution to the development of international law. Some commentators maintain the Greeks had such a racial, cultural, lingual, and religious homogeneity that the relationships among the peoples of the city-states should better be described as "intermunicipal" rather than "international."

Perhaps the most relevant of the ancient contributions to the practical and theoretical development of a law among nations came from the Romans. During the years of the republic, Rome could well have been considered as a Mediterranean power, as only one among many in a primitive system of relatively civilized political com-

munities. That era might well have been propitious for the
emergence of a rudimentary law, but that did not come
about, because the Romans moved in the direction of
monolithic imperialism. As history well attests, the Romans
achieved a takeover of the known civilized world, their
desire for political universalism providing the motivation for
conquest. The administrative talents required for ruling the
far-flung parts of an enormous political entity were
prodigious, but the Romans seemed to possess an abun-
dance of such skills and proceeded to impose order on many
different peoples or nations (*gens*) for almost three
centuries. In attempting to dispense justice, however, the
Romans encountered some problems that had to be
resolved. Initially, the laws of Rome (*ius civile*) were
applicable only to Romans themselves, with municipal
citizenship determined by birth and residency. A difficulty
soon posed itself: Could the civil law be applied to non-
Romans residing in the city (aliens or *peregrini*) and to the
peoples of the numerous tribes whom the Romans had
conquered in outlying areas? Theoretically, all such persons
were not entitled to the privileges and protections of the
*ius civile*, since Roman municipal law was considered as a
culturally exclusive body of law. To cope with the dilemma,
the Romans developed a unique feature in their legalism.
Special magistrates or judges (*praetor peregrinus*) were
appointed, whose duty it was to deal with any litigation
involving the non-Romans, that is, litigation between aliens
and municipal citizens or among the aliens themselves.
From the decisions (*praetorian edicts*) of these officials
there emerged a body of law which, from a practical point
of view, had the characteristics of a functional law of
nations, but it must be kept in mind that these rulings were
merely common to diverse cultural groups within the unified
Roman political system rather than laws that were common
to peoples of separate, sovereign states.

There has been considerable scholarly debate ever since,
over the way in which this law developed. First, did the

judges utilize elements of the *ius civile* for the cases that came before them? Second, did they seize on laws and customs that were common to Romans and other tribes? Or, third, did they create equity law from their own reasonings as to what was just under the factual circumstances with which they had to deal? Sir Henry Maine, an English legal scholar, in a work of 1861 entitled *Ancient Law*, concluded that the Romans combined the second and third options and consciously applied the term *ius gentium* (law of nations) to the new body of law which accumulated. Maine also concluded that the Romans considered the new law as a resurrection of a "lost code of nature." Maine's views found acceptance for a good many years, but they have been generally discredited by more recent legal historians. Current scholarly consensus inclines to the view that the *praetor peregrinus* applied elements of the *ius civile*, stripped of their unique Roman municipal formalities, to non-Romans and that the resulting composite of law was designated as the *ius honorarium*, a branch of Roman law conferred as an honor or privilege on others. The later Roman adoption of *ius gentium*, it is now believed, had its theoretical rootage in Aristotle's notion of general law. In the previous chapter we noted that when Aristotle discussed general law and described it as rules "common among men according to nature," he went on to say that these rules were unwritten and found their validity in custom. When the Romans applied the term in the days of waning empire, they used it, not as a substitute for *ius honorarium*, nor in reference to a lost code of nature, but rather in reference to a growing recognition of the rules and customs that were common to the Romans and to the tribesmen of outlying areas.[2]

Cicero is reputedly the first Roman theorist to have used the term *ius gentium* in the first century B.C. One could only wish that he might have elaborated on it to some extent, but, unfortunately, he did not. From the few segmented references that are contained in his writings, some have argued that he made an identification of the *ius gentium* with *ius naturale*.[3] The proponents of this stance point particularly to a statement in Cicero's *Tusculan Disputations* where he asserted, "In every matter the consent of nations is to be considered the law of nature."[4] That statement is ambiguous at best, for it could be read to mean that the common law of nations had only a relation and not an identity to natural law, and close examination of Cicero's other references indeed shows that his thought was not as conclusive as the proponents of the above stance would like to believe. In fact, even though Cicero was somewhat vague, a strong presumption could be made in favor of an argument that he did not intend to equate *ius gentium* with *ius naturale*. In the opening segment of *The Commonwealth*, in *Moral Duties*, and in a lesser work entitled *Oratorical Selections*, Cicero described the *ius gentium* as a common law of mankind, with the strong implication that it had developed through custom and was not deduced directly from first principles in nature. In *Moral Duties* he wrote of the *ius gentium* as positive human law. He did not attempt to argue for it as constituting that part of the Roman law which was applied solely to aliens. He simply drew a distinction between it and the *ius civile* and suggested that the *ius gentium* denoted legal practices which were common to all peoples and which could readily be incorporated into the corpus of civil law of each particular state. Similarly, in his *Oratorical Selections*, Cicero remarked that common legal principles were not in conflict with nature, and he went on to describe them as positive law: "Common legal principles are by nature. Particular laws are either written or those unwritten principles contained in the law of nations or the customs of our ancestors."[5] Rather than attempting to read too much into Cicero, an analyst should merely take cognizance of the fact that he conceived of the *ius gentium* as being akin to, but wider in scope than, positive civil law and that he also included in the totality of his thought a theoretical concept

of a law of nature which was immutable and not promulgated by any human authority nor developed through
custom.

Christian thought played an unavoidable role in the
historical process of legal development. The Christian
religion began within Roman culture, and its subsequent
institutional growth was wholly intermeshed with the
political and legal evolution of the West. Originating in a
far-off corner of the Roman Empire among a subject
people, Christianity reached the capitol city itself before a
century had passed. Both Peter and Paul, as church
tradition would have it, died in Rome as martyrs during the
reign of the emperor Nero. From that time forth, the
imperial city became a vital center for the incipient faith.
At first, Christianity was considered as a threat to the
solidarity of Roman civilization, but the historical progression of the faith went from repression to acceptance. By
the beginning of the fourth century A.D. it had become the
religion of the most influential Roman classes. In A.D. 337
the emperor Constantine was converted to the faith, and in
the span of another hundred years all of Roman culture
came to be generally associated with it. Paradoxically, as
Christianity ascended, the empire declined and, by the latter
half of the fifth century, after repeated invasions by
barbarian hordes from the north, the empire, along with the
control it had exercised over so large a part of the ancient
world, came to an end. Roman civilization was fragmented,
and along with it went any hope for unitary government or
law. The disappearance of empire also marked a disappearance of the need for imperial jurists. From that point
on, the churchmen who were familiar with Roman law
assumed an immediate importance. They took as their
task that of expounding on legalistic conceptions within the
framework of their particularistic theologizing and in
relation to the continued growth of the church itself.

The church represented a tie to the civilized, unitary past
and survived the empire as the one institution seemingly

capable of promoting universal values and of imposing some
measure of order throughout the politically shattered West.
By sheer historical circumstance, the chuchmen fell heir to
the Roman administrative task of trying to enforce peace
and law across a vast area. With its extensive network of
bishoprics, as established in late imperial days, the church
provided a continuity for Roman ideas and for Roman
institutionalism in what were formerly the imperial
provinces. Within the city of Rome itself, the Christian
bishop, of necessity, came to assert leadership in secular as
well as in ecclesiastical matters. Increasingly, as the
Rome-centered churchmen extended their authority over
public affairs, they promulgated the canon law which,
though oftentimes confused and contradictory, assumed the
appearance of a law common to all those within the fold. As
a potential universal law, and as a possible true law of
nations, it dealt not only with matters spiritual, moral, and
ecclesiastical but also with those matters that had previously
been considered as under the exclusive jurisdiction of
secular authority. Clearly, a confrontation was in the
making if sufficiently assertive political and legal authorities were to arise and challenge the expanding secular
influence of the church.

Following the so-called Dark Ages, feudalism became the
prevailing form of political and social organization in the
West between the eighth and twelfth centuries. It was quite
diverse in its institutional manifestations and practices but,
in general, it bestowed rudimentary political authority on
tribal leaders or "noblemen" who had established their
personal control over geographically delimited areas, and,
in function, it fostered political and legal decentralization.
Feudalism was essentially based on a hierarchical order
characterized by lordship and deference. To dispense
justice, a lord sat in council with his lesser lords (vassals),
and out of their deliberations came decisions which were
subsequently recognized and applied as customary law. The
most enduring feature to come out of feudalism was, of

course, medieval monarchy, even though at first feudal structures had been contrary to this centralization of authority. The feudalistic era also witnessed the attempt to cling to the idea of empire, a Holy Roman Empire. The hope remained for an imperial power that could impose law on all nations, that there might be a *pax Germanica* to replace *pax Romana,* but the effort proved abortive. Though aspirants to an imperial throne helped keep the idea alive for a long time, monolithic government never came into being administratively or jurisdictionally for the West and, ultimately, the claim for empire was recognized for what it was, a myth. Developing monarchies, in fact, proved to be the counterforce for any hope for universalism for secular law or for any hope for unitary government as had once been known. The monarchies in time spawned nationalisms which turned into the "European states system," as historians are now fond of calling it.

Before the monarchies were sufficiently consolidated, that is, before the monarchs themselves were secure in the exercise of centralized political power, the church, under a succession of ambitious leaders, continued to intrude into secular matters. Church theorists clung to the notion of a universal, spiritual community for the West, Christendom, with the bishop of Rome—now called pontiff or pope—as the head. The increasing aspirations for the right of the church to exercise lordship over secular affairs culminated in the claim that the bishop of Rome was indeed the supreme lord and judge of the world. Western Christendom was henceforth seen by most of the church spokesmen as composed of two orders, the temporal and the spiritual, with the latter as superior. This imagery had its origin in Augustine and in the "two swords" theory of Pope Gelasius (A.D. 492-496) and was forcefully articulated by Pope Gregory VII in his decree *Dictatus Papae* of 1075. Gregory maintained that the Roman church was divine in origin, that the Roman pontiff alone could be called universal ruler, that the pontiff could depose kings and emperors and be judged by no human powers, and that the Roman church had never erred and could not err.[6]

While the members of the official church hierarchy and other spokesmen were insisting upon the supremacy of the spiritual authority over the secular and essentially reaching out for world power, some scholars, like Thomas Aquinas, in the thirteenth century began to express ideas which eventually opened the way for challenging such a vision of power. The consequences of Aquinas' thought would be far-reaching. Ironically, while he was attempting to defend the Christian faith against the threat of a revived rationalism, he resurrected the classic concept of natural law, and by categorizing it as rational human law, paved the way for future arguments regarding the independence of secular authority from the spiritual.

An element of crucial import in the thought of Aquinas was the theoretical link he made between *ius naturale* and *ius gentium*. In elaborating upon his scheme of law, Aquinas made clear that, in his estimation, the *ius gentium* was human law, not unlike the *ius civile*, but it was basically rooted in *ius naturale*. Roman thought had suggested a relationship between *ius naturale* and *ius gentium*, implying that the latter was an aspect of human reason manifested in custom, but Aquinas, skillful theoretician that he was, went beyond this to pose a dual aspect of a law of nations, one having a direct tie to natural law, the other having only a relationship to it. Human law was described by Aquinas in part 1-2, qu. 91, art. 3, of his *Summa Theologica*:

> Accordingly, we conclude that just as, in the speculative reason, from naturally known indemonstrable principles, we draw the conclusions of the various sciences, the knowledge of which is not imparted to us by nature, but acquired by the efforts of reason, so too it is from the precepts of the natural law, as from general and indemonstrable principles, that the human reason needs to proceed to the more particular determination of certain matters. These particular determinations, devised by human reason, are called human laws. . . .[7]

In question 95, article 2, Aquinas forged ahead with a more refined analysis of human law. He stated:

> . . . it must be noted that something may be derived from the natural law in two ways: first, as a conclusion from premises, secondly, by way of determination of certain generalities. The first way is like to that by which, in sciences, demonstrated conclusions are drawn from the principles; while the second mode is likened to that whereby, in the arts, general forms are particularized as to details: thus the craftsman needs to determine the general form of a house to some particular shape. . . . Accordingly both modes of derivation are found in the human law. But those things which are derived in the first way, are contained in human law not as emanating therefrom exclusively, but have some force from the natural law also. But those things which are derived in the second way, have no other force than that of human law.[8]

Precepts derived in the first manner made up the *ius gentium* or law of nations, whereas those derived in the second manner made up the *ius civile* or civil law. Thus, he asserted in question 95, article 4:

> A thing can of itself be divided in respect of something contained in the notion of that thing. . . . Now, in the notion of human law, many things are contained, in respect of any of which human law can be divided properly and of itself. For in the first place it belongs to the notion of human law to be derived from the law of nature, as explained above (Art. 2). In this respect positive law is divided into the *law of nations* and *civil law*, according to the two ways in which something may be derived from the law of nature, as stated above (Art. 2). Because to the law of nations belong those things which are derived from the law of nature, as conclusions from premises. . . . But those things which are derived from the law of nature by way of particular determination belong to civil law, according as each state decides what is best for itself.[9]

Was Aquinas here restricting the derivation of a law of

nations to a process of direct rational deduction from first principles, or could a law of nations be manifested in some other way? He was aware of this dilemma and attempted to deal with it in article 3 of question 97, where he addressed himself to the issue of change in laws and asked whether custom could obtain the form of law. He cited St. Augustine and then set forth his own views:

> . . . Augustine says (Ep. ad Casulan. 36): The customs of God's people and the institutions of our ancestors are to be considered as laws. And those who throw contempt on the customs of the Church ought to be punished as those who disobey the law of God. I answer that, all law proceeds from the reason and will of the lawgiver; the Divine and natural laws from the reasonable will of God; the human law from the will of man, regulated by reason. Now just as human reason and will, in practical matters, may be made manifest by speech, so may they be made known by deeds: since seemingly a man chooses as good that which he carries into execution. But it is evident that by human speech, law can be both changed and expounded, insofar as it manifests the interior movement and thought of human reason. Wherefore by actions also, especially if they be repeated, so as to make a custom, law can be changed and expounded; and also something can be established which obtains force of law, insofar · as by repeated external actions, the inward movement of will, and concepts of reason are most effectually declared; for when a thing is done again and again, it seems to proceed from a deliberate judgment of reason. Accordingly, custom has the force of a law, abolishes law, and is the interpreter of law.[10]

Obviously, Aquinas here broadened Roman legal conceptualism by suggesting that the *ius gentium* could comprise principles deduced from the natural law and also principles manifested in custom. Custom was a confirmation of reason. Laws could be declared as plainly by men's actions as by their words, so "custom has the force of law, abolishes law, and is the interpreter of law."

The great import of Aquinas' formulation consisted of the

fact that he, a Scholastic churchman, had legitimized a basic source for all of the precepts of a law of nations, *and that source was independent of God's revelation through divine law*. It was here that Aquinas opened the way for others to advance a concept of separation of church and state. Even though Aquinas had intimated that secular rulers should be subject to the authority of the church in spiritual matters, it was possible for others to argue that church and state were coterminous institutions, each in its own way contributing to the ultimate fulfillment of man, but each institution had its own law, its own jurisdiction, and each could function separately from the other in respect to its own value orientation.

The rapid growth of the national monarchies from the thirteenth century onward proportionately decreased the capability of the church for actualizing a viable system of universal law. The rise of the monarchies gave evidence to new attitudes and new social and economic forces stirring across the West attendant upon the disintegration of feudalism. The monarchs themselves began to turn away from feudal notions of reciprocal obligations among landed lords and to rely increasingly upon the fast-growing commercial classes for support. The monarchs appropriated unto themselves all the prerogatives of the feudal lords and more and more assumed the kingly claim to promulgate law by arbitrary will. A further appropriation was that of the Roman concept of *imperium*; the monarchs wanted to cloak themselves with the former attributes of emperors and to assert their newly felt powers within their own kingdoms. There was one very troublesome thing with which they had to contend, however: their realms were still part of Christendom. The Christian faith cut across territorial boundaries, and the peoples within the realms were oftentimes caught in a dilemma of loyalty to new sovereign authority or loyalty to the church. In order to strengthen their positions and to promote the loyalty of their peoples, the monarchs intensified their resistance to any possible encroachments of the papacy. The sixteenth-century Reformation provided a golden opportunity for many of the reigning sovereigns to ward off potential church intrusions into their national affairs. In large measure, the vast religious upheaval which swept all of Europe helped to promote the phenomenon of nationalism. By 1560 most of the basic tenets of Protestantism had been asserted, and the changing circumstances dispelled once and for all any lingering notion that Christendom was a monolithic unity directed from Rome.[11]

Political theory had not kept pace with burgeoning nationalism prior to the sixteenth century; only later would theory become reflective of changing political realities. Niccolo Machiavelli, writing with the strongman of an Italian city-state in mind, gave the monarchs across the Alps something to ponder in the conduct of statecraft. Machiavelli's *The Prince* of 1513 was a "how to" book, a handbook of advice for a ruler on how to achieve, exercise, and retain political power. Machiavelli postulated that a stable state could be the guarantor of human happiness and that the creation and maintenance of order was the mark of high statesmanship. It followed for Machiavelli that all means appropriate to the realization of the "good" end could be justified. A ruler, therefore, could become a law unto himself, subject to no limitation other than his own strength and cunning. He could define the values for his own political society and be accountable to no external norms. Machiavelli embraced no concept of universal values; hence, there was no law and no obligations among rulers of states, since there could be no devotion to a common higher good. Further, since there was no superior human power to impose standards of behavior on individual princes, each prince remained an authority in his own right—a power above which there was no other. What this amounted to was an expressed belief that relationships among political states were unrestrainedly competitive; it was a matter of every state for itself. This was a clear articulation of "reason of state" or national self-interest as the overriding motivation for the practice of statecraft.

One who did make an effort in the latter part of the sixteenth century at rethinking important concepts in the light of the new nationalism for the West was Jean Bodin. Bodin was very much a French nationalist who was deeply disturbed by the religious factionalism and the civil strife which occurred in his country and in other states in the post-Reformation period. Bodin became convinced that the cause for internal disorder could be attributed to the as yet incomplete centralization of power in the monarch. Thus, he wrote to substantiate mounting claims for kingly power, believing firmly that the only corrective for civil chaos was concentration of authority. A king, boldly commanding, could ensure order amidst religious factionalism. Bodin dealt at length in his theorizing with the concept of sovereignty which should be embodied in a ruler. In his *Six Livres de la Republique* (*Six Books of the State*), published in 1576, Bodin tried to define and to describe this power. Sovereignty, he said, was supreme power (*summa potestas*) over citizens and subjects; it was the command of the sovereign, promulgated by royal decree and unlimited by law. Utilizing paternalistic imagery, Bodin stated that no father was appointed by his children to rule over them. This being so, he was in no way accountable to their wills. Bodin then made an analogy to kingship: family units were the source of any political society, so a kingdom was only a family writ large. The ruler was a father and his subjects his children. Rulership was a king's natural obligation imposed by God to maintain order, to protect his family, and to hold it together, and the right to command was independent of consent from the family.

Insisting upon the right of kingly rule within a political realm, Bodin, perhaps in a deliberate effort to counter the arbitrary character assigned to a prince by Machiavelli, went on to indicate that a monarch's power was not as unrestrained as his definition and discussion of sovereignty had first implied. Sovereign power, said Bodin, was not underived, for it came from God. Within his kingdom, a ruler was only the highest *human* authority; he was by no means a law unto himself, for he was always the agent of divine will, and as such was accountable to divine law. Even beyond that, a king was also accountable to natural law, the universal precepts of nature discernible by all rational beings. Finally, Bodin suggested a monarch was bound by custom and tradition, by the decrees of his predecessors and by "his own law." Custom could not be ignored, and neither could a sovereign reject any oaths he had taken. Oaths were contracts among the agreeing parties and God himself and, therefore, should not be broken. A monarch was obligated to divine law and natural law on this. Clearly, Bodin's theorizing was an effort at recognizing kingly power in a rapidly transforming West, but he revealed his deep concern for arbitrary authority by proposing limitations upon any monarchical claim for total freedom of action.

Bodin's work was a step forward for internal, domestic accountability on the part of a ruler, but the vital question which still remained was: By what rules were the interactions among sovereigns to be regulated when the sovereigns recognized no common legal superior? Wars, from the sixteenth century onward, became international in the sense that they were fought under the banners of the new monarchs. These conflicts were broad in scope and replaced the "private" wars of the feudalistic era. Religion was oftentimes involved, but it was not a single causative factor, for political, economic, and social issues entered in. Unfortunately, whatever practices or customs that had found acceptance over time in regard to intersocietal relationships came to be minimized or even ignored entirely. This growing disregard for any restraint on state behavior led monarchs to adopt Machiavellianism either by design or by default. National interest or "reason of state" was becoming the dominant theoretical and practical orientation for international conduct.

This trend compelled creative legal thought on the part of some who were theoretically inclined. They were appalled by the conflicts which raged throughout Europe and by the growing insensitivity on the part of sovereigns toward any consideration of principles of right and justice. Though history, like a giant hammer, had fallen upon the West, breaking it into numerous pieces, these theorists came to believe that the fragments could be held together in a meaningful whole with universal law serving as a bonding medium. To lay a foundation for their belief, they turned to political and legal elements of classic thought, to Roman conceptualism and law, to theology, and to practices that had survived through time. Sixteenth-century jurists like Conrad Brunus, Pierino Belli, Balthasar Ayala, and Alberico Gentili came to insist upon a need for the recognition and utilization of existing rules for controlling the behavior of sovereigns who acted for their political societies. They were of similar mind in a belief in a law of nature and in custom as a manifestation of nature for a justification of such rules. Ayala, for example, in his, *De Jure et Officiis Bellicis* of 1582, criticized the view that war knew no law and argued fervently in favor of a *ius naturale* grounded in reason and a *ius gentium* based on common consent. Gentili said much the same in his *De Jure Belli Libri Tres* of 1598, insisting that there was a law of war based on natural reason and custom. Important as these juristic contributions were, they were matched by the speculations made by sixteenth- and early seventeenth-century theologians, foremost among them being the Spanish Jesuits like Francisco Victoria, Fernando Vasquez, and Francisco Suarez. A case might well be made for these men as having a grander vision, a firmer perception of change, and a greater adeptness with issues of law than the professional jurists themselves. They were especially courageous in scorning the claims to world authority by the church hierarchy and in advocating restraints on secular sovereigns through principles that were independent of divine law and canon law. All of them rejected the medieval imagery of the papacy as having supreme authority over all of humanity, and they revealed a realistic acceptance of the transition from any concept of political universalism to multinationalism throughout the West. As early as 1557, Francisco Suarez, while acknowledging the spiritual authority of the papacy over Christendom, nevertheless denied to a pope any claim of right to exercise any authority in secular matters. In like manner, Fernando Vasquez declared that neither Christ, the pope, a Holy Roman emperor, nor any man since Adam had ever been *de jure* master of the whole world in temporal matters.

Undoubtedly, the intellectual giant of the Spanish Jesuits was Francisco Suarez. He fully exemplified the results of late medieval rationalism, and this made it possible for him to conceptualize a system of rational law capable of application to a new society of independent, sovereign nation-states. Revealing a general Aristotelian influence upon him on politics and law, and revealing certainly a Stoic influence on him in regard to universal rational law, Suarez argued that such law could be grounded in the reality of a universal human society which had existed for all time by nature and which superseded the historical developments of classical empire, medieval Christian universalism, and nationalistic separatism.[12] It was in his *De Legibus ac Deo Legislatore* (published twelve years before Grotius' *De Jure Belli ac Pacis*) that Suarez clearly set forth his version of a universal human society which was transcendent to but coterminous with the existence of diverse national societies and for which universal law was a counterpart:

> . . . the human race [Suarez wrote], into howsoever many different peoples and kingdoms it may be divided, always preserves a certain unity, not only as a species, but also a moral and political unity (as it were) enjoined by the natural precept of mutual love and mercy; a precept which applies to all, even to strangers of every nation.

Therefore, although a given sovereign state, common-wealth, or kingdom may constitute a perfect community in itself, consisting in its own members, nevertheless, each one of these states is also, in a certain sense, and viewed in relation to the human race, a member of that universal society; for these states when standing alone are never so self-sufficient that they do not require some mutual assistance, association, and intercourse, at times for their own greater welfare and advantage, but at other times because also of some moral necessity or need. This fact is made manifest by actual usage.

Consequently, such communities have need of some system of law whereby they may be directed and properly ordered with regard to this kind of intercourse and association; and although that guidance is in large measure provided by natural reason, it is not provided in sufficient measure and in direct manner with respect to all matters; therefore, it was possible for certain special rules of law to be introduced through the practice of these same nations. For just as in one state or province law is introduced by custom so among the human race as a whole it was possible for laws to be introduced by the habitual conduct of nations. This was the more feasible because the matters comprised within the law in question are few. . . .[13]

Suarez followed Thomas Aquinas on his general scheme of law but proceeded to qualify the concept of *ius gentium* while, at the same time, insisting he was being consistent with the true intent of Aquinas. The argumentation of Suarez became quite refined and complicated on this, so it is essential to examine his reasoning with great care. At the root of all law, he maintained, was eternal law, "the essential principle of divine providence." This law resided immutably and from the beginning of creation in the mind and will of God, and, though it was all-pervasive and all-inclusive, it was not promulgated in the usual meaning of the word. Thus, men were not able to obtain knowledge of it directly, but the more philosophically minded and those who obtained revelation through faith were at least able to grasp some understanding of it. The eternal law could only be known in earthly life in other laws or through them. In distinction to the eternal law, Suarez defined divine law as that which was directly promulgated by God. This law was revealed and, as such, could be classed as positive divine law. The natural law was conceived by Suarez as having been made known to men through the dictates of natural reason, and the principles of this law were unchangeable. The final category of his scheme was human positive law, and, revealing here his reinterpretation of Aquinas on the *ius gentium,* Suarez declared that the *ius gentium* did not comprise principles directly deduced from the natural law and principles manifested in the customs or practices of men, but rather the *ius gentium* found confirmation and validity *solely* in the actual customs of nations. Consent, not as manifested in the rational agreements of man, but consent as manifested in custom was to be the pre-dominating characteristic of human positive law. Secondary principles deduced from primary principles rightfully belonged to the realm of natural law, Suarez maintained, and this is what Aquinas actually intended and this was the way in which Aquinas had to be properly interpreted!

It was in chapter 17 of book 2 that Suarez advanced his case to the effect that Aquinas had been misinterpreted on the issue of the *ius gentium.* Suarez called attention to Aquinas' statement that the natural law was derived "without reflection—or at least the simplest kind of reflection" while the precepts of the *ius gentium* were deduced "by means of many and comparatively intricate references." It was precisely at this point, commented Suarez, that Aquinas had been interpreted erroneously, for even though St. Thomas had used the term "necessary" in reference to the precepts of the *ius gentium*, he nevertheless did not exclude human consent as manifested in custom as an essential condition. Principles directly deduced from the natural law were part of that law, whereas the *ius gentium* had to be exclusively part of positive law. Said Suarez:

. . . the precepts of the *ius gentium* were introduced by the free will and consent of mankind, whether we refer to the whole human community or to the major portion thereof; consequently, they cannot be said to be written on the hearts of men by the Author of Nature; and therefore they are part of the human, and not of the natural law.[14]

Again, Suarez said that Aquinas had been interpreted as saying that natural law embraced conclusions so essential that, independently of the existence of human society, or a society dependent upon human volition

. . . these conclusions would obviously follow upon natural principles; and the said conclusions would not come under the *ius gentium*; whereas there are others which also follow upon natural principles, necessarily, yet not absolutely, but rather in conjunction with the assumption of the existence of a human society and in view of certain circumstances essential for the preservation of that society; so that precepts relating to such conclusions constitute the *ius gentium*.[15]

Not so, said Suarez, for Aquinas maintained that the precepts of the *ius gentium* were dependent upon the exercise of human free will and upon usage.

. . . the *ius gentium* does not prescribe anything as being of itself necessary for righteous conduct nor does it forbid anything as being of itself and intrinsically evil, whether such commands and prohibitions are absolute or whether they involve an assumption of the existence of a particular state and set of circumstances; on the contrary, all such matters pertain to the natural law; accordingly, it is from this standpoint that the *ius gentium* is outside the realm of natural law; neither does it differ from the latter in that the *ius gentium* is peculiar to mankind, for that character pertains also to natural law, either in large part, or even entirely, if one is speaking of right (*ius*) and law (*lex*) in the strict sense.[16]

Suarez undertook the refutation of an argument to the effect that the *ius gentium*, as distinguished from the natural law, was merely concessive law rather than preceptive. Concessive law was defined as that which was promulgated by civil authority and which was applicable to man only within his social context. Suarez noted that proponents of the concessive posture credited Aquinas with saying that the *ius gentium* was socially expedient and that it was not grounded in higher law. Completely rejecting this line of argument, Suarez—defending Aquinas—acknowledged that the *ius gentium* was dependent upon the free will and consent of mankind, but this did not make it any the less preceptive or true law. When the *ius gentium* conferred the faculty to perform an act, one had always to ask whether the faculty had its source in human agreement alone or whether it had its ultimate source in natural reason.

> We conclude then that the *ius gentium* is not properly distinguished from natural law on the ground that the former is concessive only; and the latter preceptive. For one of two alternatives will apply: either the two characteristics are found in both systems of law; or else if a legal precept does pertain to natural law, then the concession duly corresponding to that precept also has its source in that same natural law.[17]

An outline summary of his views on *ius naturale* and the *ius gentium* was given by Suarez in book 2, chapter 19. These two forms of law, he said, agree in three ways:

1) Both are in a sense common to mankind. On this ground, each may be called a law of nations.
2) The subject matter of both apply only to mankind.
3) Both include precepts or prohibitions and permissions or concessions.

On the other hand, he said, they differed in these ways:

1) The *ius gentium* does not have inherent necessity as does natural law. That is to say, the precepts of the *ius gentium* were not derived from first principles, but were established by the consent of peoples through custom.
2) The *ius gentium* is not as immutable to the same degree as natural law. Immutability springs from necessity.

3) Natural law is common to all, and only through error it is not observed everywhere. The *ius gentium*, however, is not observed always and by all nations, but only as a general rule, and almost by all. Hence, that which is held among some peoples to be *ius gentium*, may elsewhere and without fault fail to be observed.[18]

Thoroughly satisfied in his own mind that Aquinas considered consent the essential characteristic of the *ius gentium*, Suarez then made this definitive observation:

Therefore, the conclusion would seem to be, in fine, that the *ius gentium* is in an absolute sense human and positive. This proposition may be inferred from the words of St. Thomas [1-2, qu. 95, art. 4] who divides positive law absolutely into *ius gentium* and civil law, saying that both are human law, derived from natural law.[19]

For further confirmation on his position, Suarez went into a long explanation, claiming an affinity with both Aristotle and Aquinas, as he himself interpreted their thought.

For law may sometimes be called human, not with respect to its author but with respect to its subject matter and because it is concerned with human affairs; and in this sense it governs the human race and directs the actions of mankind. It is thus that Aristotle (*Nic. Eth.*, 5, 7) seems to have understood the term "human law." . . . Accordingly, he divides civil law into natural and conventional, referring by the latter term to what we call positive civil law. St. Thomas (1-2, qu. 95, art. 2) also seems to have interpreted human law in this sense, for he divides it into that which derives its force from natural reasoning and that which derives its force from the free will of men; two divisions which seem to be equivalent simply to natural and positive law. Moreover, St. Thomas (ibid., art. 4) calls positive law human, and he holds every law established by men to be of this character. He also makes a subdivision of laws; for there is in his classification one branch in the form of [general] conclusions, which derives its force from the natural law; whereas the other branch exists in the form of specifications

which introduce a new law, and this form we call positive
law, in an absolute sense. Therefore, St. Thomas, in the
passage cited above, is apparently speaking of the *ius
gentium* as human and positive law in the first of these two
senses. For he clearly says that *ius gentium* exists in the form
of a [general] conclusion and derives its force from the
natural law. He appears, moreover, to maintain this same
opinion in another passage (1-2, qu. 57, art. 3, *in corpore*).
Nevertheless, the term in question may be understood
properly as referring to positive and human law, that is, to
law constituted by men; but that law is said to be constituted
in the form of a [general] conclusion, and not as a
specification, since St. Thomas does not interpret the force
of the *ius gentium* as leading to complete and concrete
specification; on the contrary, he holds that the *ius gentium*
is established with general force in the form of a conclusion
not absolutely necessary, but so in harmony with nature that
it is inferred (as it were) at the instigation of nature. This is
the interpretation given to the works of St. Thomas. . . .

. . . it suffices that law should be divided into natural and
positive, properly so called or into divine and human law,
each of these being named according to its author, since the
two branches are mutually exclusive, as is evident; but it
has been shown that the laws of the *ius gentium* are not
natural law, properly and strictly speaking, and consequently
not divine; and, therefore, they must be positive and human.

This argument is confirmed by the fact that natural law
is that law which springs not from human opinion, but from
the evidence afforded by nature, as Cicero has pointed out.
Hence, every law that is of this latter variety is positive and
human. And the *ius gentium* is of this latter variety, because
it came into existence not through [natural] evidence but
through probable inferences and the common judgment
of mankind.[20]

With all of these premises firmly established, Suarez then
proceeded to make an emphatic distinction between written
and unwritten law and to set forth a dual classification of the
latter as forms of the *ius gentium*. Written law was that
which was promulgated by civil authority—the *ius civile*,
or law peculiar to each state—but:

It is manifest, moreover, that the *ius gentium* is unwritten, and that it consequently differs in this respect from all written civil law, even from that imperial law which is applicable to all. Furthermore, unwritten law is made up of customs, and if it has been introduced by the custom of one particular nation and is binding upon the conduct of that nation only, it is also called civil; if, on the other hand, it has been introduced by the customs of all nations and thus is binding upon all, we believe it to be the *ius gentium* properly so called. The latter system, then, differs from the natural law because it is based upon custom rather than upon nature; and it is to be distinguished likewise from civil law, in its origin, basis, and universal application. . . .[21]

Hence, *ius gentium*, in the broad sense, could be taken as comprising those rules which various peoples and nations ought to observe in their relations with each other, and this was the *ius gentium* "properly called." In a restricted sense, the *ius gentium* could be taken as comprising rules which were held by all or nearly all peoples of the world but which were applied only in the internal relations of states. This *ius gentium* in the narrow sense was embodied in municipal or civil law but was not exactly identified with it, because it was unwritten. Suarez was so convinced in his own mind of this dual aspect of the *ius gentium* that he tried to affirm his argument through repetition:

I shall add that a particular matter . . . can be subject to the *ius gentium* in either one of two ways: first, on the ground that this is the law which all the various peoples and nations ought to observe in their relations with each other; secondly, on the ground that it is a body of laws which individual states or kingdoms observe within their own borders, but which is called *ius gentium* [i.e., civil law] because the said laws are similar [in each instance] and are commonly accepted.[22]

The difference between the written and unwritten law, Suarez admitted, was a very fine one, but the difference was there nevertheless. The fact he wanted to stress most, however, was that the *ius gentium*, taken in both senses, was consensual or customary law. Suarez had noted that all positive law laid down by mankind for the governance of the purely political order was called "conventional" by Aristotle.[23] The same was true for Aquinas.[24] Suarez wanted to make certain, however, that no one would overlook the uniqueness of the *ius gentium* in each of its senses. Each was distinctive in its own right and each included subject matter peculiar to it alone. He was adamant in his belief that the crucial difference between the two could be found only in the scope of application based upon the intention of the respective consent involved. There was no ambiguity in his thought when he said the *ius gentium* of the first sense was essential for the society of states as he saw it, that it was grounded in custom and had reference only to the external relations of states and that it was consonant with the law of nature. To repeat and to extend his words on the matter:

> . . . such communities have need of some system of law whereby they may be directly and properly ordered with regard to this kind of intercourse and association; and although that guidance is in large measure provided by natural reason, it is not provided in sufficient measure and in a direct manner with respect to all matters; therefore, it was possible for certain special rules of law to be introduced through the practice of these same nations. For just as in one state or province law is introduced by custom, so among the human race as a whole it was possible for laws to be introduced by the habitual conduct of nations. This was the more feasible because the matters comprised within the law in question are few, very closely related to natural law and most easily deduced therefrom in a manner so advantageous and so in harmony with nature itself that, while this derivation [of the law of nations from the natural law] may not be self-evident—that is, not essentially and absolutely required for moral rectitude—it is nevertheless quite in accord with nature, and universally acceptable for its own sake.[25]

The *ius gentium* of the second sense, by contrast, had reference only to internal relations, even though the rules may have had a common character:

The second kind of *ius gentium* embodies certain precepts, usages of modes of living, which do not, in themselves and directly, relate to all mankind; neither do they have for their immediate end (so to speak) the harmonious fellowship and intercourse of all nations with respect to one another. On the contrary, these usages are established in each state by a process of government that is suited to the respective courts of each. Nevertheless, they are of such a nature that, in the possession of similar usages or laws, almost all nations agree with one another, or at least they resemble one another, at times in a generic manner, and at times specifically, so to speak.[26]

In the formulations of an intellectual like Suarez, the stage was being set for an attempted application of theoretical concepts to practical politics and law. The tension which had been created between Machiavellianism, which saw the individual state as the highest form of political evolution, and universal idealism, which held out the hope for a higher human unity with a transcendent concept of legal obligation, brought into focus the need for a theoretical and substantive work on the subject of a law among nations. This progressive evolution in human thought was to find its culmination in Hugo Grotius.

The time was ripe [said T. J. Lawrence] for a great reformer who would combine all the scattered elements of strength . . . and bind them together by means of some principle which would be generally accepted by the thinkers of his day and generation. He came after a century of confusion in the person of Hugo Grotius.[27]

With a scholar's understanding of the course of history, with a profound grasp of past and contemporary theory, and through the creative energies of his own mind, Grotius was determined to produce a complete work, one setting forth theoretical confirmation for the identity of individual states while at the same time denying their absolute separateness through the systematic exposition of a body of substantive law reflective of the universal society of mankind which cut across all state boundaries. It would be his great accomplishment to reaffirm the persistent notion of universalism, but he would do it within the framework of a theoretical and substantive legalism which would take into account the new political system of the West.

Grotius was not yet forty years old when he began writing his *De Jure Belli ac Pacis*, but already in his lifetime he had experienced more than enough of the horrors stemming from a lawless society of nation-states. Desirous of making a lasting contribution to the cause of order and stability, he set as his task the writing of a definitive treatise that would convince statesmen they should be accountable to a higher authority than their own wills. Initially, in the Prolegomena to his great work, he expressed regret that so few persons had endeavored to produce a systematic and comprehensive treatise on laws which could govern "the mutual relations among states or rulers of states." The need for a treatise had become urgent, he felt, because of the events that had transpired in the Europe that he knew so well. To fill the need, Grotius realized he would have to produce a theoretical and substantive work which would have a minimal sectarian faith orientation but, being a theologian and a genuinely religious man himself, he felt constrained to ground his conceptions in theological premises. In chapter 3, a thorough examination was made of the manner in which he accomplished this in regard to the law of nature. A similar detailed analysis must now be made of the law of nations as he conceived it to determine whether it fits consistently into his entire conceptual scheme. As with his natural law theorizing, we will learn that his thoughts on a law of nations do not comprise a unified presentation. One cannot turn to a given section of the *De Jure Belli ac Pacis* and in a few minutes' time read a concise and well-organized rendition of his ideas on the subject. In attempting to produce a treatise that was more weighted to the substance of law than to its theoretical foundations, Grotius was once more given to an economy of words in regard to the latter. An analyst must search through his work to note the scattered references to a theory of a law of nations, and he is compelled to indulge in extensive cross-referencing and matching in order to derive meaning from them. The analyst is particularly confronted with the task of filling in the gaps where Grotius left so much unsaid. The whole process is akin to putting together the pieces of a puzzle so as to make a comprehensive picture. Where pieces are missing, the analyst must delve into the past to find them, hoping all the while that he will be able to complete a meaningful composition.

To approach a study of a law of nations as Grotius saw it, one can best begin by examining his concept of universal society and his concept of political association. In tracing these, one is struck by his Aristotelian and Stoic orientations and by the similarity of his views with those of Suarez. It has already been observed that Grotius did not consider human beings as ever having lived outside the bounds of society. Originally, all of humanity composed one vast society characterized by families and family groupings. In true Aristotelian fashion, Grotius maintained that human beings were social by nature, that from the dawn of creation they entered responsively into social relations. Nature determined that human beings should be weak; therefore, from compulsions of need and preservation they were directed toward social life. By natural reason, they were able to comprehend the advantages of social living. Grotius quoted from Lactantius to this effect:

> God, who did not impart wisdom to other animals, made them more safe from attack and from danger by natural means of defense. But because He made man naked and weak, to the end that He might the rather equip him with wisdom, in addition to other gifts He gave to man this feeling of mutual regard, that man should defend, should love, should protect man, and should both receive and furnish help against all dangers.[28]

The family was the natural unit of human association, but very quickly family groupings made up larger associations or

communities. With the broadened scope of human
relationships came the recognized need for formal institutionalized order. Grotius commented that "as soon as
numerous families were united at a common point, judges
were appointed, and to them alone was given the power to
avenge the injured, while others are deprived of the
freedom of action wherewith nature endowed them."[29] This
marked the progression from natural society to civil society.
"Public associations," distinguished by their magistracies,
were localized by territorial delimitations, and Grotius
implied that they were similar to townships, provinces,
and colonies.

The next stage of human association in the process of
naturalistic political evolution was the emergence of the
state and here, writing in terms of nationalistic separatism,
Grotius showed his theoretical confirmation of the trans-
formed political circumstances of sixteenth- and seventeenth-century Europe when he said the state "is a complete association of free men, joined together for the
enjoyment of rights and for their common interest."[30] In
book 2 he amplified this:

> An association in which many fathers of families unite into
> a single people and state gives the greatest right to the
> corporate body over its members. This in fact is the most
> perfect society. There is no lawful act of men which does not
> have relation to this association either of itself or by reason
> of the circumstances. And this is what Aristotle expressed
> in saying that "the laws prescribe concerning matters of
> every kind."[31]

A state, therefore, was a corporate community of persons
bound together under municipal or civil law. In Prolegomena 8 Grotius had remarked that the social order,
which was "consonant with human intelligence," was the
source of law. It was through an exercise of reason that
municipal law came into being. The *ius civile,* though
classed as human law, was derived from natural law;
therefore, the civil law and the society which prompted it
were both manifestations of the natural order of things. This

was set forth unequivocally where Grotius first summarily rejected the Sophistic idea that law was mere convention:

> What is said, therefore, in accordance with the view not only of Carneades, but also of others that
> Expediency is, as it were, the mother
> of what is just and fair
> is not true, if we wish to speak accurately. For the very nature of man, which even if we had no lack of anything, would lead us into the mutual relations of society, is the mother of the law of nature. But the mother of municipal law is that obligation which arises from mutual consent; and since this obligation derives its force from the law of nature, nature may be considered the greatgrandmother of municipal law.[32]

Though Grotius may have had a subjective preference, he gave no indication of favoring a "best" form of government. Human beings could agree on a wide range of possible forms, he said, from participant to absolutist. Different peoples, depending on unique circumstances, could choose the types of government most suited to their particular needs. People could exercise political and legal authority through magistrates of their choice who would be held accountable, or they could yield authority to some particular person. The actual constitution of a state determined the institutional structure of its government, as to who would rule and how he or they exercised this authority.

> Just as, in fact, there are many ways of living, one being better than another, and out of so many ways of living each is free to select that which he prefers, so also a people can select the form of government which it wishes; and the extent of its legal right in the matter is not to be measured by the superior excellence of this or that form of government, in regard to which different men hold different views, but by its free choice.[33]

Before he could deal effectively with a law of nations, Grotius had to give attention to one more facet of a state association, a facet which was actually a major prerequisite for the formulation of a theory. In defining the state as a "complete association," Grotius meant that it was self-sufficient, that is had the supreme power of sovereignty with no other human authority above it.

> That power is called sovereign [he said] whose actions are not subject to the legal control of another, so that they cannot be rendered void by another human will.[34]

In whom did this sovereignty actually reside, and in what way could it be exercised? Grotius repeated his conviction that human beings, by agreement, could establish the constitutional form of a state and thereby decide on whom they would confer the legal right to govern. This he set forth in no uncertain terms:

> All associations have this in common . . . that in those matters on account of which the association was formed the entire membership, or the majority in the name of the entire membership, may bind the individual members. In general it must be believed that it was the wish of those who united in an association that there should be some method of conducting business. But it is manifestly unfair that the majority should be ruled by the minority. Therefore, naturally, the majority has the same right as the entire body, if due exception is made of agreements and laws which prescribe the form of conducting business.[35]

The need for a "method of conducting business" called for the choice of designated agents who would be fully empowered to act on behalf of the members of the political society. These agents—"one or more persons, according to the law and customs of each nation"[36]—embodied sovereignty, and their acts, consequently, would be considered as binding on the whole people. They had to deal with matters both internal and external to the state. In the exercise of internal responsibilities the agents were obligated to act in such a manner as to guarantee the "enjoyment of rights" to all the members. In the exercise of external authority the agents conducted public relations, or relations among states, on behalf of the people they represented. In performing these functions they were agents in the fullest sense of the word, that is, they were only individuals acting by the authority entrusted to them by a collectivity of persons.

Should this be taken to mean, then, that sovereign authority was unrestrained externally in its actions so long as the interests of a state were being promoted? It was the purpose of Grotius to maintain that rulers and peoples were not without obligation in their external relationships. His basic contention was that the welfare of all human beings— their fulfillment as social creatures—could be made possible and ensured by overriding law. The state association was not a negation of, nor an escape from nature. It was just a reduction from the larger, universal, natural human society. It was a lesser manifestation, so to speak, of the greater reality. For Grotius, the state association did not cömplete the universal society; rather it was a convenience by which men could more easily pursue the natural purposes of that larger society of which they were always a part. In other words, men divided themselves into civil aggregates from motives of advantage, but the universal human society with its overriding natural obligations never ceased to exist and never lost its claims on all humankind.[37] State agents were not the fountainhead of all legal obligation. Whoever exercised the sovereign power within a state association was under liability to higher law. Just as civil law constituted the ordering authority within the individual state, so also a general law of all mankind constituted the ordering authority of universal society. If this were not true, Grotius insisted, if universal society did not have a legal character, then the laws of civil society would have no validity. Emanating from the universal human society was natural law and divine volitional law, and emanating from the political associations into which human beings had entered was civil law and —of great import—the volitional law of nations, which was rooted in the law of nature. In Prolegomena 16, Grotius had divided volitional law into divine and human law with the latter divided into municipal law (*ius civile*) and the law of nations (*ius gentium*). Both ruler and ruled were bound by these sources of law; no state association fell outside their scope. Grotius was especially emphatic on the obligations imposed on state agents by these laws for, as he said in book 1, chapter 3, " . . . observance of these is binding upon all kings, even though they have made no promise."[38] Quite clearly, the claim for laws over and above the state association revealed that the legal conceptualism of Grotius rejected the Machiavellian view that the state was the ultimate level of human experience.

Having asserted the reality of *ius gentium*, Grotius was faced with the task of defining it more carefully and of providing convincing justification for it. Both the definition and the attempted justification were woven throughout the Prolegomena and the three books of his treatise. To construct his system and to make a cogent presentation of it, Grotius first had to set definite boundaries for his thinking. He paralleled Aquinas and Suarez on a broad scheme of law, but he took issue with Suarez on the two senses of the *ius gentium*. Grotius categorized Suarez' *ius gentium* of the second sense as unwritten civil law. The unwritten laws common to all states but applicable only to internal matters were part of municipal law. Grotius referred to both written and unwritten municipal laws—the law of any separate state—as *ius civile singulorum populorum*. The unwritten laws were analytically separable but functionally the same as the written laws. He asserted his position with no equivocation whatsoever, revealing his departure from Suarez on the issue and referring to the Roman *ius gentium*, the unwritten law, as civil law. The very first line of his Prolegomena indicated his stance and his intention to concentrate on the *ius gentium* "proper," the body of law governing the relations among states:

> The municipal law of Rome [Suarez's *ius gentium* of the second sense] and of other states has been treated by many who have undertaken to elucidate it by means of com-

mentaries or to reduce it to a convenient digest. That body of law, however, which is concerned with *the mutual relations among states or rulers of states* [Suarez's *ius gentium* of the first sense], whether derived from nature, or established by divine ordinance, or having its origin in custom and tacit agreement, few have touched upon. Up to the present time no one has treated it in a comprehensive manner; yet the welfare of man demands that the task be accomplished.[39]

Later Grotius again had occasion to refer to the Roman *ius gentium*, and he proceeded to confirm the position he had taken:

This law of nations is not [*ius gentium*], strictly speaking, for it does not affect the mutual society of nations in relation to one another; it affects only each particular people in a state of peace.[40]

Pursuant to the task he had set for himself, Grotius declared that it was not his aim to devote time and space to a treatment of such "municipal" law; he wrote:

It is not our purpose to treat of the municipal law of states, for that would be an endless task, and the particular disputes relating to wars are not decided in accordance with municipal laws.[41]

To dispel any doubts that might still exist on the issue, one might turn also to book 1, chapter 1, where Grotius provided a negative approach to his subject and a negative definition of the law of nations by stating that his intention was to deal with "controversies among those who are not held together by a common bond of municipal law," and, furthermore, these controversies were "related either to times of war or to times of peace."[42] In essence, then, Grotius wanted to deal with those laws which were applicable to the relations among states and not with those which were common but relevant only to peoples within the separate nation-states, that is, Suarez's *ius gentium* of the second sense.

Grotius summarized his views on the law of nations in two sentences:

> The law which is broader in scope than municipal law is the law of nations; that is the law which has received its obligatory force from the will of all nations, or of many nations. I added "of many nations," for the reason that, outside of the sphere of the law of nature, which is also frequently called the law of nations, there is hardly any law common to all nations.[43]

His departure from Suarez on the issue of the two senses of the *ius gentium* is apparent here, but so also in his agreement with Suarez, and his disagreement with Aquinas, on the necessity of consent as the essential characteristic of a "proper" law of nations. Consent made the law of nations human law, thus distinguishing it but nevertheless giving it a relation to natural law. The consent was the same as that required for unwritten civil law. In Prolegomena 1, Grotius had stated that the mutual relations among states or rulers of states were to be regulated by laws derived from nature, from divine ordinances and from laws having "their origin in custom and tacit agreement," the latter being the law of nations. The law of nations, therefore, could not be deduced directly—i.e., "necessarily"—from the first principles of nature, but had to be grounded in the essential element of human consent as manifested in custom and usage. To forestall any objections and to dispel any doubts on the whole question, Grotius wrote:

> The proof for the law of nations is similar to that for unwritten municipal law; it is found in unbroken custom and the testimony of those who are skilled in it. The law of nations, in fact, as Dia Chrysostom well observes, "is the creation of time and custom." And for the study of it the illustrious writers of history are of the greatest value to us.[44]

Why were the divine ordinances (divine volitional law) and the precepts of nature not sufficient for regulating the mutual relations among nations? Like Aquinas, Grotius believed that the divine ordinances were more oriented to the specifics of supernatural fulfillment than to the fulfillment of the natural purposes of men, and the natural laws were too general for application to all the factual detailed circumstances of men in their multifarious relationships. The law of nature he saw as consisting of broad and unchanging principles of justice, principles that represented only the most general of general rules. In the *De Jure Belli ac Pacis* Grotius, even less than Aquinas, did not elaborate on the content of natural law in any great detail. He suggested in broad terminology that the natural law existed and that it was comprised of prohibitions and commands.[45] In book 2, chapter 20, where he had made a mathematical analogy to the law of nature, Grotius did try to illustrate his points with examples on content, but such a passage was an exception in his work.[46] If anything it showed the difficulty rather than the ease with which the law of nature might be delineated. In that passage Grotius said that the natural law consisted of first principles, precepts that were self-evident or "akin" to first principles, and deductions (inferences) from the first principles and self-evident axioms. It was a vertical scale, from certainty to probability. As one came down the scale, the rules at the lowest level became less obvious and, therefore, more obscure. The obscurity was such that the rules were often accepted only with difficulty. The further removed from their initial source, the greater was the burden of proof.

It was in connection with Grotius' exposition on volitional law that he expressed his thoughts on the subject of change. Grotius was unyielding in his conviction that the law of nature was unchangeable, even, as was learned, to the extent of directly stating that God himself could not alter it. Because volitional laws were founded on human consent—and were, therefore, subject to the vagaries of human will and changing social circumstances—Grotius was sensitive to the possibility of misunderstanding arising on the matter of change. If volitional law were grounded in natural law, and if it were granted that volitional law could undergo alteration, how could one maintain the immutability of natural law? In anticipation of such a question Grotius tried to make his position clear. In book 1, chapter 1, section 10, subsection 5, he had stated his case for the immutability of natural law. Following hard on this, he said:

> Sometimes nevertheless it happens that in the acts in regard to which the law of nature has ordained something, an appearance of change deceives the unwary, although in fact the law of nature, being unchangeable, undergoes no change; but the thing, in regard to which the law of nature has ordained, undergoes change.[47]

Not the law of nature itself, but the subject matter to which it had reference was altered, he said. That statement was simple enough, but behind it there lay a wealth of hidden meaning. That meaning can be uncovered once more only by relating the thought of Grotius to the refined arguments of Suarez who, by self-declaration, was expounding what he interpreted as the position of Aristotle and Aquinas. We have already become well acquainted with the views of Suarez on natural law as presented in book 2, chapter 6 of his *De Legibus ac Deo Legislatore*. In book 2, chapter 14 of the same work he devoted considerable space to a discussion of change in relation to natural law and to the *ius gentium* as he saw it in a dual sense. The main strength of his presentation rested on three assertions. First, he said, no human power—not even papal power—could abrogate any proper precept of natural law; neither could any power restrict such a precept nor grant a dispensation from it.

> . . . the natural law, insofar as its precepts are concerned, is by its very nature unchangeable; and men cannot change that which is unchangeable. . . . This argument is confirmed and made clear by the fact that the natural law, in all its precepts, relates to the natural qualities of mankind; and man cannot change the nature of things. . . . God is the Lawgiver; and man cannot change a law that God has

established, since an inferior cannot prevail as against a superior.[48]

## Secondly, said Suarez

. . . the precepts of the natural law which depend for their preceptive force *upon a prior consent of the human will*, and upon the efficacy of that will to issue in some action, may sometimes be subjected to human dispensation, involving not a direct and absolute abolition of the obligation of natural law but a certain remission that affects the subject matter [of the precept in question].[49]

To change or to vary the subject matter of such precepts, he continued, was not contrary to natural law, "since such a variation depends upon a change of human volition."[50]

Furthermore, once this change has been effected, not only is there no obstacle necessarily opposed to the abolition of [that particular] obligation of the natural law, but the obligation lapses even of itself, and ceases to exert a binding force. Nay, more: a private individual can sometimes do away with the natural obligation arising from a promise (for instance, by remitting it) or with the obligation arising from a loan by making it completely a gift.[51]

Suarez then took his argument to its utmost reaches in his third assertion where he said:

. . . through human law, whether it be the *ius gentium* or the civil law, there may be effected in the subject matter of the natural law a change of such sort that, by reason thereof the obligation imposed by natural law will also change. . . . The rational basis of the said assertion is the fact that such a mode of change is not inconsistent with the necessary and unchangeable character of the natural law; and that, for the rest, it is convenient and frequently necessary for men, in accordance with the various changes of estate which befall them. In this connection, too, one may fittingly apply the familiar illustration drawn from Augustine, namely, that just as the science of medicine lays down certain precepts for the sick, others for the well, certain precepts for the strong, and others for the weak, although the rules of medicine do not therefore undergo essential change, but merely become manifold, so that some serve on one occasion, and others, on another occasion; even so, the natural law while it remains [in itself] the same, lays down one precept for one occasion and another, for another occasion; and is binding previously or subsequently, and this without undergoing any change in itself but merely because of change in the subject matter.[52]

Suarez reverted to the controversial issue of private property in order to counter the possible argument that voluntary laws were actually rules that were contrary to the natural law and thereby effected changes in it. He cited the contention of Christian traditionalists who said that, before the commission of sin by man, the natural law decreed that all property should be held in common, whereas after the fall from innocence, this precept was annulled so that private property was not then contrary to the law of nature. Suarez also cited an opinion of Duns Scotus who had a variation on the above argument to the effect that the fall from innocence and the introduction of private property did not really bring any intrinsic and true change in natural law but simply resulted in a cessation of its binding force, "owing to a change made by men and therefore made in the subject matter itself."[53] To refute such views, Suarez indulged in some deft reasoning. He stated that there were two senses in which a matter came under the natural law— negative and positive.

It is said that [a given action] falls negatively under the natural law because that law does not prohibit, but on the contrary permits [the said action], while not positively prescribing its performance. When, however, something is prescribed by natural law, that prescription is said to be positively a part of natural law; and when anything is prohibited thereby, the thing thus prohibited is said to be positively opposed to natural law. Hence, a division of property is not contrary to positive natural law; for there was no natural precept to forbid the making of such a division.

Therefore, when certain legal precepts are said to be opposed to the law of nature, they are to be thought of in their negative relationship to natural law; for ownership in common was a part of natural law in the sense that by virtue of that law all property would be held in common if men had not introduced any different provision. Such is the deduction to be drawn from St. Thomas (2-2, qu. 66, art. 2, ad. 1, and 1-2, qu. 94, art. 5, ad. 3).[54]

What Suarez meant, stated more simply, was that natural law had permitted, but did not require, ownership in common. After private property came into being under human volitional law, natural precepts still applied to common property but natural law now forbade interference with anything which had come under private control.

In chapter 20 of book 2, Suarez finalized his argument on change. Having dealt thoroughly with the *ius gentium* in relation to natural law, he ventured to state:

. . . from the above discussion one may infer [the corollary] that the *ius gentium* is subject to change, insofar as it is dependent upon the consent of men; and in this respect also the *ius gentium* differs from the natural law. . . . Therefore, the corollary must be understood as referring to the *ius gentium* as a system of law that contains prohibitions or precepts. For these are of themselves subject to change; and the reason [for their mutability] is that the things prohibited by the *ius gentium* are not, absolutely speaking, evil (in themselves and intrinsically) in view of two facts: first, because the precepts in question are not deduced from natural principles by a necessary and evident inference; secondly, because the obligation imposed by the *ius gentium* does not spring from reason alone, apart from human obligation of every sort, even from that which has its source in general custom. Hence, insofar as pertains to the subject matter of that system of law, it is not absolutely inconsistent with reason that the said law should be subjected to change, provided that the change be made on sufficient authority.[55]

Hence, though a precept of volitional law may change

externally in reference to changing human circumstances, the precept in essence was still consistent with the basic principles of natural law. Not only was this true for the *ius gentium* as a law of nations, but it was also true of the *ius gentium* as the unwritten municipal law on which there was common agreement. Change was easy of accomplishment for the latter, said Suarez, because it could be done within a single nation-state; for the former, however, change was more complicated.

> In connection with the other phase of the *ius gentium* (law of nations), however, changes are far more difficult, for this phase involves law common to all nations and appears to have been introduced by the authority of all, so that it may not be annulled (even in part) without universal consent. Nevertheless, there would be no inherent obstacle to change, insofar as the subject matter of such law is concerned, if all nations should agree to the alteration, or if a custom contrary to [some established rule of this law of nations] should gradually come into practice and prevail.[56]

In book 2, Grotius revealed his agreement with Suarez on the way change is effected in regard to positive human law (i.e., Suarez's *ius gentium* of the two senses or, as Grotius saw them, the law of nations and unwritten municipal law). His brief sentences indicate that his thought was undergirded by the more extensive and complex reasoning of the Spanish Jesuit. Unwritten municipal law relates only to a particular people in a state of peace, he said; therefore:

> For this reason a single people can change its determination without consulting others, and even this happens, that on different times and places a far different common custom, and therefore a different law of nations (improperly so called) might be introduced.[57]

The *ius gentium* as the law of nations, on the other hand, required the consent of all or almost all of the nations for its validity; by the same token, the agreement of all or nearly all was required to alter that law. Once a rule had been established and was in force, it could not be changed by the unilateral action of any single nation. For any rule or for any change, it had always to be considered to what extent the nations actually reached an agreement.[58]

In the midst of his discussion on change, Grotius expressed his conviction that the law of nature, because of its generality, made allowance for a broad area of what was permissible. Once more it is of striking interest that Suarez had done the same. In his *De Legibus ac Deo Legislatore*, Suarez included this realistic passage:

> I must add, indeed, that there is a difference between the *ius gentium*, and the natural law in its strict interpretation. For the latter not only prescribes the performance of good acts but also prohibits all evil acts in such a way as to be tolerant of none; whereas the *ius gentium* may permit some evils. . . . This statement would seem to apply especially to that form of the *ius gentium* which is in point of fact civil law, but which is called *ius gentium* by analogy and owing to mutual agreement thereon among the nations. For just as certain evils are tolerated by the civil law, so also they may be by the *ius gentium*; since this very toleration may be so necessary, in view of the frailty of mankind or of business affairs, that almost all nations agree in manifesting it.[59]

Suarez went on to say that the expression "is permissible" in relation to volitional law should not be strictly interpreted:

> The expression "is permissible," then, ought to be taken in a broad sense and as relating to human judgments, in accordance with the fact that a thing is said to be permissible when it is done with impunity and tolerated by usage, which is the same as to say that it is permitted. Or else one may offer the following explanation, which amounts to very nearly the same thing: the act in question is "naturally permissible"—that is, "permissible by the *ius gentium*"— which is to say that it is "not forbidden" thereby; this permissibility being based, not on the fact that natural law in its strict sense does not prohibit the said act, but rather on the fact that the *ius gentium*, inasmuch as it is a human system of law, does not include a special prohibition as to

the point in question, decreeing on the contrary that the act
is not punishable and is not to be considered as a crime in a
human state or court of justice.[60]

Positive human law assumed a place of great importance
in the overall scheme of Grotius because he believed that
many of its rulings, both as *ius civile* and as *ius gentium*,
could be classified within the area of permissibility.
Permissible rules would in no way be contrary to natural law
but would "spell out" the laws of nature in greater detail so
that human beings would be able to strive for fulfillment of
their natural aims as social beings. The broad area for
permissible behavior within the framework of natural law
was to be filled by rules derived by "reduction," that is, a
rule for conduct could be justified as being in accordance
with natural law when it was considered as not being a law
of nature in the strict sense, but as a residual law not
prohibited by natural law. Said Grotius:

> For the understanding of the law of nature, again, we must
> note that certain things are said to be according to this law
> not in a proper sense but—as the Schoolmen love to say—by
> reduction, the law of nature not being in conflict with them;
> just as we said above that things are called just which are free
> from injustice.[61]

Later he wrote:

> . . . sometimes that is said to be permissible which is right
> from every point of view and is free from reproach, even if
> there is something else that might more honourably be
> done. . . . In another sense, however, something is said to
> be permissible, not because it can be done without violence
> to right conduct and rules of duty, but because among men it
> is not liable to punishment.[62]

By this intellectual technique, Grotius created a tie between
natural law and all rules deemed valid within the scope of
permissibility. If no prohibition of any human act could be
determined by an exercise of reason, then that act could be
considered as not being in conflict with natural law.

Actually, the law of nature, as Grotius conceived it, would have been an adequate standard for governing human relations. The law of nature was predicated upon the rational and social nature of man, and it was not essential, therefore, that any act must have a natural quality about it in the sense that it was common to all animals and men or that it had an imaginary origin in pre-civil, or natural, society. The natural qualities of men as rational beings in social contact with each other constituted the proper subject for the application of natural law. Because of the difficulties attendant upon the process of making deductions from the natural law, however, Grotius postulated the extended need for volitional laws and presented his ideas on permissibility. The purpose of volitional law was to create rules for specific factual circumstances, and these rules could be fashioned in accordance with courses of action that were possible and permissible within the framework of the natural law. In a situation where the natural law was obscure and where there was a compelling need for volitional rules to apply, then the assumption could be made that the natural law was still efficacious. Through this logic there was no lapse in law, since every human relationship could be subjected to the law of nature, no matter how vague. Grotius, in order to provide a broad "umbrella" of law, tried to anticipate every eventuality. He would grant no instance where there would be no coverage by law, either natural or volitional. With this scope of conceptualism, Grotius had formulated the intellectual basis for his deepest conviction, namely, that conflicts among states and behavior in warfare could be brought under the rule of law.

# 5.

# Grotius
# and the
# Law of War*

IN 1622 WHEN GROTIUS embarked upon the writing of his masterpiece, one of the specific aims he had in mind was to create a theoretical foundation for a law of war and to set down a body of substantive rules for the guidance of nations and individuals. The preface of his work not only signified this aim but also indicated his desire to classify the law of war under the *ius gentium* or law of nations, which, in turn, was grounded in the law of nature. In Prolegomena 28 he expressed the revulsion he felt for the lawlessness which had characterized the conflicts of history and of his own time, and in Prolegomena 3 he strongly expressed the need for a comprehensive and systematic law of nations on which the law of war could be based.

Such a work is all the more necessary because in our own day, as in former times, there is no lack of men who view this branch of law with contempt as having no reality outside of an empty name. On the lips of men quite generally is the saying of Euphemus, which Thucydides quotes, that in the case of a king, or imperial city nothing is unjust which is

* This chapter, with some changes and additions, first appeared as a published article. See Charles S. Edwards, *Journal of Public Law* (1970), vol. 19, no. 2, pp. 371-97. Reprinted by permission of the *Emory Law Journal* (formerly *Journal of Public Law*) of the Emory University School of Law.

expedient. Of like implication is the statement that for those whom fortune favors might makes right, and that the administration of a state cannot be carried on without injustice.

Furthermore, the controversies which arise between peoples or kings generally have Mars as their arbiter. That war is irreconcilable with all law is a view held not alone by the ignorant populace; expressions are often let slip by well-informed and thoughtful men which lend countenance to such a view.[1]

Grotius was indeed conscious of the fact that wars were fought and concluded from the perspective of superior political and military power rather than from the perspective of right and reason. His moral and legal sensitivities were disturbed, principally, at the prevalence of what he considered to be unjust wars. As a theorist and as a jurist Grotius was greatly concerned with justice, because if war were to be utilized as an arbitrary means for pursuing human interests or for settling human differences, then justice would be a hopeless ideal. The justice or injustice of war, he believed, had to be determined in reference to the precepts of the law of nature. He was disturbed further by the evidences he saw everywhere of the acceptance of practices in war as valid which, in his opinion, were flagrantly at odds with the law of nature. He could see no justification, for example, for the indiscriminate killing of women and children or of farmers and of prisoners during warfare. His intention was that of exposing and denouncing such practices within his total scheme of law whereby the conduct of nations and individuals could find a logical and rational relationship.

To appreciate the role which he assigned to war in his thinking, one must understand his conception of violence. Basically, Grotius felt that a resort to violence was a trait of nonrational creatures. Since man was by nature a rational being, the brutal, insensitive behavior of the primitive tribes and of pagan peoples was, to his mind, not natural. He saw violent practices as the inevitable result of evil which negated the sociability of men. By the law of nature men were meant to be social, he said, and thus, "it is an impious crime that one should be injured by another."[2] By indulging in indiscriminate violence, men only denied their true nature. In making specific reference to pagan customs on war, Grotius commented, "But we have said elsewhere that such laws were relics of the nomadic ages, in which the usages had dulled the natural social sense which exists among all men."[3] Violence, in the last analysis, was destructive of human society and the great society of states. It was highly desirable, therefore, that "good faith" (just conduct) be manifested in the behavior of nations and individuals and that peace be maintained when possible.

. . . good faith should be preserved, not only for other reasons but also in order that the hope of peace may not be done away with. For not only is every state sustained by good faith, as Cicero declares, but also that greater society of states. Aristotle truly says that, if good faith has been taken away, "all intercourse among men ceases to exist."

Rightly the same Cicero says that "it is an impious act to destroy the good faith which holds life together." To use Seneca's, it is "the most exalted good of the human heart." And this good faith the supreme rulers of men ought so much the more earnestly than others to maintain as they violate it with greater impunity; if good faith shall be done away with, they will be like wild beasts, whose violence all men fear.[4]

If violence were contrary to human nature, how then could Grotius, in the face of such a conviction, validate war as a necessary part of his scheme of law? He did it by postulating war as a tool for fulfilling the natural purposes of men. War need not be considered in the negative sense as being disruptive of order, but rather in the positive sense of promoting it. For Grotius, war was an external fact which had no inherent moral connotations. Right reason did not pronounce against it but only against force which was in conflict with the needs of society. Morality in regard to war, therefore, arose only in connection with the way in which men utilized it. War could thereby be an evil or a good. Barbaric practices in war had led many to totally condemn it, but Grotius believed that war could be brought under the rule of reason and used to serve positive human ends. Force was allowable to maintain legitimate rights,[5] and, as such, it was not irreconcilable with law. It could be resorted to for the purpose of executing justice against those who were too strong to be submitted to the courts or subjected to any judge.[6] War, correctly used, was an instrument of rational, civilized men and had as its function the preservation of society. In sum, Grotius was not a pacifist, for he believed war could be utilized as an instrument in the service of the law of nature. War could be evidence of the fact that laws were existent and operative.

> Last of all should that be admitted which some people imagine, that in war all laws are in abeyance. On the contrary war ought not to be undertaken except for the enforcement of rights; when once undertaken, it should be carried on only within the bounds of law and good faith. Demosthenes well said that war is directed against those who cannot be held in check by judicial processes. For judgments are efficacious against those who feel that they are too weak to resist; against those who are equally strong, or think that they are, wars are undertaken. But in order that wars may be justified, they must be carried on with not less scrupulousness than judicial processes are wont to be.
>
> Let the laws be silent then, in the midst of arms, but only the laws of the state, those that the courts are concerned with, that are adapted only to a state of peace; not those other laws, which are of perpetual validity and suited to all times.[7]

Grotius was following here in the tradition of some classic and Christian predecessors who had reasoned that war could be either proper or improper. He made reference to Sallust, Roman historian of the first century B.C., who asserted that war should be utilized for the maintenance of social order,

and to Aristotle, who denounced aggressive wars predicated
on self-interest, but who approved war waged in the interest
of social preservation.[8] Undoubtedly Grotius was familiar
with Cicero, who had speculated upon the justice or
injustice of war,[9] and he revealed his knowledge of
Augustine's just war theory as set forth in *The City of God*.[10]

> Sallust most truly said, "The wise wage war for the sake of
> peace." With this the opinion of Augustine agrees: "Peace
> is not sought that war may be followed, but war is waged
> that peace may be secured." Aristotle himself more than
> once condemns those nations which made warlike pursuits,
> as it were, their end and aim. Violence is most manifest in
> war; wherefore the more diligently effort should be put forth
> that it be tempered with humanity, lest by imitating wild
> beasts too much we forget to be human.[11]

Convinced, therefore, that there was "a common law
among nations, which is valid alike for war and in war,"[12]
Grotius turned to systematizing his thoughts on the subject.
He wanted no misunderstanding on the position he was
adopting; he stated at the outset that he intended to find a
compatible relationship between the ideal principles of the
law of nature and the actual customs of war which were
accepted by all the nations. Grotius seemed well aware of
the futility of playing the role of either a complete idealist
or a complete realist. His purpose was to strike the balance
so that "men may not believe that nothing is allowable or
that everything is."[13] His starting point was his definition
of war:

> As we set out to treat the law of war, then, we ought to see
> what is war, which we are treating, and what is the law which
> forms the subject of our investigation.
> Cicero defined war as a contending by force. A usage has
> gained currency, however, which designates by the word not
> a contest but a condition; thus war is the condition of those
> contending by force, viewed simply as such. The general
> definition includes all the classes of wars which it will
> hereafter be necessary to discuss. For I do not exclude

private war, since in fact it is more ancient than public war and has, incontestably, the same nature as public war; wherefore both should be designated by one and the same word.[14]

The justice or the injustice of war had to be proven, said Grotius, and it was his earnest hope to supply the criteria for such proof. As a legal scholar and historian, Grotius must have been fully cognizant of the ideas of his predecessors. Aristotle had written that war could be justified in three instances:

> Training for war should not be pursued with a view to enslaving men who do not deserve such a fate. Its objects should be these—first, to prevent men from ever becoming enslaved themselves; secondly, to put men in a position to exercise leadership—but leadership directed to the interest of the led, and not to the establishment of a general system of slavery; and thirdly, to enable men to make themselves masters of those who naturally deserve to be slaves.[15]

Cicero had argued for just causation in war, maintaining that war could be waged only for purposes of honor (to avenge wrongs or to punish for injuries received) or for purposes of safety (defense).[16] Augustine, acknowledging Cicero in *The City of God*, approved this dual justification, asserting first, "It is therefore agreed that, according to Cicero, a state should engage in war for the safety which preserves the state permanently in existence. . . ."[17] Augustine proceeded to list what he termed the "real evils" of war—"love of violence, revengeful cruelty, fierce and implacable enmity, wild resistance, and the lust of power, and such like"—and concluded that

> . . . it is generally to punish these things, when force is required to inflict the punishment, that, in obedience to God or some lawful authority, good men undertake wars, when they find themselves in such a position as regards the conduct of human affairs, that right conduct requires them to act, or to make others act, in this same way.[18]

Grotius observed that the sources from which wars arise were "as numerous as those from which lawsuits spring," but he summarized the thought of his predecessors by categorizing just causation under three headings, saying, "Authorities generally assign to wars three justifiable causes, defence, recovery of property, and punishment."[19] Most of his second book was devoted to an elaboration of this. He went into great detail to list the rights which could be maintained by the ultimate sanction of war. Since there were no institutions above the state association which could adjudicate controversies and enforce decisions among nations, the final means for obtaining or defending rights consisted of a resort to war. In advocating war as a sanction to right wrongs, Grotius gave his universal human society a legal character. Even where formal, centralized institutions for authoritative decision making were lacking, war could be utilized by moral leaders who represented common humanity and who acted under the dictates of reason. Within states, civil laws provided legal remedies for the protection of rights. In an organized political society, the individual renounced his personal right to redress wrongs committed against him. The community acted for him. States, however (that is, governments or the agents of governments), in their relations with each other had no superior authority to which to turn for a redress of wrongs. Hence, force, or just war, could be used as a means for serving justice. It was imperative, however, that a just war be waged within just limits. It had to be moral in accordance with the law of nature. The extent to which war could be used was limited by the nature and the scope of the wrong which instigated it.[20]

Wars could be of three types, according to Grotius:

> The first and most essential division of war is that into public war, private war and mixed war. A public war is that which is waged by him who has lawful authority to wage it; a private war, that which is waged by one who has not the lawful authority; and a mixed war is that which is on one side public, on the other side private.[21]

In a just war, no matter of what type, only one side could be in the right:

> In the particular sense and with reference to the thing itself, a war cannot be just on both sides, just as a legal claim cannot; the reason is that by the very nature of the case a moral quality cannot be given to opposites as to doing and restraining.[22]

Grotius made allowance for human frailty, however, and thus admitted the difficulty of making an objective judgment in some situations. There were, indeed, cases where definite just causes could be established for wars; but, on the other hand, there were more uncertain cases where just causes were not easily determinable because of the fallibility of men. Regarding the "thing itself," that is, the just war, it was always true that only one side could be just, but whether men were always able to discern this was another question. Grotius conceded that cases could arise where neither party would have a just cause, and, here too, one would have to make allowance for human fallibility. As he stated:

> Yet it may actually happen that neither of the warring parties does wrong. No one acts unjustly without knowing that he is doing an unjust thing, but in this respect many are ignorant. Thus either party may justly, that is in good faith, plead his case. For both in law and in fact many things out of which a right arises ordinarily escape the notice of men.[23]

To say who had a just cause of war according to the law of nature, then, was one of those problematical areas where the rational efforts of men to apply abstract principles of natural law to factual circumstances could be strained to the utmost. Hopefully, such instances would be rare. The fact that by age-old custom the belligerents in a formal public war had been considered as being equal in the justice of their cause presented a major difficulty for Grotius. Each party had been permitted to use extremes of violence for conducting hostilities but to hold that each had a just cause was not in accordance with nature and was, by definition, impossible. Any effort, therefore, on the part of Grotius to include such customs in his legal system would theaten the entire structure he was trying to build on the foundation of the law of nature. Yet such customs existed and could not be ignored. Above all, they could not be left outside the boundaries of the law. The question, then, was how could these customs be reconciled with his legal system? To avoid the difficulty, Grotius resorted to his argument on permissibility which pushed his rationalism to the outer limits. Grotius said that the law of nature in regard to war could be supplemented, like other provisions of that law, with rules of positive volitional law. Such rules, ideally, should never be in opposition to the law of nature, yet, he admitted, there were provisions of the law of nations which *seemed* to permit actions forbidden by natural law. This was especially true in reference to formal public wars.[24] Acts of force seemingly contrary to the law of nature were allowed because the age-old customs of nations dictated that such acts were not punishable. Any belligerent did not have to fear being called to account for them, since these actions did not represent a wrong in their outward effect. In the Prolegomena Grotius had stated that in developing his scheme of law, one main intent was to distinguish the law of nature from the law of nations as much as possible. He immediately expressed a second intention in the same passage:

> Furthermore, in the law of nations I have distinguished between that which is truly in all respects law, and that which produces merely a kind of outward effect simulating that primitive law, as, for example, the prohibition to resist by force, or even the duty of defence in any place by public force, in order to secure some advantage, or for the avoidance of serious disadvantage.[25]

By means of the legalistic artifice of permissibility Grotius once again sought to keep his system intact. He was certainly realistic in recognizing the existence of practices in the relations of nations which had the appearance of being contrary to the law of nature, but he never relinquished his idealism, since he strove to find a theoretical justification for such behavior. Grotius might be severely criticized for this aspect of his thought. It could be said that he extended his justification to the point where any behavior could be allowed under the doctrine of permissibility. It must be kept in mind, however, that Grotius was sincerely motivated to bring all human actions under the restraint of law. He in no way stated that *all* conduct was permissible; he made it quite clear that only those rules which had the *consent* of nations were to be recognized. Simply because certain actions were performed frequently and by most nations did not mean that those actions were in accordance with law. It was not sufficient to claim that tradition or the force of precedent bound men to the observance of any action. The rules of volitional law had to be accepted as obligatory by the nations which consented to them. There had to be unambiguous observance of the particular rule of law. Some mutual advantage must have impelled the nations to consent to the volitional regulation.

Aware of the possibilities of having his permissible laws of nations misconstrued, Grotius was most anxious that all of the sovereigns of his day would feel bound in conscience by the law of nature whenever they indulged in legal public wars. He tried to impress upon them that all circumstances arising out of those wars were subject to the precepts of natural law.

Because matters regarding the permissible fell within that area which was farthest removed from natural law on the deductive scale, judgments as to what was or what was not allowable were often difficult to make. Grotius was cognizant of this dilemma.

Thus it comes about that between what should be done and what it is wrong to do there is a mean, that which is permissible; and this is now closer to the former, now to the latter. Hence, there often comes a moment of doubt, just as when day passes into night, or when cold water slowly becomes warm. This is what Aristotle means when he says: "Oftentimes it is hard to decide what choices one should make." Andronicus of Rhodes states the matter thus: "It is hard to distinguish what is truly just from that which appears to be so."[26]

In this situation, said Grotius, one should follow Cicero's advice: "That is a good rule which they lay down who bid you not to do a thing when you are in doubt whether it is right or wrong." But, Grotius continued:

> This course, however, cannot be pursued where one really must do one of two things, and yet is in doubt whether either is right. In that case he will be allowed to choose that which appears to him to be less wrong. For always, when a choice cannot be avoided, the lesser evil assumes the aspect of the good. "We must take the least among evils," says Aristotle; and Cicero, "Of evil one must choose the least." Quintilian writes: "In a comparison of evils, the lesser evil takes the place of the good."[27]

Thus, wherever doubt could not be resolved and where a choice still had to be made, Grotius recommended strongly that a decision be made against war. In war too many sufferings fell upon the innocent. Peace, therefore, was to be preferred, for it was better to err on that side than on the other:

> Therefore, in the midst of divergent opinions we must lean towards peace. Silus Italicus praises Fabius, for—
> With cautious mind the future did he scan,
> Nor took delight
> To stir up war for causes
> Slight and doubtful.[28]

In pursuing this theme, Grotius suggested three methods by which disputes could be prevented from breaking into wars. The first method was by conference. This was to be desired, for, quoting Cicero, he said that arguments were characteristic of men while force was characteristic of beasts, and men should have recourse to the latter only when they were not permitted to use the former. The second method which he recommended was arbitration, and it was applicable among those who had no common judicial authority.

> Especially, however, Christian kings and states are bound to pursue this method of avoiding wars. For if certain arbiters were established both by Jews and by Christians in order that the sentences of strange judges might be avoided by those of the true faith, and this was prescribed by Paul, how much more should this be done to avoid a far greater disadvantage, that is, war? . . . Both for this and for other reasons it would be advantageous, indeed in a degree necessary, to hold certain conferences of Christian powers, where those who have no interest at stake may settle the disputes of others, and where, in fact, steps may be taken to compel parties to accept peace on fair terms.[29]

If all efforts at reasonable settlement failed, then men could resort to a third method, said Grotius, which was still far preferable to war.

> The third method is by lot. . . . Something akin to the lot furthermore, is single combat. Resort to single combat it does not seem necessary altogether to reject if two persons, whose disputes would otherwise afflict whole peoples with very serious evils, are ready to settle their dispute by arms, as in olden times. . . .[30]

None of these methods, of course, constituted a panacea for settling the differences which arose among nations or individuals. The difficulties attendant upon the use of lot or single combat were obvious and need no discussion. Regarding conference, the negotiations were to take place among parties to a dispute to the exclusion of third parties. Any solution was dependent upon bilateral obligations which embodied the risk of unilateral violation. Arbitration, in contrast, involved the creation of a new legal authority by the consent of the disputants for the purpose of promoting agreement. Grotius did not advocate any standing organization of arbitrators between states, and the limitation of his contribution to the subject was exemplified by the fact that he did not mention arbitration with respect to contractual relations, that is, the interpretation of treaties or with respect to torts. The possibility of arbitration between individuals of different nations received no attention from him. Grotius recognized the shortcomings of his modest treatment of the subject. Regarding the question of appeal of an arbitral award, he said that the process

> . . . cannot become applicable in relation to kings and peoples. For here there is no higher power, which can either hold fast or loosen the bond of promise. Under such conditions, therefore, the decision of arbitrators, whether just or unjust, must stand absolutely, so that one may rightly apply here the saying of Pliny: "Each makes the man whom he chooses the supreme judge of his case." It is, in fact, one thing to make inquiry concerning the duty of the arbitrator, and another to inquire concerning the obligation of those who promise.[31]

Lacking a process for appeal, the arbitral method merely lifted any decision of justice or injustice one level higher than the states which were involved in the claim. The possibility of a final solution was not greatly increased thereby. Another problem in arbitration centered around the enforcement of an award. The arbitrator, if he were strong enough and chose to do so, could have assumed the responsibility for executing the award. In the absence of this, the disputants could resort to war as an ultimate solution, but conflict, ironically enough, would have been the very thing which arbitration was designed to prevent. One can understand, then, why Grotius looked hopefully to the Christian powers of his time to provide a kind of informal collective enforcement of the law of nations. Periodic conferences would be advantageous, as he wrote, since by means of these, "steps may be taken to compel parties to accept peace on fair terms."[32]

Generally, it can be said that the highest hope of Grotius was to impose moderation and control upon the relations of nations and individuals by making the consciences of men sensitive to the law of nature and by expounding a system of volitional law common to them all. The common law, in turn, was not to receive its validation from mere custom as expressed in arbitrary will, but rather it would receive its validation from custom genuinely based on natural law, which established limitations for behavior. Even in a situation where a just cause could not be determined objectively, the parties to a dispute were still responsible by the law of nature for any consequences emanating from their actions. Though Grotius reflected a realistic bent in his thought, he nevertheless made a simultaneous appeal for humanitarian sensitivity to mitigate the brutalities of war. Throughout the third book of his treatise he interjected rules of moderation, *temperamenta*, which the law of nature required of those who made use of the rights of war. These rules were especially applicable, he urged, in situations where war was initiated and conducted under the permissible laws of nations. He wrote:

> I must retrace my steps and must deprive those who wage war of nearly all the privileges when I seemed to grant, yet did not grant them. For when I first set out to explain this part of the law of nations, I bore witness that many things are said to be "lawful" or "permissible" for the reason that they are done with impunity, in part also because coactive tribunals lend to them their authority; things which, nevertheless, either deviate from the rule of right . . . or at any rate may be omitted on higher grounds and with greater praise among good men.[33]

The chapter and section headings throughout his third book indicate the deprivations he had in mind for those who would have been tempted to excesses on the "seeming" privileges of the permissible laws of nations.[34] These chapters and sections detail the provisions of moderation which limit the legal rights of war.

One function of volitional laws, Grotius had said, was to bring clarity to nebulous and confusing conclusions that were drawn from the natural law. As men gained in their social experience, volitional laws could undergo reinterpretation so as to be fully in accord with changing circumstances and to be more harmonious with the true law of nature. By this reasoning Grotius made provision for progressive growth in the law of nations. Hence, there was no obstacle to improvements that might be introduced into the rules of war by the consent of nations. The laws of war were, indeed, volitional laws created by mutual consent. By similar consent, either express or implied, these laws could be changed or superseded entirely. Grotius, no doubt, envisioned his *temperamenta* as potential improvements in this regard. By adopting the moderations which he recommended, the nations would be able to achieve a higher level of civilization and refinement in their relations. The burden for progressive growth, Grotius believed, was actually upon the more civilized nations. He sincerely hoped that his ideas would be heeded by those who had the power and capacity to turn them into practice. His closing words in book 3 were in the form of an earnest prayer, entreating men to exercise sufficient wisdom in the future to perfect their sociability and to preserve life:

> May God, who alone hath the power, inscribe these teachings on the hearts of those who hold sway over the Christian world. May He grant to them a mind possessing knowledge of divine and human law, and having ever before it the reflection that it hath been chosen as a servant for the rule of man, the living thing most dear to God.[35]

A discussion of the laws of war would not be complete without giving some consideration to the ideas which Grotius had on the justice of resistance to authority.[36]

J. B. Scott maintained that Grotius, an erstwhile diplomat badly in need of employment, did not want to offend the reigning monarchs of his day by identifying himself with a bold and uncompromising endorsement of popular sovereignty and a doctrine of resistance. Scott gives the impression that Grotius avoided these topics at all costs, but, in fact, he embraced these ideas in a very tactful, comprehensive, and legally persuasive way.[37] So as not to stir antagonism, particularly on the subject of resistance, Grotius apparently developed his thought in successive stages, beginning with a doctrine of nonresistance justified under municipal law, then making allowance for passive and forceful resistance, also justified under municipal law, then proceeding finally to a justification for intervention and even tyrannicide under the law of nature and the law of nations.

After developing his conception of just war, Grotius said:

> The question to be considered here is simply this, whether it is permissible for either private or official persons to wage war against those under whose authority they are, whether this authority be sovereign or subordinate.[38]

Initially, Grotius seems to deprive subjects of the right of forcible resistance.

> By nature all men have the right of resistance in order to ward off injury. . . . But as civil society was instituted in order to maintain public tranquility, the state forthwith acquires over us and our possessions a greater right to the extent necessary to accomplish this end. The state, therefore, in the interest of public peace and order, can limit that common right of resistance. That such was the purpose of the state we cannot doubt, since it could not in any other way achieve its end. If, in fact, the right of resistance should remain without restraint, there will no longer be a state, but only a non-social horde, such as that of the Cyclopes. . . .[39]

Social stability, clearly, was the reason for the existence of civil society, and, on this basis, Grotius predicated his doctrine of non-resistance to sovereign authority. In advocating such a doctrine, Grotius was not arbitrarily creating a legal justification for his own personal preference on the matter. Though non-resistance was not a conclusion drawn "necessarily" from the law of nature nor a precept of divine volitional law, it had firm validation in human volitional law. The doctrine was pertinent to the existence and well-being of a state and was confirmed by the approval of those who were bound by it. Its existence was not dependent upon a necessary agreement with rational and social nature but upon social need, a better regulation of human affairs within the area of permissible actions which contributed to public tranquility and the general good. To support his view, Grotius utilized his usual methodology of citing the testimonies of many persons, thus summarizing all the theoretical, theological, and historical evidence at his command in order to point to what he called a "universal cause." By this procedure he concluded that the doctrine was valid almost everywhere. But it did not come under his law of nations, the *ius gentium*; it came, rather, under unwritten municipal law. Its application was internal; it had meaning for the relations between ruler and ruled. It was, therefore, one of the "laws common to many people separately" and had to be distinguished from those laws which received their obligatory force "from the will of all nations or of many nations."[40]

In the face of such a presentation one might easily conclude that Grotius was indeed the advocate of a rigid doctrine of non-resistance. Further reading reveals, however, that Grotius had some further categorizations, which were not in any way destructive of his fundamental principles. In weighing the relevance of his distinctions, one must always be alert to the fact that Grotius kept the maintenance or preservation of civil society in the forefront of his thinking. Hersh Lauterpacht says that the exaltation of "public tranquility" in Grotius' theory could best be understood in consideration of the needs of his day, for "at a time of general uncertainty and of loosening of traditional ties, national and international order was looked upon as the paramount dictates of reason.[41] Nevertheless, Lauterpacht continues, the exceptions which Grotius made to his doctrine of non-resistance were "so comprehensive as to render the major propositions almost theoretical."[42] This is an unfortunate overgeneralization on the part of Lauterpacht, for Grotius did not advocate "comprehensive" exceptions to his doctrine in any way. His doctrine of non-resistance was categorical and remained unalterable. Grotius did proceed, however, to make distinctions and to elaborate on when resistance would be allowed against a sovereign who, in the legitimate performance of his duties, did commit some crimes.

In book 1, Grotius made an argument for passive resistance:

> Among all good men one principle at any rate is established beyond controversy, that if the authorities issue any order that is contrary to the law of nature or to the commandments of God, the order should not be carried out. For when the Apostles said that obedience should be rendered to God rather than to men, they appealed to an infallible rule of action, which is written in the hearts of all men and which you may find in Plato expressed in about as many words. But if from any such cause, or under other conditions as a result of caprice on the part of him who holds sovereign power, unjust treatment be inflicted on us, we ought to endure it rather than resist by force.[43]

Having said that, Grotius then attempted to draw the line as to where passive resistance ended and where active, forceful resistance began. In situations of extreme and unavoidable necessity, he argued, passive resistance was inadequate. "Self defense against atrocious cruelty" constituted full justification for individuals or groups to resist sovereign authority with the caveat, however, that "a greater evil, such as the destruction of a great many innocent people" does not result. The justness of resistance depended upon whether the righting of a wrong was "of greater importance" than the right which was being violated. Grotius elaborated on his position in compelling words:

> Now this law which we are discussing—the law of non-resistance—seems to draw its validity from the will of those who associate themselves together in the first place to form a civil society; from the same source, furthermore, derives the right which passes into the hands of those who govern. If these men could be asked whether they purposed to impose upon all persons the obligation to prefer death rather than under any circumstances to take up arms in order to ward off the violence of those having superior authority, I do not know whether they would answer in the affirmative, unless, perhaps, with this qualification, in case resistance could be made without a very great disturbance in the state, and without the destruction of a great many innocent people. . . .[44]

He goes on to say:

> Barclay . . . concedes to the people and to a notable portion of the people, the right of self-defence against atrocious cruelty, despite the fact that he admits that the entire people is subject to the king. I readily understand that in proportion as that which is preserved is of greater importance, the equity of admitting an exception to the letter of the law is increased. But on the other hand I should hardly dare indiscriminately to condemn either individuals, or a minority which at length availed itself of the last resource of necessity in such a way as meanwhile not to abandon consideration of the common good.[45]

In other words, if the resistance of an individual or a group to sovereign authority would in itself be a threat to "public tranquility," then such resistance would be destructive of its purpose and should be abandoned. The preservation of the social order must be maintained above all other considerations. The justification for active resistance must always be kept within the limits of self-defense, he cautioned. Using a Biblical illustration, he said that David was

one who lived in accordance with law. Even when wronged
by Saul, David did not seek to destroy the kingdom but
limited himself to proportionate defensive measures. At all
costs, said Grotius,

> . . . the person of the king must be spared. Those who
> think David conformed to this role not from a sense of duty,
> but from a higher purpose, are mistaken. For David himself
> openly said that no one who laid hands on the king could
> be innocent.[46]

It was in reference to situations where sovereigns
committed such excessive wrongs as to place in jeopardy the
continuance of civil society that Grotius granted approval
to intervention or tyrannicide. A distinction, it seems, had
to be made between a legitimate ruler who committed some
wrongs and a ruler who had become so evil as to lose all
legitimacy, thus descending to the level of a tyrant.
Tyrannical sovereigns were not performing their primary
functions and were, in effect, no sovereigns at all. In this
sense, then, those who resisted the sovereigns were not
really opposing lawful authority but were opposing instead
poseurs who had repudiated their right to rule. Grotius
likens a sovereign who has lost or alienated his grant of
power to one who has reverted to "the position of a private
person." A sovereign could reduce himself to such a position
in a number of ways, and in successive sections of book 1,
Grotius enumerates these clearly:

> First, then, if rulers responsible to the people, whether
> such power was conferred at the beginning or under a later
> arrangement, as at Sparta—if such rulers transgress against
> the laws and the state, not only can they be resisted by force,
> but, in the case of necessity, they can be punished
> with death.[47]
>
> In the second place, if a king, or any other person has
> renounced his governmental authority, or manifestly has
> abandoned it, after that time proceedings of every kind are
> permissible against him as against a private person.[48]

In the third place, Barclay holds the opinion that if a king alienates his kingdom or places it in subjection to another, the kingdom is no longer his.[49]

In the fourth place, says the same Barclay, the kingdom is forfeited if a king sets out with a truly hostile intent to destroy a whole people.[50]

Fifthly, if a kingdom be granted under the condition that upon the commission of felony against the overlord, or the violation of a clause inserted in the grant of power, that if the king do thus and so, the subjects are released from all duty of obedience to him, in such case also the king reverts to the position of a private person.[51]

Sixthly, in the case the sovereign power is held in part by the king, in part by the people or senate, force can lawfully be used against the king if he attempts to usurp that part of the sovereign power which does not belong to him, for the reason that this authority does not extend so far.[52]

Seventhly, if in the conferring of authority it has been stated that in a particular case the king can be resisted, even though such an agreement does not involve the retention of a part of the authority, some natural freedom of action, at any rate, had been reserved and exempted from the exercise of royal power. For he who alienates his own right can by agreement limit the right transferred.[53]

If Grotius' doctrines of non-resistance and of passive and active resistance were applicable under the aegis of unwritten municipal law, i.e., to internal relations of a state, then the query arises as to what importance any part of the doctrines may have had for relations *among* nation-states. Since Grotius conceived of law as any rule which created an obligation as to what was right and since he considered all men as members of one vast human society, it obviously did not matter to which category a rule belonged, whether common to all nations or to each nation separately. Though he possessed this broad perspective, Grotius nevertheless propounded another distinction which was quite pertinent to relations among nation-states, and this distinction was related to the right to punishment which Grotius justified under the law of nature and the law of nations. If the ruler of a state unjustly denied to his subjects their rightful claims or injured them with some wrong, then he had committed an "evil of suffering" for which he deserved punishment. Now, since the unwritten municipal law of non-resistance precluded the wronged subjects from forcibly defending their rights or from punishing their rulers in most cases, a vacuum of justice would occur if no restitution were made for the wrongs committed. Someone else, therefore, could take up the cause of the injured subjects. In allowing others to interfere and to punish criminal rulers, Grotius extended his just war doctrine to the defense of subjects of another state, and, in so doing, he gave legal vindication to international intervention by third states as an "exercise of the rights vested in human society" if it were done properly and for humanitarian reasons.[54]

There were grave subjective dangers, of course, in advocating intervention, and Grotius was not unmindful of them; consequently, he exerted himself to delineate the limitations within which such an action could apply. In a situation where subjects resorted to passive resistance to assert their grievances and where no restitution was made to right the obvious wrong, justice would demand that an outside agent should inflict punishment. Also, intervention would be allowable in situations where the subjects were entitled to resist by force—"self-defense for atrocious cruelty"—but where such resistance was of no avail because of the preponderant strength of the oppressing sovereign. Here again justice would demand an external sanction to right the wrong. Humanitarian intervention was fully justified, said Grotius, under the law of nature, and, beyond that, redress could also be extracted for injuries that were in violation of the law of nations.

> The fact must also be recognized that kings, and those who possess rights equal to those of kings, have the right of demanding punishments not only on account of injuries committed against themselves or their subjects, but also on

account of injuries which do not directly affect them but excessively violate the law of nature or of nations in regard to any persons whatsoever. For liberty to serve the interests of human society through punishments, which originally, as we have said, rested with individuals, now after the organization of states and courts of law is in the hands of the highest authorities, not, properly speaking, insofar as they rule over others but insofar as they are themselves subject to no one. For subjection has taken their right away from others.[55]

Grotius spelled out the principle of his position on the whole subject in book 2, chapter 25, entitled "On the Causes of Undertaking War on Behalf of Others":

This, too, is a matter of controversy, whether there may be a just cause for undertaking war on behalf of the subjects of another ruler, in order to protect them from wrong at his hands. Now, it is certain that from the time when political associations were formed, each of their rulers had sought to assert some particular right over his own subjects. . . . But all these rights have force in cases where subjects are actually in the wrong, and also, you may add, whether the cause is doubtful. For such purposes, in fact, this division of authorities was established.

If, however, the wrong is obvious, in case [a ruler] should inflict upon his subjects such treatment as no one is warranted in inflicting, the exercise of the right vested in human society is not precluded. . . .

If, further, it should be granted that even in extreme need subjects cannot justifiably take up arms (on this point we have seen [that many authorities] are in doubt), nevertheless it will not follow that others may not take up arms on their behalf. For whenever the check imposed upon some action arises from the person concerned and not the action itself, then what is refused to one may be permitted to another on his behalf, provided that the matter is such that the one may therein be of service to the other. . . . The restriction, in fact, which prevents a subject from resisting, does not arise from a cause which is identical to the case of a subject and of one who is not a subject, but from the personal condition which is not transferred to others.[56]

At this highest stage of his thought on resistance, then, Grotius was reminding rulers that their authority was not absolute. With consummate skill he reached the apogee of his theorizing on the subject and told the monarchs of his day that they were not free to commit crimes and to perpetrate injustice either internally or externally. Tyrannous acts within their own state associations indicated that the rulers were not performing their duties. This constituted crimes for which these rulers were liable to punishment. Neither could they commit injustices against aliens or against rulers and peoples of other states. Acts could not be performed that were contrary to humanity and the rights of mankind. Whoever exercised the sovereign power in a state association remained a human being under liability to the higher law, whether natural or volitional. In elaborating on this liability, Grotius came closest to fulfillment of the primary purpose for which he had undertaken his work.

# 6.

# Conclusion

In final evaluation there are several questions that might be asked about Grotius. First and foremost, where can he actually be placed in the history of natural law theory? In attempting to classify him, it may be easier to state initially what he was not. The general conclusion of this study is that, regarding natural law, Grotius was not the proponent of a modern theory, and he certainly was not the secularist that many have made him out to be.[1] Modernism, like rationalism, can be subjected to many shades of meaning, but Grotius was assuredly not of any school of modernism that advocated a functional, existential reason tied to a mechanistic explanation of the universe. He certainly was not a pure secularist, for even though he wanted to sever natural law from its traditional medieval association with Christian claims of revelation, he clearly wanted to retain theological premises for his conceptualism. His own faith preference led him to believe that revelation provided valid knowledge of reality, and he, like Thomas Aquinas, gave revelation a place in his scheme of law. Reason, however, was a separate and independent source of knowledge and could provide understanding for human fulfillment; hence, he sought to formulate his theory of rational natural law on the naturalistic side of religion.

Grotius might be called a late medieval rationalist largely

because of the role he assigned to reason in his theorizing, and, on this account, it might be said that he *tended* in the direction of modernism, but it would be wholly inaccurate to conclude that his rationalism automatically thrust him into the ranks of modern secularists. His treatise revealed, much in the manner of Aquinas, his dependence upon the Stoics and upon Cicero who embraced basic Stoic concepts for his ideas on the origin and the nature of law in general and upon Aristotle for his ideas on law in particular. In keeping with the Stoics and Cicero, he held to the belief that within every man was a spark of the divine which enabled him to discover universally binding rules of right conduct. Man was essentially a rational creature whose wisdom was shown by his inclination to live by nature. For Grotius the world was created and permeated by divine reason. He always viewed the universe in terms of ultimate mind and purpose. He grounded all his definitions in a transcendent reality and certainly rejected any effort toward metaphysical explanation based upon a semantic consensus or upon a sensation calculating reason. Though he did not explicitly describe natural law as an "irradiation" or a reflection of an eternal law, as did Aquinas, there was nevertheless implicit throughout his work the conviction that all true laws had to be a manifestation of the essential principles of things. True laws, he firmly believed, existed from the beginning of creation in God as divine reason and were employed through God's ultimate will and providence as rules for the governance of all creatures. He thus renounced the dogmatics of traditional medieval Christian orthodoxy in favor of rationalized natural law, but his doctrine still required God. He did not cast away theological presuppositions, because he made recourse to the reason of God as a grounding for first principles.

In attempting to identify Grotius with a later brand of rationalism, many commentators have attributed to him theoretical conceptions that were not there, thus yielding to definitional and conceptual confusions which influence their overall understanding of him. Correctly analyzed, the conceptual work of Grotius on natural law must be recognized as a significant addition to legal theory. He certainly was not a radical innovator in that he made a drastic break with the past, but he was sufficiently creative to produce a new synthesis embodying many aspects of classicism and late medieval thought. To be sure, Grotius has earned a place for himself among western political and legal theorists, and his writings have been the object of extensive commentary over the past three-and-a-half centuries, drawing both criticism and praise. With deeper perception on the part of contemporary and future scholars, however, the ideas of Grotius, especially on natural law, should be given a more rightful place in the history of western thought and should earn for him more genuine and well deserved plaudits in view of his contribution at a specific period in time.

Can Grotius be credited as the "father" of "modern" international law, as so many commentators have done over the years? On his thinking in regard to a law of nations Grotius clearly reached back into classical history. He utilized classical theory and legalism for his purposes, but again he emerged very much as a later medieval synthesizer, attempting to apply theory and practice to the rapidly changing political system of the West. In his contribution to the evolution of a law of nations Grotius, in many ways, followed the lead of others, especially scholars like Aquinas and Suarez. Though he differed with these men in some respects, he nevertheless was in full agreement with them on a grand hierarchical scheme of law, on a conceptualization of a universal human society existent from the dawn of human experience, and on a system of law which developed as a counterpart to that society. That body of law, in Grotius' view, had commonality and remained applicable to the particularistic political entities into which human beings had divided themselves.

Appalled at the prospect of disorder among sovereign

independent nation-states, Grotius came forth with his masterpiece on theory and substantive law, his unique and enduring contribution to the evolution of a law of nations. The time was indeed ripe for such a work, but that work was an edifice built upon a foundation laboriously constructed by others. We have discovered that, for Thomas Aquinas, the *ius gentium* was looked upon as human law, like the municipal law of any given society, but the *ius gentium* was rooted in *ius naturale* which, in turn, emanated from eternal law, the reason of God, which was the source of all law. Aquinas went beyond Roman legal conceptualism, which had grounded the *ius gentium* in custom, and he proceeded to postulate a dual aspect for the law of nations, the one having a direct tie to natural law, the other having only a relationship to it. The first was directly deduced by reason from first principles in nature; the second was validated through custom, which was a manifestation of reason in accordance with nature. Obviously, for Aquinas, laws could be declared by men's "actions" as well as by their word. As he wrote, ". . . when a thing is done again and again, it seems to proceed from a deliberate judgment of reason."[2] Both aspects of the *ius gentium* were conceptualized within the category of human law, but the deduced precepts were perceived as being on a slightly higher level in the hierarchy of law than those which were confirmed by custom. Human law was human by its orientation to earthly fulfillment or earthly "happiness," but all law was viewed as on a descending order from its author, God. Aquinas' deduced *ius gentium* did not fall outside the confines of human law, but it was on a higher level than customary law in its approximation to natural law and eternal law.

Suarez made distinctions in regard to the *ius gentium*, insisting all the while that he was presenting an accurate interpretation of Aquinas. Suarez, in effect, tried to impose his own imagery on the mind of Aquinas by arguing that the distinctions represented the true intent of the thirteenth-century scholastic. Suarez contended that the *ius gentium* was not a combination of principles deduced directly from nature and principles manifested in custom, but rather that the *ius gentium* found validity solely in custom. The law of nations, therefore, was exclusively human law. Principles deduced directly from the *ius naturale* rightly belonged to that category. Further, Suarez insisted that, even though the law of nations received validity solely through consent (usage), it could still be considered as preceptive law, that is, law derived from the will of him who commanded it. The law of nations, therefore, was linked to God in the vertical hierarchy. It was in the category of human law, but it had a relation to natural law, and, ultimately, to eternal law.

In still further refinement Suarez discussed the distinction between written and unwritten law. Both were within the category of human law, but the former was legislated law, brought into being through civil institutionalism and civil processes and applicable only to the particularistic internal relations of specific political societies. Unwritten law, on the other hand, was that which was manifested in custom, and it could be conceptualized in two senses because of external and internal application. The first sense embraced law which was common to universal society. It was validated by the consent of all mankind. Its scope of application was universal because it was binding upon all. This, said Suarez, comprised the *ius gentium* "properly so called."[3] It was distinguishable from municipal law by its origin and orientation. The second sense embraced law which was introduced within diverse societies and was applicable only to the internal relations of those societies, but it was law which was common to them all. Commonality made it a *ius gentium*, but its scope of application identified it with municipal or civil law. Thus for Suarez, each of the senses was distinctive and each included subject matter peculiar to it alone. The *ius gentium* of the first sense was essential for order within the new society of nation-states. It was relevant to the external relationships of sovereign political entities and was fully consonant with the law of nature and eternal law in a hierarchical scheme. The *ius gentium* of the second sense was essential for order within societies, and it too was consonant with natural law and eternal law.

Grotius, as we have learned, followed through on all this. He recognized the identity of individual nation-states but wanted to negate any claim for atomistic separateness— each society for itself with no obligations to higher morality or to higher law. He wanted to give a systematic exposition of a theory and a body of substantive law reflective of a concept of a universal society of mankind. Grotius fully subscribed to universal imagery and to a hierarchy of law, and the hierarchy included a law of nations fundamentally rooted in natural law and eternal reason. Like Suarez, Grotius conceptualized municipal law and the law of nations as falling within the category of human law, but he then took issue with Suarez on the two senses of the *ius gentium*. Grotius categorized Suarez's *ius gentium* of the second sense as unwritten municipal law. It was identifiable with municipal law since it was peculiar to each civil society and was applicable only to internal relations. Such unwritten law may have been common to diverse societies, but the scope of application logically made it part of municipal law. Grotius, as we have noted, referred to both written and unwritten municipal law as *ius civile singulorum populorum* (the law of a separate, identifiable nation-state). This law was not applicable to the relations among nation-states; it was not the law of nations "strictly speaking." The intent of Grotius, as he made clear in his masterpiece, was to deal only with those laws which were applicable to external relations and not with those laws that were common but relevant only to people within separate societies. For Grotius the scope of application was crucial to his choice, but his refinement in no way affected his own or Suarez's conception of the *ius gentium* as human law.

Grotius disagreed with Aquinas and agreed with Suarez

on consent or custom as the necessary element for the true law of nations. It was custom that made the law of nations human law and gave it a relation to natural law. The law of nations, therefore, did not include precepts directly deduced from first principles in nature. Any precepts attempted through deduction could suffer from uncertainty. As one came down the scale from first principles, to precepts akin to first principles, to deductions or "inferences" on the lowest level, vagueness or obscurity could be the result. Grotius placed his confidence in time-tested reason, on that which had proven acceptable or workable, as a stronger confirmation for that which was in approximation with nature. Essentially, he believed that many voices over time were more trustworthy than the speculative abstractions or the logical constructs of any one person or the few at any point in time. Custom gave greater evidence of certainty than did precepts derived through unverified speculation. Abstractionism, disassociated from usage, was to be held suspect, for it was under a greater burden of proof.

In relation to all of the above, it is necessary to ask once again, Can Grotius be credited as the "father" of modern international law? It has already been determined that Grotius' law of nature and his law of nations were not forms of law which regulated the relations of nation-states conceived as abstract juristic personalities. He saw those forms of law as applicable to individual persons, most notably those who acted as agents of the collective political associations. It must not be forgotten for a moment that when Grotius wrote about the "free will of man" or even the "will of all nations," he was writing in reference to the will of individuals, or rulers, and not in reference to the general wills of reified, personalized nation-states. The precepts of the law of nature and of the law of nations could only be understood and observed by rational human beings. The "will" of any one nation-state was inherent in the actions taken by the duly selected agent or agents who represented the entire political association. Furthermore, the consent so necessary to validate the law of nations had to be manifested by the peoples of separate nation-states who, taken together, made up the universal human society. Said Grotius:

> But just as the laws of each state have in view the advantage of that state, so by mutual consent it has become possible that certain laws should originate as between all states, or a great many states; and it is apparent that the laws thus originating had in view the advantage, not of particular states, but of the great society of states. And this is what is called the law of nations, whenever we distinguish that term from the law of nature.[4]

For international law in the modern sense—a corpus of law pertinent to states as volitional entities—Grotius did not even try to invent a phrase because he did not conceptualize it. P. P. Remec has written:

> Grotius never uses the expression "international law" or its Latin counterpart "jus inter gentes." He writes widely about the law of nations or "jus gentium." . . . He states that the object of his work is to write about the law that concerns the mutual relations among states or rulers of states. . . . But mutual relations among states are not in any way limited to the dealings of abstract juristic personalities called states or nations. They are made by individual persons acting either in their private or public capacity. The sphere to which an "international law" would apply, if Grotius used this term, is therefore human relations taking place outside the bonds of municipal law (*jus civile*).[5]

Roscoe Pound, writing on international legal theory, said that, even though Grotius had a conception of sovereignty, he did not think of states as abstractions. Pound states:

> . . . When Grotius thought of the duties of sovereigns as the duties of individual men he was not thinking metaphorically. He was thinking in terms of the moral and legal duties that rested on Ferdinand and Louis and Philip

and James as completely as upon Titius and Seius and Maevius, and for the same reason, namely, that in each case they were men and hence moral and rational entities with power to do the things which reason and conscience prescribed as the course which they should take.[6]

When legal responsibility shifted from the king to the sovereign people, when kings began to reign but not to rule, it was then that a transformation began to take place, Pound continued. The juristic assumption evolved through time to the effect that each population was a collective "person" and was accountable and amenable to legal reason as such.

Along with the personification of the state came a change in terminology with reference to *ius gentium*. The English translation of law of nations underwent a conceptual change. "International law" gained in usage and eventually acquired the specific connotation of an exclusive law among sovereign entities. Richard Zouche, in 1650, had been the first to use the term *ius inter gentes*, but at that time he did not intend it as a separate category of law applicable to personalized states.[7] Emerich Vattel utilized the term *droit des gens* in 1758, and he clearly used it in the context of a law regulating the relations of moral personalities in the guise of states.[8] It was Jeremy Bentham who coined the English term "international law" in 1780,[9] and from the eighteenth century on into the twentieth both political and legal theorists began to exalt the state as a reified subject of discourse and to exalt the "will" of such states as the source of law. They expanded their abstraction so as to personify the state completely and to elevate it to a level where it became the apogee of all human volition. The culmination of this trend was to be found in G. W. F. Hegel who, in the early nineteenth century, posited the state as a supreme, almost mystically divine, entity.[10] Once the fiction of the state as a personalized abstraction became firmly entrenched in political and legal conceptualism, Grotian thought was in danger of being superseded. The Grotian theoretical system had barely been acknowledged before a conception of personalized states as actors in international politics was well on the way toward being actualized in law. The Grotian system was not so much in danger of failure by default as it was in danger of change through theoretical progression, a progression which Grotius would have abhorred.

This study would be incomplete without examining the question of why, since Grotius obviously agreed with many basic political and legal conceptions of Suarez, did he not give to the Jesuit theologian more adequate recognition? Grotius has been recorded as saying of Suarez that "he had hardly an equal, in point of acuteness, among philosophers and theologians."[11] If this be true, why, then, did Grotius avoid making any acknowledgment of indebtedness to Suarez in the theoretical portions of the *De Jure Belli ac Pacis*? Where Grotius does mention Suarez (there are four marginal citations in connection with matters of substantive law),[12] he reveals that he had read the Jesuit's *De Legibus ac Deo Legislatore* (1612) and most certainly must have been familiar with his political and legal thought, but the seeming reluctance on the part of Grotius to express openly any further dependence on the Jesuit is a source of puzzlement. No one as yet has been able to provide a sufficient explanation for this mystery, but four possibilities might be offered.

In the first place, Grotius, out of sheer scholarly pride, may have been reluctant to admit to all posterity that he had to rely heavily upon someone else for assistance on fundamental theoretical formulations. This may be a remote possibility, but, at the same time, it is of a kind which is not unknown in the history of scholarship.

In the second place, Grotius may have hesitated publishing to the world that he gave credence to Roman Catholic thinkers on political and legal matters. In order to produce a treatise with broad appeal, Grotius would have taken special pains to avoid any sensitive issues that might have compromised his aim. He had very adroitly criticized those of his predecessors who had written in the interests of their "sect, their subject or their causes." He would not want in any way, therefore, to give the impression that he had fallen victim to the same limitation. It must be remembered that Grotius wrote at a time when religious partisanship was extreme; in fact, as had been noted, many of the conflicts which he would like to have had regulated by law had arisen in part from religious differences. Consequently, in order to promote peace and stability in the West as he knew it, he did not want to stir sectarian sentiments any more than was necessary.

In the third place, Grotius did not specifically set out to write an extended theoretical exposition of his views on politics and law. He was more concerned with a treatise on substantive law which could serve as a guide for the embattled monarchs of his day. This he made evident in Prolegomena 59 where he explained his paucity of words on many matters and where he made clear that his work was directed primarily at statesman by saying:

> I have therefore followed, so far as I could, a mode of speaking at the same time concise and suitable for exposition, in order that those who deal with public affairs may have, as it were, in a single view both the kinds of controversies which are wont to arise and the principles by reference to which they may be decided.[13]

Hence, in terse, general sentences he summed up complex theoretical issues for which late medieval thinkers like Aquinas and Suarez had required vast tomes to contain their arguments.[14] Perhaps Grotius may have assumed also that the learned men of his time had possessed a common knowledge of all the theoretical issues that had been fought out in medieval and late medieval disputations and that he himself need not repeat the arguments at length, especially since he had more pressing matters to attend to. At any rate, because of his desire to skim over theoretical concepts and to hasten on to what he considered things of greater

import, Grotius may have felt that it was most unnecessary
to pause even for an instant to give others adequate credit
where credit was due.

Lastly, in his introduction to the works of Suarez, J. B.
Scott presents what he considers as a strong reason for the
failure of Grotius to give proper recognition to the Spanish
theologian. Scott refers to an article by Jan Kosters,
Dutch scholar and jurist, who claimed that, upon examining
the original text of Grotius' *De Jure Praedae*, he had
discovered evidence of a summary of Suarez's twofold
conception of the *ius gentium*.[15] Grotius had written the
*De Jure Praedae* in 1604, however, and the *De Legibus ac
Deo Legislatore* of Suarez was not published until 1612, so
the question was, How could an earlier work contain a
summary from a later one? Kosters maintained that the
summary was written on a small sheet of paper that had been
inserted into the original text of Grotius' work, and close
scrutiny showed that the handwriting on the former varied
considerably from that in the latter.[16] Kosters concluded,
therefore, that when Grotius had read Suarez's *De Legibus
ac Deo Legislatore*, he wrote in his own words a summary of
the distinction between the two senses of the *ius gentium*
and inserted it into the appropriate place in his unpublished
manuscript.[17] When Grotius later wrote his *De Jure Belli ac
Pacis*, said Kosters, he apparently incorporated the
distinction of Suarez into his text—but without ever
mentioning the Jesuit. The summary in the *De Jure Praedae*
was reproduced by J. B. Scott in his introduction to Suarez.
Grotius, evidently, had interjected his few sentences at a
point where he had been discussing examples of the law of
nations, for he stated:

> These examples [of the *ius gentium*], moreover, are of two
> kinds. For some have the force of an international pact, as
> have those just mentioned; others have not that force, and
> these examples I should prefer to classify under the head of
> custom rather than law. Even the latter, however, are

frequently spoken of as being part of the *ius gentium*, as in the case of those relating to servitude, or to certain kinds of contract, or to order of succession, which all or at least a majority of peoples have adopted in identical form, whether by imitation or by chance, when this was expedient for them [respectively] as individuals. Wherefore it is permissible for individual states to depart from such practices, since the latter have been introduced not by action in common but [by the respective states] acting singly.[18]

Kosters believed—and Scott agreed—that Grotius was obviously following Suarez in making a distinction between the *ius gentium* of the two senses. What Kosters and Scott failed to realize, however, was that Grotius was already evidencing a departure from Suarez on the *ius gentium* of the second sense, a departure that would be confirmed in the *De Jure Belli ac Pacis* of 1625. In the summary above, Grotius was already indicating his preference for placing Suarez's *ius gentium* of the second sense under the classification of unwritten municipal law. Even though there were practices common to states, these practices, Grotius pointed out, "have been introduced not by action in common but [by the respective states] acting singly." In his *De Jure Belli ac Pacis* Grotius repeated more clearly his belief that, since these practices were applicable to internal matters only, they should be considered as coterminous with municipal or civil law. Because of this fundamental difference, Grotius may have hesitated to give direct credit to Suarez for his conceptualism on a law of nations, but J. B. Scott proceeds to argue that the reluctance on the part of Grotius was due to differences between the two men on political doctrines. Scott says:

From internal evidence there is little doubt that he [Grotius] was influenced by Suarez not only in his conception of the *ius gentium* but also, as Dr. Kosters points out, in his theories on natural law. It would seem that Grotius, although appreciating Suarez as a jurist and a philosopher and profiting from his writings, had some reason for not invoking the authority of the Spaniard. What that reason was we may only surmise, but there is some justification for suggesting that it had to do with certain political doctrines professed by Suarez.[19]

Scott then proceeds to review Suarez's doctrine of consent and his conception of civil society with the implication that Suarez was the bold liberal of his day and that Grotius refrained from dealing with such matters. Suarez insisted, says Scott, that any form of government depended upon human choice, for civil power "in the nature of things, resides immediately in the community."[20] Regarding monarchy, especially, said Suarez:

> . . . the monarchical nature of the government of such a state or province is brought about by human disposition, as has already been shown; therefore, the principate itself is derived from men. Another proof of this derivation is the fact that the power of the king is greater or less, according to the pact or agreement between him and the kingdom; therefore, absolutely speaking, that power is drawn from men.[21]

Even after a civil society had been created and the sovereign power had passed through succession or election to many persons, the people of the community remained as the true possessors of that power. Furthermore, since the people had the right to bestow political power, they also had the residual right to withdraw it at any time for good cause, particularly in a situation where a monarchy had degenerated into tyranny. Scott says that, in another treatise,[22] Suarez went so far as to approve deposition and tyrannicide under certain conditions. The people were always superior to the monarch, and, if he did not govern for the public good, he could be deposed and for just cause even killed.

Such bold doctrines were not favorably received in the leading monarchies of Grotius' day, Scott says. In fact, Suarez's treatise was publicly burned by James I of England

and by Louis XIII of France. Grotius, after his escape from prison, lived in France and received a meager pension from the royal treasury. Scott makes the contention, already referred to in Chapter 4, that Grotius, who experienced increasingly straitened economic circumstances and who began to nurture the hope of entering into some form of public service, could not afford to bring the wrath of any monarch down on his head. He could not risk being as independent and forthright as Suarez. He therefore expediently avoided anything which might have offended the rulers, and, as Scott says:

> . . . it is not unlikely that for similar reasons he deemed it unwise to make anything more than a few casual citations of Suarez, thus relegating to the position of a minor authority, as it were, the Spanish theologian whose writings had roused the ire of reigning monarchs.
>
> In any event, whatever his motives may have been, the fact remains that the great Dutch jurist was acquainted with the *De Legibus* or he would not have cited it. And in view of this fact, as well as of the marked similarity between certain of his own conceptions and those of the Spaniard, it is difficult to believe that, in preparing his treatise *On the Law of War and Peace*, Grotius failed to avail himself fully (though without due acknowledgment) of Suarez's masterly treatment of natural law and the law of nations.[23]

Scott's conclusions cannot be accepted without challenge, because, as has been noted, Grotius embraced political views quite similar to those of Suarez, and Grotius also endorsed resistance to authority, including a doctrine of tyrannicide. Inherent in his thought was a basic concept of popular sovereignty and of residual power. A people could exercise sovereignty by delegation of authority to magistrates who could be held fully accountable, or the people could yield authority by consent to some particular person (a ruler) who, if he became tyrannous, could be deposed and killed. In both instances the people were sovereign from a constitutional point of view. Like Suarez,

Grotius adopted a clear distinction between a legitimate ruler who degenerated into tyranny and a usurper who never held rightful title, but the distinction led to greater theoretical refinement in regard to tyrannicide. In contrast to Suarez, who approved tyrannicide by private action for defense of life against either type ruler, Grotius objected to such action against one who held just title, and, reminiscent of Aquinas, he advocated caution in taking private action against a usurper. It seems that Grotius had a concern for public order that extended beyond that of Suarez, and he expressed his caution when he wrote:

> . . . as civil society was instituted in order to maintain public tranquility, the state forthwith acquires over us and our possessions a greater right, to the extent necessary to accomplish this end. The state, therefore, in the interest of public peace and order, can limit that common right of resistance.[24]

His concern was further expressed in another passage where he indicated that resistance would be unwise if it created a greater evil of irreversible social injury.

> . . . it may happen that he who holds the sovereign power by right would prefer that the usurper should be left in possession rather than that the way should be opened for dangerous and bloody conflicts, such as generally take place when those who have a strong following among the people, or friends outside the country, are treated with violence or put to death. At any rate, it is not certain that the king or the people would wish that matters should be brought to such extremities, and without their known approval the use of violence cannot be lawful.[25]

Then, in section 20, Grotius recommended that, when the question of legitimacy or usurpation was arguable, where there was no easy resolution of the matter, discretion should lie in favor of the possessor of sovereignty. Private persons should not hastily resort to extreme and potentially destructive action, for judgment should always be inclined in favor of social stability.

Possibly the most significant difference between Suarez and Grotius on the subject of resistance centered on the question of whether a ruler who had departed from the Christian faith (heresy) could be deposed. In a *Defense of the Catholic and Apostolic Faith*, Suarez concluded his discussion of resistance by insisting that a prince who had been declared heretical by his own community or by the papacy and who tried forcibly to retain political power should be considered a usurper and subjected to the penalties thereof.[26] The pope had the power of deposition for the sake of the spiritual well-being of any realm. Grotius for his part, assiduously avoided this entire matter. His difference with Suarez was one of omission rather than one of substantive assertion. Here again, this might be attributed to the fact that Grotius wrote primarily as a political theorist and legalist in the post-Reformation period of western Christendom, and he wanted to produce a treatise that would find maximum acceptance among diverse religious groups, whereas Suarez, a Jesuit churchman, could not fully disassociate himself from his ecclesiastical affiliations. Grotius apparently made a special effort to avoid a sensitive issue that could have been a cause for dissension and disunity in his day, and, overall, he may have taken particular pains not to be too closely identified with the name of Suarez.

# 7.

# The Grotian Quest: Significance for Our Time

THIS STUDY SHOULD NOT be abandoned without an inquiry into whether the thought of Grotius can be construed in any way so as to credit him with having made a contribution to the evolution of international institutionalism. It is worthwhile, from a contemporary interest, to ponder this, because some might be inclined to make an argument for him on this score. One could point, for example, to the proposal which Grotius made for periodic conferences of Christian rulers to forestall resort to war, a proposal which clearly revealed the confidence he had in human reason for imposing order on a system of independent nation-states.[1] Perhaps a hint of international organization might be read into his suggestion, but any statement of Grotius must always be measured within the total context of his thought. It is true that Grotius advocated conferences of Christian rulers, but such conferences were looked upon by him only as an informal instrumentality of his natural universal society. He saw Christian rulers—the more "civilized" among men—as having a special responsibility thrust upon them by nature for maintaining law and order. In conferring together they were simply performing a natural function relative to the common society of all mankind. Hence, Grotius considered their role in terms of responsibility without relating this role to any formal artificial organization. An intellectual transition could easily be made, no doubt, from Grotius' proposal to possibilities of international organization, but Grotius did not himself make the transition. He theorized consistently within the conceptual bounds of his universal human society. Grotian scholars of repute reject any effort to read thoughts of international organization into the *De Jure Belli ac Pacis*. Referring to Grotius' suggestion for Christian conferences, C. van Vollenhoven has stated forthrightly:

> Does this mean that Grotius conceived a new order of things in the political sphere? He does not even dream of such a thing. . . . Only with difficulty have people succeeded in culling six lines, not more than that, from his book of six hundred pages in which he gives his imagination the reins and draws the faintest outline of what, at present, one would call a league of nations. His book does not project or perfect; it merely states what he considers the present duty of all nations, if they would escape their own destruction and that of all Europe. That duty is to avoid crime, even if, at a lucky moment, crime should augment their paramount power.[2]

Actually Grotius himself resolved the issue quite satisfactorily. In book 2, chapter 2, he revealed that he considered any efforts toward world institutionalism in his own time as fruitless because of the practical problems of efficient administration. He did not deny the theoretical possibility of world institutions, but he did feel that any move in the direction of international organization or of world government would be rife with difficulties, so much so that it would be better not to make the attempt in the first place. "For as a ship may attain such a size that it cannot be steered," he observed, "so also the number of inhabitants and the distance between places may be so great as not to tolerate a single government."[3] Thus, in conceptualizing his system of law for all mankind, Grotius kept his thought within the framework of a natural human order and avoided any theorizing on matters of international organization of independent, sovereign states.

Finally, one might ponder the question of whether Grotius, if he were alive today, would synthesize his thought into new institutional forms as a result of continuing political-technological transition. It is impossible, of course, to attribute posthumous thoughts to a man long gone from this earth, but one might logically speculate on this and also on the corollary question of whether Grotius would alter his posture on the use of war as an instrument of justice. There is little doubt that the work of Grotius marked an epoch in the political and legal history of the world, but many believe that the supreme and continuing value of his theorizing lies in the realm of the inspirational and idealistic. That judgment may ring true in recognition of the basic premise of Grotius that heads of states, even though immediately accountable to the peoples of their own communities, should nevertheless be ultimately accountable to law and morality representative of the common society of all mankind. Grotius was idealistic in his conviction that every ruler should be responsive to this overriding obligation for international conduct and that just causation should be soberly consulted before any decision was made to resort to war. It was here, however, that his conceptual system became most tenuous, because he was in full confrontation with the problem of perception: Whose reason would prevail on contentious legal issues? Who exactly would make a decision as to when a just cause for war existed, or how could resolution be made in the event of conflict of opinion? Grotius, as we know, had placed great confidence in human reason. Rational, responsible, moral men would act in good faith to abide by the universal precepts of the law of nature and the law of nations and thereby serve the well-being of all humanity. Grotius fervently believed that national leaders could rise above their own political parochialisms to embrace a larger view and a greater sense of commitment in order to make his system operative. Tragically, that is precisely where his theorizing foundered—on a human inability or a human unwillingness to embrace a breadth of vision that would have served all mankind. Time, indeed, has shown that international politics became saturated with the principles of Machiavellianism, with heads of states inclined to make decisions on the basis of expedient national interest rather than on the basis of universal precepts of law and morality. How many national leaders since Grotius have even resorted to the deceptive claim that God and natural law were on their side in order to justify their own self-serving nationalistic aims? This was a brand of power politics which Machiavelli himself did not contemplate. Human moral weakness undermined the Grotian system, and the actualization of "reason of state," oftentimes under the aura of religion and natural law, as a standard for international behavior became commonplace. This, to say the least, would have saddened the great Dutchman.

Grotius would certainly have been very unhappy over the theoretical progression which came to accept nation-states as juristic personalities. When social abstractions are reified and looked upon as volitional entities, as having minds and wills of their own, then moral consequences do flow. The result of reification is to shift the burden of individual human responsibility for acts done in the name of the state to the state itself as a "person." It is not difficult to comprehend how this effort at psychological delusion would tend to make national leaders morally insensitive and irresponsible. Those who make decisions for the state psychologically absolve themselves from moral accountability and enjoy legal immunity for anything they do. Guilt is projected onto the social collectively envisioned as a functional unit, and individual guilt is minimized, if not eradicated. Even a Machiavelli in his theorizing conceived of human beings as the actors in politics, albeit actors who defined their own state goals and who deemed any action as good if it served to achieve those goals. His was a limited morality, one which was unrelated to any concept of a universal good and which came to dominate international life, but theory went one step beyond Machiavelli to postulate the social abstraction of the state as the volitional entity which acted within a political context.

The persistent inclination down to the present day to dichotomize private mind and public mind, private morality and public morality, is a troublous phenomenon for human behavior. Peoples in national societies today will normally condemn what they consider as heinous conduct in private persons, yet they express little or no moral indignation when the same persons as officeholders indulge in similar conduct. Governmental leaders themselves might hesitate to do certain things in their private capacities while they might hesitate not a moment when they do those things on behalf of their nation-states. The more sensitive may be bothered in conscience by this moral dilemma, but most leaders seemingly are not. The latter can compartmentalize their minds and sleep untroubled at night after having made decisions that would have shocked their own sensibilities if made as private persons. "Thou shalt not kill" is a moral commonplace for western civilization, and responsible, rational people agree that to protect and to sustain life is a universal value that should be observed, but how many national leaders, with the apparent approval of their peoples, justify indiscriminate mass killing or assassination as wholly acceptable in the day-to-day practice of statecraft? The dichotomization of moral responsibility contributes heavily to anarchy on the world scene, and there is a disturbing complacency for tolerance of it. Woodrow Wilson once suggested in an address that there should be a single standard of justice for individual and state action; what was wrong for the state should not be right for the individual, and what was right for the individual should not be wrong for the state. Wilson expressed that as an ideal. The fact is, that kind of double standard does exist and seems to enjoy widespread approval. What is wrong for the individual is too frequently tolerated as right for the state, at least right in the sense that no person is held morally or legally accountable for what is done. Hugo Grotius, as a moral being, would have openly condemned such moral duplicity among men with its consequence for lack of world order.

Modern technology might lead Grotius, if he were writing today, to reevaluate his approval of war as a sanction for law, particularly under the circumstances for decision making which he had advocated. Weaponry in the time of Grotius was still rather primitive. Military hardware was hand-wielded and hand-operated. Gunpowder was useful only for crude musketry and cannon, and transport was done by draught animals and wind-driven ships. The waging of war demanded less than the total effort of any society, and armed conflict posed no ultimate threat to all of humanity nor to earth's environment. In short, national wars in Grotius' day had advanced little beyond the so-called "private" wars of medievalism. The twentieth century, in marked contrast, has witnessed the development of nuclear power and biological-chemical weapons and also the development of technological carriers for weaponry which stagger the mind. Current techniques for warfare could indeed spell the demise of the human race through outright destruction or through impairment of the physical environment to the point where it would be incapable of sustaining life. We are now compelled to distinguish between the "conventional" weaponry of old and the new weaponry which, if used, could bring about a greater evil which Grotius feared—in fact, an evil not just of social disintegration but of social obliteration. Advancing technology with frightful armaments have moved national leaders to the anomalous logic of deterrence, the belief that massive arms buildups will make all possessors hesitate to resort to their use. The hope is that a balance of power will be achieved with relative political stability for the world arena. Deterrence, thus far, has seen only madcap arms races for equivalence or for superiority, and, rather than having a reassuring feeling of balance of power, the people of the world live under an uncertain balance of terror. Much idealistic rhetoric is heard, of course, from national spokesmen about world order, world peace, law, morality, and universal human brotherhood, while the usual business of naked power politics for national self-interest goes on. The horrifying prospect is that deterrence can fail by accident or by design, and the nuclear Armageddon will be loosed upon the world. If history has shown anything, it has shown that armaments acquired are armaments eventually used.

In desperation many may look to arms control and arms limitation, even disarmament, for an answer to the human prospect. Every effort, certainly, ought to be made in those directions, but the record thus far has been one of failure. Incredible political complexities as well as practical complexities regarding the number, type, and qualitative character of weapons surround any negotiations for arms control. Even while negotiations take place, events rush on to overwhelm whatever progress is being made. International crises mount in number and severity, and what guarantee can there be that agreements, once concluded, will be observed? In a states system where a premium is placed upon duplicity and national self-interest, where time has shown that national leaders are little inclined to act in good faith as far as law and morality are concerned, how much can anyone hope for in any international agreements? Problems are so great as to allow for little optimism here. A Harvard-M.I.T. study group has speculated that nuclear war will be likely if present values, images, and present trends continue. The minute hand of the clock on the cover of the *Bulletin of the Atomic Scientists* moves ever closer to nuclear midnight. Would Grotius today continue to place his confidence in national rulers as regards the use of war as an instrument of justice? One might question his rationality if he did.

The "court" to which Grotius appealed to forestall international anarchy—universal human reason—and the concepts of the law of nature and a law of nations can be retained in the twentieth century as inspirational idealisms, but the problem of perception for decisionmaking remains. What might Grotius now recommend in the realization of his misplaced faith in rational princes? The hope Grotius had for world order rested fully on national leaders who might live and move within a broader orientation than that of their own singular states, who might respond to the legal character of a common human society; but, since his dream for order did not materialize, Grotius, one might believe, would be compelled today to ascend to another level of political and legal conceptualism. As a proponent for some method of control over the use of force, and with a candid assessment of the magnitude of war for modern times, Grotius, were he here today, might be constrained to speak out with great urgency. Not just logical consistency, but also a large measure of pragmatism, might move him to advocate some kind of international institutionalism as a formal counterpart to his natural universal society. Plato had speculated on the possibility of philosopher kings, and Rousseau had written of a superior Legislator who would provide wisdom for the governance of mortals; since no all-wise beings have ever appeared in human history, and in all likelihood will never appear, a more practical step might consist of looking to a collective wisdom of humanity as distilled from an international institution mandated to adhere to universal law. Formal institutional ties to the idea of a common humanity might hold out the possibility of cultivating a sincere sense of dedication to universal law and morality. Those who identified with and labored within such an institution might develop the larger view and the larger commitment so necessary to fulfillment of purpose. These functionaries could be liberated to a significant extent from the status quo of nationalistic politics and given the opportunity to serve a higher mission. If it be true that human beings psychologically focus upon and develop a loyalty to that which is within the immediate range of their obligations, then reason would seem to dictate that obligations should be expanded and interests broadened so that a sense of commitment might grow correspondingly. It is not enough to dream dreams; idealisms require supportive pillars. Henry Thoreau wrote in *Walden*, "If you have built your castles in the air, your work need not be lost; that is where they should be. Now put the foundations under them."[4] Grotius had built his castles, but the foundations proved to be insubstantial, as he himself would probably acknowledge. The task now would be to structure the supportive pillars for his idealistic edifice for world order, and these pillars might be an international institution correlative to his universal natural society and which could make it a functional reality. But what kind of institution might he recommend?

Despite the scope of his mind and despite the accelerative transformations of modernism, Grotius might not be so presumptuous as to embrace world government as such. He might be hesitant to do so now for the same reason that he offered in his *De Jure Belli ac Pacis*, namely that the administrative difficulties for political universalism would be beyond human capability. The task of governing would be administratively prohibitive, since the "ship" would always be too large for steering. Geographic vastness, Grotius might conclude, would always spawn cultural diversity and political fractionation. Humanity, it is true, is not now separated into relatively isolated civilizations, as it once was in a time of primitive transportation and communication. The earth has shrunk, so to speak, with the advances of technology, yet humanity most likely will continue for some time to come being divided into "lesser units," into nation-states as a political reductionism from the natural human society to better fulfill human needs. Rejecting world government, but facing the problems of a sovereign states system, Grotius might tend toward approval of some kind of international machinery with some coercive authority for controlling the resort to war. His mind would be adaptable to the transformations of the modern age so as to make theoretical accommodation. He might reason that, if limited national leaders cannot discipline themselves to an observance of higher law, then perhaps they might be sufficiently persuaded to create an institution which would enable them to overcome their individual shortcomings. The psychological reinforcement of group identification might assist them in breaking away from their confining nationalistic roles and in submitting themselves to larger obligations. Eventually it would be accepted as a matter of course that some national sovereignty on serious issues would have to be yielded for the sake of human survival, that the state was not really the "complete association" that could meet all human needs. With an increasing awareness that the state was not the highest form of political association, there might then be a frank admission that states are incomplete in not guaranteeing the greatest need of all, survival, against which all other needs pale into insignificance. States would be seen as "lesser units" in the truer sense that they would have to be placed in a lower order on the scale of political organization. If the parts could not necessarily safeguard the whole (universal society), then the latter would require institutional forms to save the parts.

Grotius might favor a collective security organization similar to, but far more effective than, the current United Nations. This organization would have to have some sovereign power on decisionmaking for international behavior, most pointedly on the use of force as a sanction for law. The charter mandate for such an institution would have to provide effective procedural techniques for determining when a threat to international peace existed and for designating the "outlaw" government or governments responsible for the threat. In addition there would be an absolute necessity for giving to the organization a monopoly on force with a viable military arm to perform peace-keeping functions. Without this, any hope for international order would be illusory. Grotius might even advocate that his collective security organization be given authority to deal with any situation within a territorial nation-state that might lead to an international confrontation. The present United Nations has heretofore played a very restrictive role in that it could only deal with one sovereign power in conflict with another, if such were deemed as threatening to international peace and security, and it has had severe procedural problems for even defining aggression, for deciding on unified action, and for gathering military contingents adequate to its task. For the sake of meaningful world order, Grotius might readily recommend that a collective security organization be empowered to reach inside the boundaries of a single state to deal with any internal political, economic, or social tensions which could lead to external violence. In this way internal threats, as potential international conflict, could be brought to the attention of the world community, and every effort could be made to solve such problems before they provoke international catastrophe. To strengthen his machinery for order, Grotius might further advocate judicial proceedings whereby any governmental officials could make appeal to a world court for adjudication of any case involving a question of international peace, with the collective security organization having sufficient executive authority to enforce a court decision. Such proposals might be shocking to staunch defenders of national independence and sovereignty, but the logic of Grotius might contend that it would be better to sacrifice some national pride than to sacrifice all of mankind on the altar of armed conflict with the possibility of nuclear escalation.

Undoubtedly, Grotius would be a proponent of an improved law of nations as an important step to world order. He would be among the first to admit that historical transformation would require an updating of the substance of such law. When Grotius wrote his masterpiece, he addressed himself primarily to the peoples of the West, because they comprised the most advanced civilization of the time, and they were the hope for moral leadership. Even though he lived within a dominant Christian culture, however, it can be said of him, as of so few, that he truly possessed a universal mind and a universal knowledge. His breadth of mind was manifested in many ways throughout his work, for careful reading shows that he disapproved of racial discrimination among states, whether civilized or barbarian, of white or non-white, or of Christian or non-Christian. He freely advocated treaties among different peoples,[5] and, for his entire treatise, he drew his precedents and arguments from many sources. He dealt with justice or injustice in relation to individuals the world over rather than in relation to select persons, groups, or cultures. Whatever references he made to less-advanced or even uncivilized states were made with an objective appreciation of cultural differences among human beings and not with any intent to discriminate or to exclude anyone from his concept of universal society. In view of all this, Grotius would have been quite disturbed over the fact that the law of nations, in its expedient and oftentimes grudging development, took on a decided western arrogance. The attitude seemed to be that, since westerners made up the most advanced civilization of the world, their law, as it had evolved from capital-producing, capital-exporting states, must be superior. There was little difference in ideology in the time of Grotius, for most states were characterized by monarchies and growing capitalist economies. Whatever international norms had developed reflected this and bolstered the attitude of what was good for the West was good for the entire world. As technology progressed and as exploration and communication with other cultures grew, most westerners arrogantly assumed that they could take their laws and customs with them wherever they went and impose them on inferior peoples. This, to a large extent, has continued down to the present day. There is a marked resistance toward change or accommodation even though the state system has expanded far beyond its western origins and even though there is great diversity in ideology. This reluctance for legal transformation, as a consequence, has made the law of nations something less than universal. Many of the western norms are offensive and are considered as not directed toward the well-being of peoples in noncapitalist states and to peoples in the so-called developing societies. These peoples fear the heritage of western political and economic domination with a rather blatant record of imperialism, colonialism, and material exploitation. This fear engenders a rejection of any claimed system of law and certainly encourages a retreat into political and legal separatism with deepened attitudes of national self-interest and suspicions toward proposals for international institutions. Distrust is evidenced in the question of order for the benefit of whom? Grotius, without a moment's reluctance, would insist upon the need for eradicating the western bias so as to create a genuinely viable corpus of law that would be acceptable to all national societies. All peoples, he would believe, would want to feel that a legal system was oriented to their best interests rather than to their exploitation, otherwise that system would fail through contemptuous non-compliance. Chances for world order can be maximized only through improved law, for that law would be the very essence of any effective international institutions. Grotius would plead for new values, new attitudes, because he knew in his own day that stability could be achieved only by eliminating, not perpetuating, the root causes for international tensions. He would see the absurdity of clinging to images of the past simply because they provided selfish advantage, when survival was the actual issue. Adaptation, not resistance, must become the commanding motive. Westerners, he would insist, must seize upon the actuality that the law of nations must be modernized in order to cope with the problems of international politics which have increased, not diminished, since the publication of his treatise. The "time lag" in legal development must be overcome, else any dream for international order would remain purely visionary.[6]

On past record, is there any optimistic promise for future functional world order? The present mood may seem quite discouraging. Most people harbor an ingrained cynicism and an almost helpless resignation toward the modern states system. Even among students one can sense a feeling of submission to naked power politics with the fatalistic attitude of "that's the way it is, and that's the way it will always be." There seems to be an uncritical acceptance of the independent, sovereign nation-state as representing the highest level of human political evolution with a parallel hostility to international institutionalism as posing a threat to national self-interest. Most disturbing is an almost subconscious, but prevalent subscription to a Sophistic-Machiavellian-Hobbesian view of human nature. So many appear to accept as a given fact that the individual human being is a wholly self-oriented and aggressive creature, that human character is what it is and cannot be improved. From that evaluation of human nature, it is too easy to proceed to the conclusion that political society has to be structured from flawed material. Government is created for fearful, selfish individuals who desire some form of coercive authority to prevent themselves from injuring each other, while guaranteeing them the freedom of action to engage in a rat race for unlimited acquisition. Government, in short, exists to perform a police function for the sake of minimal security so self-interest can be served. Thomas Hobbes certainly utilized that kind of thinking in his political theorizing and went further to apply it to his view of international relations. Since organized societies were only collectivities of selfish individuals, then these societies as political entities behaved in the same manner in their interactions with each other. Hobbes, however, did not carry all the way through on his logic; he did not make a consistent application to the international system. Whereas a domestic political society did have authoritative decisionmaking institutions for the sake of order, the international system with states as actors did not. The people of any society defined their own "goods," and their political leaders were duty bound to pursue them relentlessly with no reference to a common good. Said Hobbes:

> And every Sovereign hath the same Right, in procuring the safety of his people, that any particular man can have, in procuring the safety of his own Body.[7]

Thus, there was no international society as such, no world sovereign to impose order, but rather there was a condition of lawlessness, a world of anarchy and disorder.

If one accepts a negative concept of human nature and subscribes to a cynical attitude toward international life, then it is not difficult to understand how this leads to the conclusion that might makes right, that superior strength serves interest, that all of human life is a record of endless power struggles for advantage. Out of this comes a philosophy of history according to which civilizations rise and fall with no essential meaning to the cyclical process. All of nature holds no enduring purpose; life is incessant questing with futility and frustration, possibly with universal destruction as the end of it all. What has fearful, paranoid, predatory man really accomplished other than a steady progression from stones and clubs to nuclear bombs, from boiling oil to bacterial weapons, and the peak of this madness has not yet been reached. Shall a cynical appraisal of human nature carry us to that summit?

Conceptions of universal law and morality have been decried by the so-called realists who, it must be noted at once, reach their own conclusions about reality from their assumptions about individual and social nature. It is only reality as they perceive it. Spokesmen for this kind of realism have not masked their views. They openly endorse blatant power theory in international politics and are scornful of any foreign policy which, to them, smacks of crusading moral righteousness for idealistic ends. Realistic morality proclaims any action as good if it promotes national interest, however that interest may be defined. Any foreign policy aimed at that goal is "realistic" in a world system of competitive states. Realists cannot bring themselves to see the world in terms of community, and, as confirmed Hobbesians, they cannot see international life in terms of cooperation or harmony of interests. Nicholas J. Spykman, a Dutch-born Yale professor of the 1920s and 1930s, was a staunch advocate of such "realistic" values. His commitment to a negative view of human nature and to national self-interest in a world of endless competition was set forth succinctly in a book published in 1942 under the auspices of the Yale Institute of International Studies. His basic theme was set forth in the introduction to that work:

> International society is . . . a society without a central authority to preserve law and order, and without an official agency to protect its members in the enjoyment of their rights. The result is that individual states must make the preservation and improvement of their power position a primary objective of their foreign policy.[8]

Spykman's view of human nature and of intersocietal relations was then set forth in this way:

> All civilized life rests . . . in the last instance on power. . . . Distrust of the moral character of power which echoes out of the Christian conscience has not prevented man from pursuing it with a whole-hearted devotion. . . . Strife is one of the basic aspects of life and, as such, an element of all relations between individuals, groups, and states. A world without struggle would be a world in which life had ceased to exist.[9]

Spykman made the expression, "the struggle for power" a veritable cliché for international discourse, and this struggle was inevitable in an anarchic world arena:

> Any association, however simple its purpose, which depends for the realization of its objectives on the actions of other men or groups, becomes involved in the struggle for

power, and must make not only self-preservation but also improvement of its power position a primary objective of both internal and external policy.[10]

The notion of power position was stated repeatedly in his text. Spykman elevated the concept of balance of power to the level of an unchallenged truism.

> . . . the struggle for power is identical with the struggle for survival, and the improvement of the relative power position becomes the primary objective of the internal and external policy of states. All else is secondary, because in the last instance only power can achieve the objectives of foreign policy.[11]

It does not require an especially incisive mind to grasp the basic assumptions which undergirded Spykman's statements. He believed, in effect, that all foreign policies would be "unrealistic" until national leaders accepted the facts of life, namely, that individuals and social collectivities were driven on by competition and self-interest and that armed conflict was only another means to an end. Since there was no international authority to impose order, force was feasible as diplomacy for the realization of interest. Material force was the *sine qua non* for survival. Force meant the ability of one society to impose its will upon another; it meant the capacity to dictate to those with lesser power. The struggle for power, thus, was essentially a struggle for war power, and this meant a succession of arms races with an obsession for predominance, not balance.

> The truth is that states are interested only in a balance which is in their favor. Not an equilibrium, but a generous margin is their objective. There is no real security in being just as strong as a potential enemy; there is security only in being a little stronger. There is no possibility of action if one's strength is fully checked; there is a chance for a positive foreign policy only if there is a margin of force which can be freely used. Whatever the theory and the rationalization, the practical objective is the constant improvement of the state's own relative power position.[12]

Policymakers could not be concerned with universal moral values. Morality should be a consideration of policy only to the extent that governmental leaders took it into account to favor their own societies. "The search for power," said Spykman, "is not made for the achievement of moral values; moral values are used to facilitate the attainment of power."[13] Spykman did not think in terms of human community nor in terms of harmony of interest. Even though he recognized an existent body of customs as comprising a rudimentary international law, this law had little effect on or little meaning for the interactions of governments. Governments need only obey such norms voluntarily, or need only appeal to international law if it served national goals. In keeping with this, Spykman gave little credence to international institutionalism. The League of Nations, created at the Versailles Conference of 1919, was only a "forum for debate"; it was utopian and a failure as far as world order was concerned, because, in the international system as it was, governments could use force at will to achieve national objectives. Spykman's "realism" was underlined in this frank comment:

> It is, therefore, not surprising that international relations are conducted to the constant accompaniment of the drums of battle. There is a tendency to look upon peace as normal and war as abnormal, but this is because of our intellectual confusion resulting from emotional reactions to war. War is unpleasant, but it is an inherent part of state systems composed of sovereign independent units. To forget that reality because wars are unwelcome is to court disaster.[14]

Spykman wrote largely in reaction to the idealism of Woodrow Wilson, developing his views during a crisis period in world politics. Though Wilsonian idealism had been manifested in the creation of the League of Nations and in much rhetoric for international law, peace, and brotherhood, it seemed that national societies were not yet ready for these things. Unrestricted nationalism remained as a paramount value. Peoples the world over saw themselves primarily as Englishmen, Frenchmen, Japanese, Russians, Americans, Germans, Italians, etc., and not as citizens of a common humanity. They expected their governmental leaders to advance their own interests and not to yield sovereignty to any international organization which might supersede the individual nation-state. Inevitably a wave of disillusionment with the League and with international law and diplomacy swept the world as a result of the intense dedication to nationalism, especially in one of its most undesirable forms. European and Asian fascism came to the fore in the 1930s, and the fascists, more than any others, exhibited a disdain for any notion of international community, law, or morality. People became deeply cynical and lost what little faith they may have had in the League of Nations as an instrument for order. As a consequence, the thesis of Spykman found receptive minds. He spoke to the growing cynicism and disillusionment of the time. Many came to believe that he was describing the real world. Spykman was widely read and quoted. His books became standard fare for courses on international politics in colleges and universities and were even seen on the desks of government officials in the 1930s and 1940s.

Another academician, the Englishman E. H. Carr, wrote in reaction to Wilsonian idealism and helped promote the resurgence of realism. In his well-known book, *The Twenty Years' Crisis, 1919-1936,*[15] Carr expressed his scorn for "utopians" as he called them, those detached visionaries who, in his opinion, refused to come to terms with reality as he, Carr, saw it. Carr called Wilson "the impassioned admirer of Utopian dreams" who spread idealism across the world and, unfortunately, made it a factor in human affairs for two decades. Carr saw "the exposure by realist criticism of the hollowness of the Utopian edifice" as "the most urgent task of the moment." Carr published his book just after the outbreak of World War II in 1939, and his aim was to try to bring humanity to its senses by a general recognition of the failure of idealism in the inter-war years. In the preface to his work Carr stated it was of great importance to examine the underlying causes which made World War II a certainty, and these causes were grounded in the unreality of Wilsonian idealism. Carr traced the roots of idealism all the way back to some of the thinkers of classical antiquity and brought his analysis forward to what he felt was the persistence of it in twentieth-century thought. He found its culmination in Woodrow Wilson who believed in rational men capable of discerning universal moral precepts in nature, in the possibility of moral judgments for world order, and in the viability of universal law and international institutions for peace. Wilson's ideas dominated world attention in the years after World War I, and this, said Carr, was unrealistic, for such ideas ignored the real nature of man and of politics, In fact, Carr commented bitterly, those who accepted Wilsonian values leaned toward "a hypothesis of stupidity," and their attempt to build a basis for a better world failed in the inter-war period as a result of their "muddled" thinking. Idealism could in no way be squared with what was; said Carr: "Much comment on international affairs . . . has been rendered tedious and sterile by incessant girding at a reality which refuses to conform to utopian prescriptions."[16] The bulk of Carr's book was devoted to an exposition of his realism, and two chapters were of particular interest: the first, "Power in International Politics," of which, for Carr, there was aplenty; the second, "Morality in International Politics," of which there was very little. The only morality for Carr, as for Spykman, lay in the efforts of any government to do that which was advantageous to national interest and which might create a balance of power for stability.[17]

With the idealistic proponents dispirited by the disappointments of the 1930s and by World War II, the field for exhortation was left pretty much to the realists. Idealism was not completely eclipsed however, for out of World War II came the United Nations with the possibility of concerted action to achieve world peace and the continued hope that rational human beings might seek just solutions for world tensions through law and diplomacy. When the limitations of the United Nations quickly became apparent, however, and when world politics degenerated into the ideological competitions of the "Cold War," world opinion once more seemed to weigh heavily on the side of realism. Power politics and international politics were construed as one and the same, and the struggle for power assumed a new theoretical as well as practical vitality. Realist assumptions comprise the dominant theoretical guide for policymaking at present. Realism furnishes the conceptual orientation and the motivation for decisionmakers. Even though lip service is given to the idealisms of international community, peace and brotherhood, of law and morality, and even though the United Nations exists and is operative, national leaders overwhelmingly formulate their policies and strategies in conformity with the sovereign states system, power struggles, and national self-interest.

The greatest challenge of our time is to overcome the mood of complacency and resignation, if cynicism and negativism toward human nature and social nature are to be reversed. Transformations in thought occur when traditional images become irrelevant or when prevailing values no longer serve primal human aspirations. If a shift is to be achieved, then, people must be made to understand that the pessimistic stance is less life-sustaining in the twentieth century than it ever has been in all of prior history. Since human beings live by their images and are moved by their beliefs, they must be convinced that a new set is in order. There is a dire need for an optimistic outlook, for a belief that human character is perfectible and can be conditioned by a higher law and a higher morality which transcends a ritualistic devotion to values which have made the modern states system what it is. A conviction must be cultivated worldwide that human beings can evolve to higher levels of political and moral development. The task is enormous but not insurmountable. Enlightenment is a pre-condition for change, and experience has already demonstrated that human life has made 180° turns when more relevant ideas replace the old. There is an almost desperate need today to understand fully the evolution of the modern states system so that its character as a "war system" becomes readily apparent. Understanding creates awareness; it can open the mind to a consideration of new values, almost with a feeling of exultation akin to that of Keats when he first encountered Chapman's translation of Homer. Wrote Keats:

> Then felt I like some watcher of the skies
> When a new planet swims into his ken.[18]

Every new insight can be an incitement for new directions in human behavior. An awareness of the problems of the practices within the modern state system can summon an inner determination for necessary political and legal transformation.

It is not necessary for human beings to wallow in a sense of helplessness as though they are victims of impersonal natural or historical forces which are beyond their control. Humans do not live in a deterministic universe. They are volitional creatures who can make moral choices. Heretofore, moral choice has been heavily on the side of negativism, and this has made human history what it has been and the present what it is now. A transition must be made to a higher, more positive moral outlook for human behavior. Human beings can make and can alter history through normative choices. If political change is to be accomplished and if a commitment to universal legalism is to find validity for the future, then people the world over must adopt a life-fulfilling moral attitude toward international relations and the use of power. Heightened moral sensitivity can strengthen the capability for realizing better values for the future.

A great responsibility rests upon the educated, the

informed, who believe that such values can be inculcated in humanity if world order is to be even a remote possibility. The educated must seize the initiative and provide leadership. They must exercise the power of persuasion for new image-building as never before. Enlightenment is vital to attitudinal change, and only through attitudinal change can value transformation and institutional change be achieved. Most human beings are too absorbed in obtaining the material necessities of life. Existing on the periphery of history and seldom penetrating into the very center of things, they tend to have segmented views of reality. These persons must certainly be turned away from an attitude of fatalistic cynicism to a more optimistic view that history can be better directed and controlled to guarantee human survival. A burden of responsibility rests all the more on the informed because there can be little expectation for meaningful change from contemporary national leaders. Political officeholders are too mired in the status quo values of the nation-states system. They themselves have too great a vested interest in the games of power, and most of their energies are devoted to winning their political offices, in retaining them, and in catering to nationalistic needs and objectives. Seldom do they ever rise above their own political orientations. It is imperative, therefore, for others to become assertive and to lay the foundation for change.

Is it too much to hope that human minds can be stimulated to grander visions and values than those that currently prevail? Is it too much to believe that people can be turned from predation to become more altruistic, more magnanimous, more sensitively humanitarian? Is it too much to believe that people can be turned away from narrow nationalisms to see themselves as citizens of a common humanity? The hope for perfectible human character is not to be scorned when one seriously considers the alternative for the future. Why should political and moral conceptualism stop dead at prevailing images and values, as though intellectual barriers had been thrown up to thwart human progress for all time? Why should people "freeze" their minds in the status quo? Change is possible. Edwin Reischauer has written somewhere that human society usually meanders like a great river across the plains of time, but occasionally the water plunges over a great waterfall of change. Such change occurs, he said, when the prevailing values of a rigid social system grow too remote from basic human aspirations and bring a widespread alienation and despair. One would like to think that we are in a period of history when such a change is imminent. At base value, sheer self-interest should move people toward social transformation if it could mean survival. This would be change stemming from the wrong motivation, however. It should come, not from self-interest, but preferably through moral sensitivity and humanitarian concern. It should not come from paranoia and selfishness, but from a deep-seated belief in perfectible human nature. No change can be universally beneficial unless it is built upon universal moral conviction.

Human progress, it seems, has been heavily dependent upon the very few who have dared to dream dreams and raise visions of new eras for all mankind. They are the ones who have lifted their eyes from earth to the expansiveness of the heavens; they are the ones who have provided the inspirations which have thrust humanity forward into areas of greater achievement. They have dared to challenge and to reject, thus opening up new windows of the mind and spirit. Some have suffered castigation and condemnation, even martyrdom. They were perhaps too far ahead of their contemporaries, who in their historical limitations were resistant to the new ideas that were being presented. Time, however, has vindicated the visions of the few, and today they are frequently proclaimed as the great men of history. Their inspirations may well be described from the adaptation of the words of George Bernard Shaw: "Some men see things as they are and say 'Why?' I dream of things that never were and say 'Why not?'"

Hugo Grotius was one who dreamed of things as they never were and said "Why not?" He understood the values which human beings had dominantly embraced; he knew how people had behaved through history and realized the portent of such behavior for the future. He postulated a system of universal law to bring about world order, but people since have been resistant to his vision. Should we today not heed his message as that of a prophet who saw the need for change? Andrew Dickson White said that Grotius, with his great mind, was wholly aware of the travail of human experience and of the painful theoretical and practical efforts that were made on behalf of order through time. Grotius nevertheless bent his creative genius to the task of expounding a legal system that might bring order out of chaos, and, said White,

> . . . his main guide through all this labyrinth of difficulties was his own earnestness and unselfishness, his nobility of mind, heart, and soul. He fused together right and authority on every fundamental question and with precious results.[19]

His work, White concluded, was "a new treasure for humanity." The spirit of Grotius might now be resurrected in our own day to provide inspiration for a thrust forward to a new era. We are confronted with the question, Do we want to be world warriors marching on to a nuclear Armageddon or do we want to become world citizens fulfilling new values for the preservation of life on our beautiful planet? That is the question all of humanity must seriously ponder and answer.

# Notes

## Notes to Chapter 1

1. "Hugo Grotius" was the Latinized version of Huig de Groot. Latin was the scholarly language of the time, and the precocious young Dutchman himself utilized "Hugo Grotius" in authorship of his earliest and of all his subsequent scholarly works.

2. The inhabitants of the so-called Low Countries, which consisted of seventeen provinces, had been under Spanish rule and had been staunchly loyal to the Church of Rome, but through time the people of the seven northern provinces began to chafe under what they believed was the religious and governmental tyranny of their Catholic king, Philip II of Spain. Revolt occurred and by 1581, under the leadership of William of Orange, independence was declared. All of Europe was torn with conflict in the latter half of the sixteenth and in the first half of the seventeenth centuries, and the Dutch revolt was but an episode in the general disorder that prevailed. The seven northern provinces gained recognition as a unique state in a truce of 1609, but independence was not formally recognized until the Treaty of Münster in 1648, which ended one phase of what historians now call the Thirty Years' War.

3. Grotius became renowned as a poet, dramatist, classical scholar, historian, theologian, and as a political and legal theorist. In practical affairs he was to distinguish himself as a lawyer, a diplomat, and a statesman. Jérome Bignon, a contemporary and a legal official of France, called Grotius one of the most learned men since Aristotle. W. S. M. Knight has stated categorically, "Huig de Groot, better known as Hugo Grotius, ranks among the

183

world's greatest men." See Hugo Grotius, *De Jure Belli ac Pacis*, selections translated, with an introduction by W. S. M. Knight (London: Sweet, 1922).

4. In 1597, when he was fourteen, Grotius had written a critical study of the *Satyricon* of Martianus Capella, but publication had been delayed because of his journey to France. In 1599 Grotius produced a Latin translation, with an introduction, of Stevin's treatise on navigation, *The Haven-Finder*, and that same year he published a new edition of the *Phenomena* of Aratus. Then, in 1604-1605, he wrote a treatise of particular import, entitled *De Jurae Praedae* (*The Law of Prize*). This work concerned the question of rights on the high seas and was his first effort at dealing with legal conflicts among nation-states. Only a part of this treatise (Chapter 12) was published in 1609 under the title of *Mare Liberum* or *Freedom of the Seas*. The complete manuscript of *De Jure Praedae* disappeared until 1864, when it was rediscovered in a book sale at The Hague. It might also be mentioned here that Grotius wrote two Latin dramatic tragedies between 1599 and 1609, considerably adding to his reputation.

5. In 1610 Grotius published a history of "old" Holland, and then in 1612 he finished a larger endeavor and published it under the appropriate title *History of the Netherlands*. The States-General, we should note, had become the most important federal organ for the Dutch republic. It was not a highly centralized sovereign body, however, because national powers were ill-defined, and the delegates—most of them "stadtholders" or regent-magistrates of the cities in the provinces—were dominantly accountable to their own local governments.

6. Oldenbarneveldt (1547-1619) was the eminent and venerable Dutch statesman who, more than any other, was credited with having forged the provinces of the Netherlands into a united nation-state. Having come into life as the son of an obscure burger, he rose to become the grand pensionary (legal counselor) of Rotterdam and the lord advocate of Holland to the States-General, where his leadership made him a kind of chief magistrate and minister of foreign affairs. He exercised more influence over the provinces than any other man of his time, and he conducted all foreign negotiations. Oldenbarneveldt supported William of Orange as a national leader who could rally Dutch patriotism in the struggle against Philip of Spain. It was through

Oldenbarneveldt's insistence that Maurice, son of William, was proclaimed a stadtholder and appointed chief of the armed forces after William's assassination in 1584. Oldenbarneveldt negotiated the truce of 1609 which, for all purposes, gave the seven northern provinces an identity as a national sovereign entity. Maurice opposed the truce, and this marked the beginning of his political opposition to Oldenbarneveldt. Of interest for the Arminian controversy was the fact that Oldenbarneveldt had been influential in the appointment of Arminius as professor of theology at Leiden, and Oldenbarneveldt came to support fully the Remonstrant position. This increased his differences with Maurice. See Peter Geyl, *The Netherlands in the Seventeenth Century* (New York; Barnes and Noble, 1961), pp. 18-83. See also K. H. D. Haley, *The Dutch in the Seventeenth Century* (New York: Harcourt Brace Jovanovich, Inc., 1972), pp. 100-12.

7. It was rumored within the synod that both Grotius and Oldenbarneveldt had entered into collusion with the Spanish, allowing themselves to be bribed to betray the Netherlands. For their Remonstrant activities, they were seen as conspirators against the peace and security of their country. The reasoning was: resistance to Spanish tyranny was due to the steadfast Calvinist faith; both Grotius and Oldenbarneveldt were undermining the faith; therefore, the two were aiding and abetting the Spaniards. For an interesting treatment of this episode, see Jan den Tex, *Oldenbarneveldt*, translated from the Dutch by R. B. Powell (Cambridge: Cambridge University Press, 1973).

8. Grotius married Maria van Reigersberg in 1608. They had a total of seven children, four sons and three daughters.

9. Theology also commanded his interest. It was during this period that Grotius produced *The Truth of the Christian Religion*, one of the first notable efforts at Christian apologetics and one which would be translated into many languages. His *Introduction to the Jurisprudence of Holland,* a treatise on Dutch law, was also written in prison. Grotius further whiled away his time by writing poetry.

10. Evidently there were no serious repercussions against the wife of Grotius for her part in the dramatic escape.

11. Feeling somewhat more financially secure, Grotius rented a larger accommodation, but, as it turned out, the pension was paid

irregularly, and Grotius occasionally found himself on the edge of poverty.

12. Grotius had evidently read widely and reflected in great depth on a law of nations and then proceeded to write almost nonstop. Legalist that he was, he had become greatly concerned over the increasingly anarchistic attitudes with which heads of states approached their dealings with each other. Grotius was convinced there already was a valid law of nations grounded in human reason (natural law) and in custom, which was a manifestation of reason. This law should be recognized and rulers should be obligated to its observance. Grotius was filled with the determination to justify a law of nations in theory and to systematize it in a substantive treatise. Since there had been differences of opinion over time as to what constituted this law, Grotius concluded that superior reason—his reason—had to assert itself for the sake of world order. He took the title for his treatise from Cicero's *Oratio pro Balbo* in which he found a summary of the "subjects" of laws common to nations.

13. Entreaties had also been made to Grotius by Cardinal Richelieu to forswear his Dutch allegiance and enter French diplomatic service, but Grotius was not yet ready for such a decision. See Hamilton Vreeland, *Hugo Grotius* (New York: Oxford University Press, 1917), pp. 178-79.

14. Grotius served as a diplomat during the turbulent years which witnessed multinational negotiations relating to the complexities of the latter stages of the Thirty Years' War, with the Swedes themselves directly involved. He performed skillfully and well, but there were those who thought his effectiveness as a statesman was hampered by his unshakable integrity. One commentator, Jac. ter Meulen, has said that the contests of a political career "did not cause him to deviate a hair's breadth from the path of honour and recititude." See *Hugo Grotius: Essays on His Life and Works*, selected by A. Leysen, with preface by Jac. ter Meulen (Leyden: A. W. Sythoff's Publishing Co., 1925).

15. Vreeland, *Hugo Grotius*, p. 228.

16. The vital organs were later sent to Delft and entombed with the body.

17. "This is Hugo Grotius, captive and exile of the Dutch, but envoy of the great kingdom of Sweden."

## Notes to Chapter 2

1. A. P. D'Entreves, *Natural Law* (London: Hutchinson House, 1951), p. 50. Pufendorf was a seventeenth-century German jurist and theorist. As a scholar he was particularly interested in Grotius and Hobbes, and he formulated a theory of universal law. In the latter part of his life he served as the royal historian of Sweden.

2. Anton-Hermann Chroust, "Hugo Grotius and the Scholastic Natural Law Tradition," *The New Scholasticism,* vol. 7, no. 2 (April 1943), p. 118.

3. Ibid., pp. 121-22.

4. Jean Barbeyrac, *An Historical and Critical Account of the Science of Morality* (London, 1729), sec. 29, p. 79. No publisher cited.

5. Ibid., p. 79. Inherent in this statement is the assumption that a modern theory of natural law must be devoid of classical elements.

6. Ibid., sec. 30, p. 81.

7. Ibid., p. 81. Pufendorf had gone to Denmark to serve as governor to the children of a nobleman who was the ambassador of Sweden to Denmark. Shortly afterward hostilities resumed between these two countries and Pufendorf, the ambassador, and his family were imprisoned. While confined, "he took a Resolution to meditate on what he had read in Grotius and Hobbes; and having collected his Meditations together, he compos'd a short System of what he liked best, which he turn'd and explain'd his own Way; handling such Matters as those Authors had omitted; and adding to the whole some new Thoughts of his own, as they occurr'd" (p. 81).

8. Ibid., p. 81.

9. Ibid., sec. 31, p. 84.

10. Leonard Krieger, *The Politics of Discretion* (Chicago: University of Chicago Press, 1965), p. 263.

11. Ibid.

12. Barbeyrac may have overidentified Pufendorf (and, in turn, Grotius) with Hobbes because of the fact that Pufendorf incorporated some of Hobbes' conceptualism into his *De Naturae et Gentium.* Paul Sigmund maintains that Pufendorf had a combined Hobbesian-Grotian view of man. On the one hand,

man was aggressive, driven on by self-love; on the other, man was inclined by nature toward sociability. Pufendorf resolved the contradiction, says Sigmund, by asserting that self-love created an awareness of and prompted a motivation to love others. "Pufendorf's writings thus combined the individualism and pessimism about human nature of Hobbes with the belief in man's potential rationality and sociability of the older tradition. During the century after its publication, his theory was one of the best known systematic presentations of natural law." See Paul E. Sigmund, *Natural Law in Political Thought* (Cambridge, Mass.: Winthrop Publishers, 1971), p. 81.

13. This writer has examined with great care Pufendorf's major political works, namely: *Elementorum Jurisprudentiae Universalis; De Jure Naturae et Gentium;* and *De Officio Hominis et Civis.* Nowhere could be found the phrase "Father of Natural Law" in reference to Grotius. An inquiry was sent to Leonard Krieger, whose familiarity with all of Pufendorf's writings is extensive, and Krieger replied that, to his knowledge Pufendorf never used the term "Father of . . ." for Grotius. Krieger added that Pufendorf said Grotius developed a new conceptualism for natural law which was to be distinguished from *earlier medieval* versions (emphasis mine), and "The clearest statements are in his *Eris Scandica,* and within this collection in his chapter 'On the Origin and Progress of the Discipline of Natural Law.'" The edition of it to which he had access, said Krieger, was the Latin Frankfurt edition of 1744, where the *Eris Scandica* was appended to the *De Jure Naturae et Gentium.* (Personal letter from Leonard Krieger, 16 March 1966.)

Even if any of the interpreters or commentators on Grotius would attempt a justification of the title "Father of Natural Law" on the ground that he was a "modernist" for having secularized natural law, they would be open to challenge. The major contention of this study will be that Grotius was far from being a secularist. He embodied late medieval concepts in his thinking and very decidedly retained theological premises for his natural law theory as, indeed, did Pufendorf.

14. See the following works: Sir Frederick Pollock, "The History of the Law of Nature: A Preliminary Study," *Columbia Law Review,* vol. 1; no. 1 (January 1901); idem, "The History of the Law of Nature: A Preliminary Study II," *Columbia Law*

*Review,* vol. 2, no. 3 (March 1902); idem, "The Sources of International Law," *Columbia Law Review*, vol. 2, no. 8 (December 1902); Hersh Lauterpacht, "The Grotian Tradition in International Law," *The British Yearbook of International Law* (London: Oxford University Press, 1946); idem. *An International Bill of Rights of Man* (New York: Columbia University Press, 1945); Arthur Nussbaum, *A Concise History of the Law of Nations* (New York: Macmillan, 1954).

15. Sir Frederick Pollock, "The Sources of International Law," *Columbia Law Review,* vol. 2, no. 8 (December 1902), p. 518.

16. Idem, "The History of the Law of Nature: A Preliminary Study, "*Columbia Law Review*, vol. 1, no. 1 (January 1901).

17. Idem, "The Sources of International Law," *Columbia Law Review,* vol. 2, no. 8 (December 1902), p. 518.

18. Idem, "The History of the Law of Nature: A Preliminary Study," *Columbia Law Review,* vol. 1, no. 1 (January 1901), p. 11.

19. Idem, "The History of the Law of Nature: A Preliminary Study II," *Columbia Law Review,* vol. 2, no. 3 (March 1902), p. 131.

20. Idem, "The History of the Law of Nature: A Preliminary Study," *Columbia Law Review*, vol. 1, no. 1 (January 1901), p. 26. It is to be noted that by "more secular" Pollock means the disassociation of natural law from canon law or divine law (Scripture). He does not say that the revival of classical texts resulted in a total separation of natural law from theological premises. In fact, Pollock says that Grotius did not show any disrespect for the medieval doctors. "On the contrary, he ascribes the greatest weight to their agreement on questions of moral principle. . . ." (p. 26).

21. Hersh Lauterpacht, *An International Bill of Rights of Man* (New York: Columbia University Press, 1945), p. 41.

22. Idem, "The Grotian Tradition in International Law," *The British Yearbook of International Law* (London: Oxford University Press, 1946), p. 76. Lauterpacht openly praises Grotius as the first jurist who produced a treatise on international law which was both comprehensive and systematic.

. . . However incomplete—when judged by the present scope of international law—*De Jure Belli ac Pacis* may appear to be, it was the first comprehensive and systematic treatise on international law. Grotius was not the first writer on the law of nations. Belli

in 1563, Ayala in 1581 and, above all, Gentilis in 1598 wrote
learnedly on the laws of war; Vittoria about 1532 and Suarez in 1612
laid the foundations of the jurisprudential treatment of the problem
of the international community as a whole. But no one before
Grotius attempted the treatment of the subject in its entirety. There
is in *De Jure Belli ac Pacis* a good deal of matter which is not and
never has been within the proper sphere of international law, but
there is in it all the international law that existed in 1625. (p. 17).

Lauterpacht concluded that the controversy as to who was the
"founder" of international law was in essence "one of words," for
"no one denies to Grotius the representative quality of preemi-
nence." (p. 19).

23.  Arthur Nussbaum, *A Concise History of the Law of Nations*
(New York: Macmillan, 1954), p. 112.

24.  Ibid., p. 113. Hamilton Vreeland also states forthrightly
that Grotius cannot be credited with having created the law of
nature; but when Vreeland turns to the question of whether
Grotius deserved the title of father of international law, his
answer is in the affirmative. Though Grotius did not create the
doctrine of the law of nature, said Vreeland, he did use it in a
significant way. To wit:

> . . . he combined with it and to a great extent founded upon it the
> law of nations, and in that manner constructed principles which
> remain remarkably true today. In this sense, he may be called the
> Father of International Law, although some have preferred to
> speak of him as its Discoverer.

See Hamilton Vreeland, *Hugo Grotius* (New York: Oxford
University Press, 1917), pp. 171-72. Vreeland, actually, is not very
helpful on the whole issue, He makes reference to classical
sources for natural law but offers no extended treatment of the
subject.

25.  T. A. Walker, *A History of the Law of Nations* (London:
C. J. Clay and Sons, 1899), p. 333.

26.  Ibid., p. 334.

27.  Ibid., p. 336. Walker concluded, "The prophet had
appeared . . . the message was delivered, and found growing
acceptance." In an earlier work in 1893, Walker had given Grotius
recognition as the "father of international law." A science of
international law, he said, had to be a science of territorial
sovereignty.

> It was this science which the Peace of Westphalia made real-
> isable; and it was this science which Grotius expounded. . . .
> Modern International Law sets out the conduct, in the varying
> circumstances of life, or Territorial Sovereignty touched and
> softened by the improving influences of all the agencies which go to
> create, or the facts which constitute, the mysterious evolution
> which men term Civilization. And of that Law Grotius was "the
> Father."

See T. A. Walker, *The Science of International Law* (London:
C. J. Clay and Sons, 1893), pp. 91-92. By 1899 when he published
*A History of the Law of Nations,* Walker had apparently modified
his judgment on the matter.

28. L. F. Oppenheim, *International Law* (London: Longmans,
Green, 1928, p. 1.

29. Ibid., p. 2.

30. Ibid.

31. Ibid.

32. P. P. Remec, *The Position of the Individual in International
Law According to Grotius and Vattel* (The Hague: Martin Nijhoff,
1960), p. 55. Remec refers to Prolegomena 1 of Grotius's *De Jure
Belli ac Pacis.*

33. Ibid., p. 55.

34. James Brown Scott, *The Spanish Origin of International
Law* (Washington, D.C.: Georgetown University, The School of
Foreign Service, 1928), p. 9. The quotation is taken from the
foreword by Edmund A. Walsh. In the main text, Scott quotes
Coleman Phillipson to the effect that "he [Grotius] was the
veritable 'father' of international law we certainly shall not admit,"
but comments that Phillipson could not rid himself of the idea that
Victoria and his Spanish countrymen were "precursors." (p. 22).

35. Ibid., p. 90. Scott also says, "After Suarez's contributions
to international law the world found itself in the presence of a
clean-cut distinction between the law of nature on the one hand
and the law of nations on the other. . . . Last but not least the
writers after Suarez knew why there was a law of nations. His
passage on the international community had become classic,
showing at one and the same time the independence and the
interdependence of the states composing the international
community" (pp. 101-2). Scott's general conclusion is that Grotius

was heavily influenced by the basic political and legal conceptions of Suarez.

36. James Brown Scott, *The Spanish Origin of International Law* (Oxford: The Clarendon Press, 1934), p. 159. *Mare Liberum* was the chapter from the larger work entitled *De Jure Praedae*. In commenting upon Robert Fruin's analysis of *De Jure Praedae*, Scott cites a sentence of Grotius from *Mare Liberum* to the effect that "In this controversy we appeal to those jurists among the Spanish themselves who are especially skilled in both divine and human law . . . we actually invoke the law of Spain itself." See Scott, *The Spanish Origin of International Law* (Washington, D.C.: Georgetown University: The School of Foreign Service, 1928), p. 115. See also Robert Fruin, "An Unpublished Work of Hugo Grotius, "*Bibliotheca Visseriana*, 20 vols. (Leyden: 1925), vol. 5, pp. 1-74.

37. Scott, *The Spanish Origin of International Law,* pp. 160, 196. In fact, Scott says Victoria was not merely the founder of the modern law of nations but was the "prophet" of the "newer" law of nations.

38. See "Introduction," by Coleman Phillipson to Alberico Gentili, *De Jure Belli Libri Tres,* vol. 2, translated by John C. Rolfe (Oxford: Clarendon Press, 1933), p. 9a.

39. Gentili was an Italian jurist and Protestant who had fled Italy and became professor of civil law at Oxford. Sir Frederick Pollock says that if any person other than Grotius deserves to be called the pioneer of international law, that person is Gentili. See Pollock, "The Sources of International Law," *Columbia Law Review,* vol. 2, no. 8 (December 1902), pp. 521-22.

40. Phillipson, "Introduction," p. 11a.

41. Ibid., p. 12a. Phillipson added " . . . because of the greater affinity between his [Gentili's] point of view and that of modern states and jurists he is, in that respect, as much as, if not more than Grotius, the progenitor of the existing law of nations." Having said that, Phillipson offered an immediate retraction:

> Strictly speaking, however, no writer can be truly described as the "progenitor" or "forerunner" or "creator" of international law. . . . Indeed, Gentili and Grotius and all the earlier writers on the law of nations constantly appeal to the classical times for

authority, for rules and principles, for practices, for analogies, and for all kinds of illustrations. (p. 12a)

42. G. H. J. van Der Molen, *Alberico Gentili and the Development of International Law* (Amsterdam: H. J. Paris, 1937), p. 197.

43. Prolegomena 38, *De Jure Belli ac Pacis.* "Knowing that others can derive profit from Gentili's painstaking, as I acknowledge that I have, I leave it to his readers to pass judgment on the shortcomings of his work as regards method of exposition, arrangement of matter, delimitation of inquiries, and distinctions between the various kinds of law."

44. G. H. J. van Der Molen, *Alberico Gentili and the Development of International Law* (Amsterdam: H. J. Paris, 1937), p. 198.

## Notes to Chapter 3

1. The spectrum of thought may well have been exemplified in the fifth century B.C. in the opposing views of Anaxagoras and Democritus. Anaxagoras argued that nothing was self-generated. Over and above material substance, there had to be something (a first cause, a first principle) that had a force and an intelligence all its own. *Nous,* or mind, explained everything and was the eternal governor of all things. *Nous* was independent of matter and was the source of all life and movement in the cosmos. It organized everything with design and according to purposeful fitness. The logical consequence, then, was that human beings should be able to discern purpose and accommodate themselves to natural design. Democritus, on the other hand, insisted that the basal constituency of the universe was purely material. Things moved because of a motion inherent in them and not imparted to them. Everything in creation was the result of chance. There was no force external to substance, no *nous* to arrange or to impose order. The cosmos was in no way purposive or reflective of design. The logical consequence of this was that human beings, of necessity, had to define their own values from the context of their own humanity and association. There was no backdrop of nature to serve as a referent for ethical behavior.

2. There were logical and social implications which flowed from this Sophistic posture, implications that were part and parcel

of the growing Greek distinction between *physis* (nature) and
*nomos* (convention). *Physis* postulated nature (the ordered
cosmos) as the source of values or norms. All of reality was
permeated with purpose and unifying principles, and these were
relevant to human relations as well as to physical phenomena.
Human experience could be "harmonized" with nature. Here was
the germinal idea for a formal doctrine of natural law: whatever
man's reason convinced him was true about all things could be
termed "natural" and if there were sufficient agreement among
reasonable men as to what constituted "first principles," these
norms could be considered as having adequate affirmation.
*Nomos* postulated a restrictive view of what could be deemed as
natural. Values were manifested only in custom and in positive
(legislated) law which were predicated upon an understanding of
human nature unrelated to a transcendental order. Values were
relative only to any given society at any given time and place.
Values were transient, expedient, arbitrary, finding confirmation
in utility or usage. This was dominantly the Sophistic approach,
and it is most significant that Grotius would later single out the
Sophists as his philosophical opponents and that the Sophists were
the philosophical forerunners of Thomas Hobbes. Grotius would
contend that utility alone was too narrow an argument for
morality and law. Human need, he would admdit, was a factor
which impelled human beings to social living, but it was not an
exclusive nor even a dominating factor. Man was social by nature,
filled with a desire for life spent in community with his fellowmen.
Unique among all creatures, man was governed not by physical
demands alone but by reason. Reason tied man to conscious,
intelligent purpose in the universe. There were external, universal
principles—norms that were permanent, "fixed"—to which all
men could conform. These principles were implicit in man's
makeup as a social being and were made explicit by reason.
Human social institutions and laws had their rootage in these
universal precepts. The social impulse of man, the gregarious and
vicarious nature of man, was the source of law. Hobbes would
later attempt to ground morality and law in the selfish yearnings
and fears of men unrelated to transcendent universal values. He
would describe the founding of human society as a contract of
forbearance whereby paranoid individuals would endure law for
the sake of self-preservation. Morality and law would emerge, not

as derivations from natural social relations, but from the sub-jective concerns of insulated, isolated individuals who grudgingly bound themselves into artificial community. See W. K. C. Guthrie, *The Sophists* (London: Cambridge University Press, 1971). See also Thomas Hobbes, *Leviathan* (Oxford: The Clarendon Press, 1965).

3. "Protagoras," translated by W. K. C. Guthrie, in *The Collected Dialogues of Plato,* edited by Edith Hamilton and Huntington Cairns (Princeton, N. J.: Princeton University Press, 1961), p. 308.

4. "Gorgias," translated by W. D. Woodhead. Ibid., p. 229.

5. "The Republic," translated by Paul Shorey. Ibid., p. 575.

6. Ibid., p. 575.

7. The doctrine of Forms was spelled out in the minor dialogues and also major Socratic dialogues, especially *The Republic*. Afterwards, in medieval disputation, the doctrine that universals existed separate from things seen in the phenomenal world came to be designated as "extreme realism." The posture was described by the formula *universalis ante rem*.

8. See Glenn R. Morrow, "Plato and the Law of Nature," *Essays in Political Theory,* edited by Milton R. Knovitz and Arthur E. Murphy (Ithaca, N. Y.: Cornell University Press, 1948), pp. 17-44.

9. In his *Metaphysics,* Aristotle said pointedly, "Now evidently the Forms do not exist," and then he added:

> Above all, one might discuss the question: What in the world do the Forms contribute to sensible things, either to those that are external or to those that come into being and cease to change in them? But again, they help in no wise either toward the knowledge of other things (for they are not even the substance of these, else they would have been in them), or toward their being, if they are not in the individuals which share in them. . . . But further, all other things cannot come from the Forms in any of the usual senses of "from," and to say that they are patterns and the other things share in them is to use empty words and poetical metaphors.

Aristotle, *Metaphysics,* a revised text with introduction and commentary by W. D. Ross (Oxford: Clarendon Press, 1924), book 1, chapter 9, nos. 6-12. The Aristotelian conclusion that universals, while having a real existence, existed only in individual objects came to be known in medieval disputation as "moderate realism," described by the formula *universalia in rem*.

10. Aristotle, *The Nichomachean Ethics,* translated and introduced by David Ross (London: Oxford University Press, 1954), book 5, chapter 7, nos. 1134b-1135a.

Aristotle, *The Art of Rhetoric*, translated by John Henry Freese (Cambridge: Harvard University Press, 1959), book 1, chapters 10, 13, and 15, nos. 1368b, 1373b, and 1375a-b.

11. The Stoic concept of God was traceable, with much change over time, back to the argument of Anaxagoras that the universe was governed by *nous*, or mind. The evolution to monotheism had seen a tendency to identify reason with a personified deity. See Mulford Q. Sibley, *Political Ideas and Ideologies* (New York: Harper and Row, 1970), pp. 114-15. Sibley erred, however, in crediting Democritus rather than Anaxagoras as the source for the Stoic concept.

12. Cicero, *On the Commonwealth*, translated with an introduction by George H. Sabine and Stanley B. Smith (New York: Bobbs-Merrill, 1929), book 3, chapter 22, pp. 215-16. The translated title of this work is the choice of the translators.

13. From the *Digest of Justinian,* translated by Charles Henry Monro (Cambridge: The University Press, 1909). Quoted by Paul E. Sigmund, *Natural Law in Political Thought* (Cambridge, Mass.: Winthrop Publishers, 1971), p. 32.

14. A. P. D'Entreves says the heritage of Roman law was a reality, and the revival of Roman law in later centuries was to have a great impact on the transformation of Europe. See A. P. D'Entreves, *Natural Law* (London: Hutchinson House, 1951), chapter 1, pp. 17-32.

15. Williston Walker says, "For Tertullian, Christianity was a great divine foolishness, wiser than the highest philosophical wisdom of men, and in no way to be squared with philosophical systems." See Williston Walker, *A History of the Christian Church* (New York: Charles Scribner's Sons, 1948), p. 68.

16. Augustine wrote:

. . . lest men should complain that something had been wanting for them, there hath been written also in tables that which in their hearts they read not. For it was not that they had it not written, but read it they would not. There hath been set before their eyes that which in their conscience to see they would be compelled; and as if from without the voice of God were brought to them, to his own inward parts hath man been thus driven, the Scripture saying, *For in the thoughts of the ungodly man there will be questioning.* Where questioning is, there is law. But because men, desiring those things which are without, even from themselves have become exiles, there hath been given also a written law: not because in their hearts it had not been written, but because thou wast a deserter from thy heart, by Him that is every where thou art seized, and to thyself within art called back. Therefore the written law, what crieth it, to those that have deserted the law written in their hearts? *Return ye transgressors to the heart.*

This is quoted in *The Political Writings of St. Augustine*, edited by Henry Paolucci (Chicago: Henry Regnery Co., 1962), p. 154.

17. The word "canon," derived from Greek, meant a rule or measure. In Christian tradition the word came to be applied to the doctrines formulated in the early church councils, but in time the application was extended to all official church rulings.

18. Gratian's work became more familiarly known as the *Decretum*. Though never officially endorsed by the church, the *Decretum* became the basis for instruction in canon law in the emerging universities of the late medieval period. Those who taught from it and commented upon it were known as the "Decretalists." Gratian's collection eventually constituted the core of Roman Catholic church law and remained so down to the twentieth century, when the current code of Canon Law was brought into being.

19. Translated from the *Decretum* by Paul E. Sigmund. See Sigmund, *Natural Law in Political Thought* (Cambridge, Mass.: Winthrop Publishers, 1971), p. 48.

20. R. R. Palmer, *A History of the Modern World* (New York: Alfred A. Knopf, 1959), p. 37.

21. Aquinas' treatment of law can be found in volume 1, part 1-2, qus. 90-97. For a good edition of the *Summa Theologica* in three volumes, see the translation by the Fathers of the English Dominican Province, *Summa Theologica* (New York: Benzinger Brothers, 1947).

22. John B. Morrall writes:

The term "positive law" which was to have an important future before it, had been known in French legal and philosophical circles of the twelfth century, by way of Chalcidius's fourth-century Latin translation of Plato's *Timaeus*. In the early thirteenth century, it had penetrated into the legal school at Bologna and this may have been the milieu from which Thomas Aquinas received the term. See his *Political Thought in Medieval Times* (New York: Harper and Row, 1958), pp. 74-75.

23. Aquinas' acceptance of naturalism was reinforced by his rationalized conception of government. Man was naturally gregarious, and political society was within the totality of nature as God had created it. Government was not ordained after the fall to serve as a coercive instrument to repress corrupt mankind. Even though man had fallen, reason nevertheless recognized that government had utility for achieving natural ends. Political society had a value apart from any conception of a Christian common-wealth. In harmony with universal values, government could serve a positive purpose, that is, to assist man in his search for a virtuous life on earth.

24. In chapter 2 attention was called to the conclusions of Jean Barbeyrac regarding Grotius as a modern secularist. More current scholars such as Otto Gierke, Ernst Cassirer, George Sabine, A. P. D'Entreves, and Carl Friedrich have contributed greatly to the evaluation of Grotius as a modernist. All of them, either directly or implicitly, attributed to Grotius a methodology akin to that of seventeenth-century empiricism, and three—Ernest Barker, Cassirer, and Sabine—made a specific analogy of Grotius to Hobbes. See the following works and page citations: Otto Gierke, *Political Thought of the Middle Ages,* translated by Frederick William Maitland (Boston: Beacon Press, 1958), p. 174, note 256; idem, *Natural Law and the Theory of Society,* translated by Ernest Barker (Cambridge: The University Press, 1958), p. 36; Ernest Barker, *Traditions of Civility* (Cambridge: The University Press, 1948), p. 11; Ernst Cassirer, *The Myth of the State* (New Haven: Yale University Press, 1946), pp. 165-72; A. P. D'En-treves, *Natural Law* (London: Hutchinson House, 1951), p. 52; George Sabine, *A History of Political Theory* (New York: Holt, Rinehart and Winston, 1961), pp. 416-26; Carl Friedrich, *Inevitable Peace* (Cambridge: Harvard University Press, 1948), pp. 117-18. Cassirer was generous with his words in ascribing scientific method to Grotius, and Sabine, in support of the same contention, stated that "he [Grotius] intended to do for the law just what, as he understood the matter, was being done in mathematics or what Galileo was doing for physics" (*A History*

*of Political Theory*, p. 46). None of the above scholars allowed much latitude for a broad understanding of rationalism; indeed they all gave the impression that rationalism should be bound within the confines of strict definitional limitation. By bracketing their type of rationalism with secularism, they led their readers to believe that the one followed inevitably as a corollary to the other. They cited Grotius as the fullest exemplification of this. Gierke suggested that Grotius helped to "emancipate" natural law from religious ideas; Barker included Grotius among those writers from 1500 to 1800 who rescued natural law from "theological trammels"; Cassirer imputed to Grotius a rejection of "moral theology" in that Grotius, under the sway of seventeenth-century scientism, accepted a kind of Stoic "autarchy" of human reason and emphasized the humanistic aspect of founding the law of nature upon a propelling rational impulse in man; D'Entreves went so far as to assert that Grotius *proved* a theory of natural law could be constructed without theological presuppositions and that his seventeenth-century successors only finalized the process of secularization; Sabine argued that Grotius "detached law" from its "entanglements" with religious authority; and Friedrich remarked that Grotius "abandoned" the basis of divine law for both reason and natural law, thus making the latter predominantly a "secular affair." Friedrich had alleged that Grotius rose above the theologies of his day by embracing a *natural* religion and a right reason "which harked back to the Stoics," and simultaneously he credited Grotius as being a "secularist" of the seventeenth- and eighteenth-century variety. This shows a selective definition of secularism on Friedrich's part. He made the categorical distinction between revealed religion ("divine law" for him) and natural religion, and he labeled that person as a "secularist" who separated natural law from the former but not from the latter.

25. The nominalist posture was described by the formula *universalia post rem*, and the medieval opposition between realists and nominalists was summed up in the expression *universalia sunt realia v. universalia sunt nomina*.

26. D'Entreves, *Natural Law*, p. 70. Nominalism was here equated with voluntarism by D'Entreves, but the two were not necessarily synonymous.

27. Ibid., p. 71.

28. Cassirer identified Grotius with voluntarism in the sense that law emanated from the will of a human legislator. Sabine made reference to the two statements of Grotius that were directly pertinent to a denial of voluntarism, but he used them, not in relation to the rationalist-voluntarist controversy, but as evidence to substantiate his case for Grotius as a "pure" rationalist and secularist. See Sabine, *Political Theory,* p. 424. The statements of Grotius to which he referred were: (1) Prolegomena 11—"What we have been saying would have a degree of validity even if we should concede that which cannot be conceded without the utmost wickedness, that there is no God, or that the affairs of men are of no concern to Him." (2) Book 1, chapter 1, section 10, subsection 5—"The law of nature, again, is unchangeable—even in the sense that it cannot be changed by God. . . . " Cassirer, Gierke, and Friedrich utilized one or both of these statements for the same purpose. All the quotations of Grotius are taken from Hugo Grotius, *The Law of War and Peace,* translated by F. W. Kelsey with introduction by J. B. Scott (New York: Bobbs-Merrill, 1925).

29. Grotius, *The Law of War and Peace*, Prolegomena 59:

> As regards manner of expression, I wished not to disgust the reader, whose interests I continually had in mind, by adding prolixity of words to the multiplicity of matters needing to be treated. I have therefore followed, so far as I could, a mode of speaking at the same time concise and suitable for exposition, in order that those who deal with public affairs may have, as it were, in a single view both the kinds of controversies which are wont to arise and the principles by reference to which they may be decided. These points being known, it will be easy to adapt one's argument to the matter at issue, and expand it at one's own pleasure. (p. 30)

It is interesting to note here that Grotius considered his work as having been written primarily for statesmen and jurists; he did not consider it necessary, therefore, to elaborate extensively on philosophic conceptions.

30. Ibid., book 1, chapter 2, section 1, subsections 1 and 2, p. 51.

31. Ibid., Prolegomena 7, p. 12. Since man, by his reason was the only creature capable of applying general principles, he, apart from all other animals, was alone capable of law. See book 1,

chapter 1, section 11, subsection 1, p. 40. Grotius had undergone a change of thought on this matter. In his earlier work, *De Jure Praedae*, he had extended natural law to beasts as well as to men, but in *De Jure Belli ac Pacis* he excluded inferior creatures. See book 1, chapter 1, section 11, p. 40. The commitment of Grotius to Aristotelian thought was strongly expressed in Prolegomena 42:

> Among the philosophers Aristotle deservedly holds the foremost place, whether you take into account his order of treatment, or the subtlety of his distinctions, or the weight of his reasons. Would that this pre-eminence had not, for some centuries back been turned into a tyranny, so that Truth, to whom Aristotle devoted faithful service, was by no instrumentality more repressed than by Aristotle's name!

In Prolegomena 42 Grotius said that he intended "to make much account of Aristotle," but he also stated that he reserved the right to take exception whenever he believed it was necessary. (p. 24).

32. Ibid., Prolegomena 6, p. 11.

33. Ibid., Prolegomena 16, p. 15.

34. Ibid., Prolegomena 15, pp. 14-15, and book 1, chapter 1, section 14, subsection 1, p. 44. Grotius did not postulate consent as legalistic, contractual agreement at a specific point in time—as later would Hobbes and Locke. Grotius considered consent as recognition by rational men of their social inclinations and an acquiescence to the naturalistic progression from natural society to civil society.

35. Ibid., book 1, chapter 1, section 9, subsection 1, p. 38.

36. Ibid., subsection 2, p. 38. Grotius took liberty with Aristotle on this. He cited the *Nichomachean Ethics* where Aristotle made reference to natural *justice*. Grotius, being foremost a legalist, may well have equated justice with law, and he attributed rationally deduced principles from nature to Aristotelian method, which would have to be qualified.

37. Ibid., book 1, chapter 1, section 15, subsection 1, p. 45.

38. Ibid., book 1, chapter 1, section 14, subsection 1, p. 44: "The civil power is that which bears sway over the state. The state is a complete association of free men, joined together for the enjoyment of rights and for their common interests . . . ."

39. Francisco Suarez, *De Legibus ac Deo Legislatore*, in *Selections from Three Works*, edited by James Brown Scott

(Oxford: Clarendon Press, 1944), book 2, chapter 6, p. 187.

40. Ibid., book 2, chapter 6, section 2, pp. 188-89. The parentheses in the quotation are those of Suarez.

41. Ibid., p. 190.

42. Ibid.

43. Ibid., p. 194.

44. Ibid., p. 196.

45. Ibid., p. 198.

46. Ibid., p. 199.

47. Ibid.

48. Ibid., p. 206.

49. In addition to his other accomplishments, Grotius, as was noted in chapter 1, was a renowned Bible scholar. He wrote numerous works on religion, but his reputation as a Christian apologist rested primarily on his treatise entitled *The Truth of the Christian Religion*. This treatise reveals that Grotius did not fully adhere to the creedalistic orthodoxy of the middle ages, but that he was nevertheless a fervent Christian with a very deep and genuine belief in God. Hugo Grotius, *The Truth of the Christian Religion*, translated by J. Clarke (London, 1800). No publisher cited.

50. Grotius, *The Law of War and Peace*, book 2, chapter 20, section 45, pp. 510-11.

51. Ibid., Prolegomena 12, p. 14.

52. Ibid., Prolegomena 16, p. 15.

53. Aquinas and Grotius basically agreed that divine law constituted an independent source of law and that it was essential for spiritual fulfillment. They also agreed that the truths of revelation could not be attained by reason, nor could they be contrary to reason. Aquinas, however, was more specific in stating that divine law was given to man in a supernatural way for transcendent purposes. It dealt, he said, with inner motivations and dispositions, and by also regulating those matters that had to do with spiritual fulfillment—the establishment of the church, sacraments, correctness of doctrine, etc.,—it made possible a life of grace. Grotius, a Protestant scholar, was not as concerned with the relation of divine law to Roman Church doctrine. His treatment of the subject, therefore, was more general.

54. Grotius, *The Law of War and Peace*, book 1, chapter 1, section 15, subsection 1, p. 45 (italics mine).

55. Chrysostom, *On First Corinthians,* xi. 3. Grotius also quoted from his third book *On the Gods*: "No other beginning or origin of justice can be found than in Jupiter and common nature; from that source must the beginning be traced when men undertake to treat of good and evil." For Chrysippus Grotius cited Plutarch, *On the Contradictions of the Stoics*, ix = Morals, 1035c.

56. Ernest Barker, introduction to Gierke, *Natural Law and the Theory of Society* (Cambridge: The University Press, 1958), p. 38.

57. Grotius, *The Law of War and Peace*, Prolegomena 11, p. 13.

58. Ibid., chapter 1, section 10, subsection 1, pp. 38-39.

59. Ibid., section 10, subsection 2, p. 39.

60. In his earlier work, *De Jure Praedae*, written at age twenty-one, Grotius revealed an acquaintance with the rationalist-voluntarist controversy and was apparently inclined toward voluntarism, even though he did not indulge in extended argumentation on the issues involved. His voluntarism was detectable in that he acknowledged divine reason but asserted that law had its source in the will or command of God. For example, on page 8 of chapter 2 he stated: "Accordingly, let us give first place and preeminent authority to the following rule: What God has shown to be His will, that is law. This axiom points directly to the cause of law, and is rightly laid down as a primary principle. . . . Anarchus has correctly inferred (even though he does put the conclusion to an improper use) that a given thing is just because God wills it, rather than that God wills the thing because it is just." See Hugo Grotius, *De Jure Praedae Commentarius,* (Oxford: Clarendon Press, 1950).

In another passage Grotius again revealed his inclination toward voluntarism by asserting that the law of nature was eternal and immutable in the sense that it was always consonant with divine will. God's will was arbitrary, capable of change, but it was subject to no higher will. Whatever God willed, therefore, was eternal and immutable until God simply willed otherwise. To illustrate this, Grotius wrote on page 33 of chapter 3: "For the law of nature—that is to say, the law instilled by God into the heart of created things, from the first moment of their creation, for their own conservation—is the law for all times and all places, inasmuch as the Divine Will is immutable and eternal." Hence, at this period of his thought Grotius did not want to identify natural law with the rational nature of God separate from any element of will, as did the "extreme" rationalists. Neither did he want to make natural law merely indicative of the reason of God as commanded through will, as did the "moderate" rationalists. He seemingly wanted to relate natural law to the primacy of will, as did the voluntarists.

With maturity, with deepening scholarship, and with the need for a firmer intellectual stance on rationalism-voluntarism in relation to his own growing theories on law, Grotius adapted the "median" position of Aquinas and Suarez and incorporated it into his *De Jure Belli ac Pacis* of 1625. Again, he did not elaborate on his chosen posture, but, by piecing his reasoning together, the analyst can see his agreement with Aquinas and Suarez emerging quite clearly.

61. The rest of Prolegomena 11 reads:

> The very opposite of this view has been implanted in us partly by unbroken tradition, and confirmed by many proofs as well as by miracles attested by all ages. Hence it follows that we must without exception render obedience to God as our Creator, to whom we owe all that we are and have; especially since, in manifold ways, He has shown Himself supremely good and supremely powerful, so that to those who obey Him He is able to give supremely great rewards, even rewards that are eternal. We ought, moreover, to believe that He has willed to give rewards, and all the more should we cherish such a belief if He has so premised in plain words; that He has done this, we Christians believe, convinced by the indubitable assurance of testimonies. (p. 13)

62. Grotius, *The Law of War and Peace,* book 1, chapter 1, section 10, subsection 5, p. 40.

63. Ibid.

64. Ibid., Prolegomena 39, p. 23.

65. Ibid., book 2, chapter 20, section 43, subsection 1, p. 507.

66. Ibid., Prolegomena 57, p. 29.

67. Ibid., Prolegomena 58, pp. 29-30.

## Notes to Chapter 4

1. J. G. Starke, in *An Introduction to International Law*, fifth edition (London: Butterworths, 1963), p. 5, restricts modern international law to a time span of 400 years. He writes:

It grew to some extent out of the usages and practices of modern European states in their intercourse and communications, while it still bears witness to the influence of writers and jurists of the sixteenth, seventeenth and eighteenth centuries, who first formulated some of its most fundamental tenets. Moreover, it remains tinged with concepts such as national and territorial sovereignty, and the perfect equality and independence of states that owe their force to political theories underlying the modern European state system.

2. For some more recent evaluations on Roman law, see Hans Julius Wolff, *Roman Law: An Historical Introduction* (Norman, Okla.: The University of Oklahoma Press, 1951); see especially chapter 3, "The Evolution of Law," pp. 79-90. See also Barry Nicholas, *An Introduction to Roman Law* (Oxford: The Clarendon Press, 1962); see especially chapter 1, "History and Sources of the Law," pp. 1-59. See also Fritz Schultz, *History of Roman Legal Science* (Oxford: Clarendon Press, 1946).

3. Moritz Voight is one who argues strongly for this point of view. See his *Romische Rechtsgeschichte* (Leipzig: A. C. Liebeskind, 1892-1902). So also does Barry Nicholas in his *An Introduction to Roman Law*.

4. Cicero, *Tusculan Disputations*, translated by J. E. King (Cambridge: Harvard University Press, 1950), book 1, chapter 13, no. 37.

5. Cicero, *On the Commonwealth*, translated, with an introduction by George H. Sabine and Stanley B. Smith (New York: The Bobbs-Merrill Company, 1929), book 1 chapter 2.

Cicero, *Moral Duties*, translated with notes by Cyrus R. Edmonds (New York: Harper and Brothers, 1880), book 3, chapters 5 and 17.

Cicero, *Orationes. Selections*, translated with an introduction by Michael Grant (Harmondsworth, Middlesex: Penguin Books, 1973), chapter 37, no. 130.

6. Pope Boniface VIII, in his decree *Unam Sanctam* of 1302, reinforced the claim of papal superiority. Otto Gierke, in his *Political Theories in the Middle Ages*, translated by Frederick Maitland (Boston: Beacon Press, 1958), pp. 11-12, describes the church claim in this fashion:

If mankind be only one, and if there be but one State that comprises all mankind, that State can be no other than the Church that God Himself has founded, and all temporal lordship can be valid only insofar as it is part and parcel of the Church. Therefore, the Church, being the one true State, has received by a mandate from God the plenitude of all spiritual and temporal powers, they being integral parts of One Might. The Head of this all-embracing State is Christ, but, as the unity of mankind is to be realized already in this world, His celestial kingship must have a terrestial presentment. As Christ's Vice-Regent, the earthly Head of the Church is the one and only Head of all mankind. The pope is the wielder of what is in principle an Empire (*principatus*) over the Community of Mortals. He is their Priest and their King; their spiritual and temporal Monarch; their Law-giver and Judge in all causes supreme.

7. All quotes of Aquinas are taken from *Summa Theologica*, 3 vols., translated by Fathers of the English Dominican Province (New York: Benzinger Brothers, 1947), vol. 1.

8. Ibid.

9. Ibid.

10. Ibid.

11. James Brierly declares forthrightly that the Reformation was not a religious revolution as such but a rebellion of the new national societies against the church. Geographically, he says, the Protestant revolt made many conquests, but more than that:

It declared the determination of the civil authority to be supreme in its own territory; and it resulted in the decisive defeat of the last rival to the emerging unified national state. Over about half of western Europe the rebellion was completely and evidently successful, and even in those countries which rejected Protestantism as a religion, the Church was so shaken that as a political force it could no longer compete with the state.

James Brierly, *The Law of Nations* (Oxford: Clarendon Press, 1955), p. 5.

12. James Brown Scott, in the introduction he wrote for his translation of some works of Suarez, provided an excellent summation of the Jesuit's political ideas. In brevity Brown's summation cannot be improved upon; therefore, for the sake of convenience, it is reproduced here in full:

[Suarez] conceived of government with appropriate powers as being not only just but "in complete harmony with human nature."

Harking back to Aristotle, he declared that man was a "social animal" with a natural and proper desire for a communal form of life. This desire manifested itself first in domestic unions, but since these were insufficient to meet expanding human needs, men were led to form political groups. Now a political group is not an unorganized mob, "a kind of aggregation, without any order, or any physical or moral union." If it is to assume a truly political character, to become what Suarez terms "a perfect community," it must possess the qualities of unity and order, and these in turn can be obtained only through some form of organization and government. And a fundamental requisite of government is, according to Suarez, "the existence of some common power which the individual members of the community are bound to obey."

As a theologian he maintained that the power of political dominion is of divine origin, but this view did not lead him to subscribe to the theory of the divine right of kings. It was his opinion that the Creator had lodged the power in question, not in any particular individual or series of individuals, but in mankind as a whole. Viewed thus, political power may be termed a natural and inherent attribute of humanity, which remains a dormant, or rather a potential, quality until human beings gather together for the purpose of forming a political community. But it is obvious that power cannot be effectively exercised by the community as a whole. There is, therefore, the need of an agency in which the exercise of such power will be vested—an agency which we shall term government.

There are various forms of government, and the selection of any particular form—monarchy, aristocracy, democracy, or a mixture of any two or three of these—is in each instance, so Suarez maintained, "dependent upon human choice." Having chosen the form of government which they preferred, the members of the community in their united capacity bestowed upon one or more individuals the powers necessary for the effective functioning of the government. In other words, as has already been indicated, the full consent of the community was necessary in transferring the governing power to a ruler. . . .

Francisco Suarez, *Selections from Three Works,* edited with an introduction by James Brown Scott, Carnegie Endowment for International Peace (Oxford: The Clarendon Press, 1944), pp. 21a-22a.

13. From the work cited, as contained in Suarez, *Selections from Three Works*, book 2, chapter 19, section 9, pp. 348-49.

14. Ibid., section 8, p. 332. All square brackets and parentheses in the quotations of Suarez are his.

15. Ibid., section 9, p. 332.

16. Ibid., section 9, p. 333.

17. Ibid., book 2, chapter 18, section 9, p. 341.

18. Ibid., book 2, chapter 19, section 2, p. 342.

19. Ibid., section 3, p. 343.

20. Ibid., sections 3 and 4, pp. 343-44.

21. Ibid., section 6, p. 345.

22. Ibid., section 8, p. 347.

23. Ibid., section 5, p. 345

24. Ibid.

25. Ibid., section 9, p. 349.

26. Ibid., section 10, p. 349.

27. T. J. Lawrence, *The Principles of International Law*, 6th. ed. (New York: D. C. Heath and Co., 1910), pp. 227-28. One statement which Grotius made might be taken as his own rejection of Machiavellianism. He made a plea for justice on the part of rulers in their relationships with each other and penned this warning (square brackets mine):

> Therefore let them [the rulers] not doubt that those who instill in them the acts of deception are doing the very same thing which they teach. For that teaching cannot long prosper which makes a man anti-social with his kind and also hateful in the sight of God.

Hugo Grotius, *The Law of War and Peace*, translated by F. W. Kelsey with an introduction by J. B. Scott (New York: The Bobbs-Merrill Co., 1925), book 3, chapter 25, section 1, p. 861.

28. Grotius, *The Law of War and Peace*, book 1, chapter 5, section 2, subsection 2, p. 165.

29. Ibid., book 2, chapter 20, section 8, subsection 4, p. 473.

30. Ibid., book 1, chapter 1, section 14, subsection 1, p. 44.

31. Ibid., book 2, chapter 5, section 23, p. 253.

32. Ibid., Prolegomena 16, p. 15.

33. Ibid., book 1, chapter 3, section 8, subsection 2, p. 104. Grotius in his younger years was a constitutional "liberal," but as he matured he more and more became a defender of the prevailing political order. Some even refer to him as a reactionary because he showed an acceptance of established government by kings and princes. He rejected any conception of hierarchical

power, however, maintaining that political legitimacy was based on a contractual relationship. He elaborated on a justification for absolutist rule in subsection 1 of book 1, chapter 3, section 8:

> To every man it is permitted to enslave himself to any one he pleases for private ownership, as is evident both from the Hebraic and the Roman Law. Why, then, would it not be permitted to a people having legal competence to submit itself to some one person, or to several persons, in such a way as plainly to transfer to him the legal right to govern, retaining no vestige of that right for itself? And you should not say that such a presumption is not admissible; for we are not trying to ascertain what the presumption should be in case of doubt, but what can legally be done. (p. 103)

He added in subsections 3, 4, and 5:

> In truth it is possible to find not a few causes which may impel a people wholly to renounce their right to govern itself and to vest this in another, as, for example, if a people threatened with destruction cannot induce anyone to defend it on any other condition; again, if a people pinched by want can in no other way obtain the supplies needed to sustain life. . . . Further, as Aristotle said, that some men are by nature slaves, that is, are suited to slavery, so there are some peoples so constituted that they understand better how to be ruled than to rule. . . . Some, again, cannot fail to be impressed by the example of nations which for a number of centuries have lived happily enough under a form of government clearly monarchical. . . . For these and similar reasons, then, it not only can happen, but actually does happen, that men make themselves subject to the rule and power of another, as Cicero also observes in the second book of his treatise *On Duties*. (pp. 104-5)

Plainly, the choice of government was very much a relative matter. The terminology which Grotius employed in his original Latin text was indicative of the distinctions he drew in reference to political institutionalism. When referring to a monarchy he used the term *rex* (*regnum imperium*), and when referring to a democratic republic he used the term *populus liber*. In most other cases he simply used *populus*. There were numerous passages, however, when he lapsed into broader terminology to designate all forms of political organization under the common heading of civil society. In these instances he used *civilis societas, civilis communitas,* or *civitas* or *res publica*, and there were times when he even used the word *imperium* or *populus* in connection with any type of state or nation. For a discussion of this whole subject of terminology with many citations from the *De Jure Belli ac Pacis,* see C. van Vollenhoven, *The Framework of Grotius' Book De Iure Belli ac Pacis* (Amsterdam: Noord-Hollandsche Uitgever-smaatschappij, 1931). Whatever the form of the political institutions, Grotius did try to make clear that a state was always a composite of individuals. He in no way alluded to a state as an abstract entity with a personality of its own.

34. Ibid., book 1, chapter 3, section 7, subsection 1, p. 102.

35. Ibid., book 2, chapter 5, section 17, p. 249.

36. Ibid., book 1, chapter 3, section 7, subsection 3, p. 103.

37. Grotius was consistent in advocating the natural society of all mankind as the paramount bond of human experience. In his original text he referred to his society of mankind in numerous ways: *communitas societas generi humani; humana societas; communis illa ex humano genere constans societas; magna illa communitas; magna illa universitas; maior illa gentium societas;* and *muta gentium inter se societas.* In his *De Jure Praedae,* written when he was but twenty-one years of age, Grotius called it *illa mundi civitas societas orbis.* There he justified the need for states because of human weakness but asserted the precedence of the universal society which bound all persons into a common humanity. He stated:

> When it came to pass, after these principles [of good faith] had been established, that many persons (such is the evil growing out of the corrupt nature of men!) either failed to meet their obligations or even assailed the fortunes and very lives of others . . . there arose the need for a new remedy, lest laws of human society be cast aside as invalid. . . . Therefore the lesser social units began to gather individuals together into one locality, not with the intention of abolishing the society which links men as a whole, but rather in order to fortify that universal society by a more dependable means of protection, and at the same time, with the purpose of bringing together under a more convenient arrangement the numerous different products of many persons' labour which are required for the uses of human life.

See Hugo Grotius, *De Jure Praedae Commentarius* (Oxford: The Clarendon Press, 1950), chapter 2, p. 19. In all instances Grotius conveyed the belief that his society of mankind was not a formal superstate but a natural association which preceded and which coexisted with all forms of civil society. No matter what kinds of civil associations people entered into by their own consent, they were still "fellow-citizens of that common society which embraces all mankind." Grotius, book 3, chapter 11, section 16, subsection 4, pp. 741-42.

38. Grotius, *The Law of War and Peace*, book 1, chapter 3, section 16, subsection 1, p. 121. Grotius fervently believed that the common human society was ruled by law. Not being a superstate, the society of mankind had no formal organization of its own, but it nevertheless comprised a legal community. Walter Schiffer has analyzed Grotius' natural law as undergirding a true legal order. Writing in *The Legal Community of Mankind* (New York: Columbia University Press, 1954), pp. 37-38, Schiffer states:

> In Grotius' theory . . . the unity of the legal system is supposed ultimately to result from the existence of a law which is higher in kind than that created in the various political bodies into which the greater community is divided. The higher law is regarded as pervading the whole legal structure and as applying even in the sphere which generally is recognized as that of the rules of inferior type. Through the doctrine of war waged for just causes . . . Grotius attempts to liken the global community to a state in which the law is enforced through legal procedures.
>
> But Grotius' legal community of mankind is not a state. In the community there is no common authority above the various political units which can decide the question as to whether a particular act is just or unjust in the light of the higher law. Grotius' theory is significant as an attempt to conceive of the higher law as a purely natural order unsupported by any special organization of the type which made it possible to consider the medieval Christian world as a state in which all individuals belonging to the Catholic faith were united. In the legal system conceived by Grotius, pure natural law imposes itself directly on the conscience of men who, in case of a violation of law, react against the wrongdoer spontaneously and without being diverted by a higher authority.

39. Grotius, *The Law of War and Peace*, Prolegomena 1, p. 9. The bracketed and the italicized commentary in this passage are mine.

40. Ibid., book 2, chapter 8, section 1, subsection 2, p. 295. Francis Kelsey, the translator of the Bobbs-Merrill edition of the

*De Jure Belli ac Pacis,* used the term "international law" in this passage. This is a mistranslation of the original Latin of Grotius. It is the only place in the translation where such usage occurs. Therefore, to avoid confusion, the term *ius gentium* is added in brackets into the quotation.

41. Ibid., book 2, chapter 7, section 1, p. 267.

42. Ibid., section 1, p. 33.

43. Ibid., book 1, chapter 1, section 14, subsection 1, p. 44.

44. Ibid., book 1, chapter 1, section 14, subsection 2, p. 44.

45. In the work of his younger manhood, *De Jure Praedae* (1604), Grotius did elaborate on the content of natural law and clearly set forth many precepts in chapter 2 entitled "Prolegomena, Including Nine Rules and Thirteen Laws." See Grotius, *De Jure Praedae Commentarius* (Oxford: The Clarendon Press, 1950).

Carl Friedrich in his *Inevitable Peace* (Cambridge: Harvard University Press, 1948) commented on the content of natural law in Grotius' *De Jure Belli ac Pacis.* If one were to ask precisely what rational nature asked of man, said Friedrich, Grotius gave the answer that it consisted of those fundamental rules of law which the maintenance of society called for. Grotius enumerated the rules as follows: 1) Abstaining from taking what belongs to another; 2) Restitution of whatever we possess that belongs to another; 3) The obligation to fulfill our promises; 4) The reparation of damage caused; and 5) The imposition of penalties upon those who deserve them. See Friedrich, p. 122. Friedrich is justified in his criticism regarding the lack of content in Grotius' presentation of natural law in the *De Jure Belli ac Pacis,* but when he goes on to say that Grotius was vague on the subject of obligation he is far afield. Said Friedrich, ". . . Grotius remains very vague as to just why human beings follow these fundamental rules, or what are the grounds for their validity, except simply that they are rational. Curiously enough, it was precisely this vagueness which greatly contributed to Grotius' success as a writer on law, as it did to his success as a theologian." (p. 122) Friedrich, we recall, had categorized Grotius as a "secularist" and was unaware of the complexity of Grotius' ideas on natural law and on obligation.

46. Grotius, *The Law of War and Peace,* section 43, subsection 1, p. 507.

47. Ibid., book 1, chapter 1, section 10, subsection 6, p. 40.

48. Suarez, *Selections from Three Works,* book 2, chapter 14, section 1, p. 271.

49. Ibid., section 11, p. 274. Italics mine. All square brackets and parentheses in the quotations from Suarez are his.

50. Ibid.

51. Ibid.

52. Ibid., section 12, p. 275.

53. Ibid., section 13, p. 276.

54. Ibid., section 14, pp. 276-77.

55. Ibid., section 6, pp. 354-55.

56. Ibid., book 2, chapter 20, section 8, p. 356.

57. Grotius, *The Law of War and Peace,* chapter 8, section 1, subsection 2, p. 295.

58. Grotius subscribed to the same view as Suarez on change in regard to private property, summing up the entire argument of the Jesuit in two short sentences in book 1, chapter 1, section 10, subsection 6, p. 40:

> Furthermore, some things belong to the law of nature not through a simple relation but as a result of a particular combination of circumstances. Thus the use of things in common was in accordance with the law of nature so long as ownership by individuals was not introduced.

In other passages the identity of the thought of Grotius with that of Suarez with respect to change is not readily apparent, but these passages reveal that both men were in agreement with what were, perhaps, the ethical commonplaces of their day.

59. Suarez, *Selections from Three Works,* book 2, chapter 19, section 3, pp. 353-54.

60. Ibid., section 4, p. 354.

61. Grotius, *The Law of War and Peace,* book 1, chapter 1, section 10, subsection 3, p. 39.

62. Ibid., book 3, chapter 4, section 2, subsections 1 and 2, pp. 641-42.

## Notes to Chapter 5

1. Hugo Grotius, *The Law of War and Peace,* translated by F. W. Kelsey with an introduction by J. B. Scott (New York: Bobbs-Merrill, 1925), Prolegomena 3, p. 9.

2. Ibid., book 2, chapter 15, section 5, subsection 1, p. 393.

3. Ibid., book 3, chapter 9, section 18, subsection 1, p. 713.

4. Ibid., book 3, chapter 25, section 1, p. 860.

5. Ibid., book 1, chapter 2, section 1, subsections 4 and 5, pp. 52-53. In sections 3, 4, and 5 Grotius went on to argue that war was not in conflict with the law of nature, the law of nations, and divine volitional law.

6. Ibid., Prolegomena 25, p. 18.

7. Ibid., Prolegomena 25 and Prolegomena 26, pp. 18-19.

8. See Aristotle, *The Art of Rhetoric*, translated by John Henry Freese (Cambridge: Harvard University Press, 1959), book 1, chapter 4. See also Aristotle, *The Politics*, translated with an introduction, notes, and appendixes by Ernest Barker (New York: Oxford University Press, 1958), book 7, chapter 14, no. 1333a.

9. See Cicero, *On the Commonwealth,* translated with an introduction by George H. Sabine and Stanley B. Smith (New York: Bobbs-Merrill, 1929), book 3, chapter 23, pp. 216-17.

10. See Henry Paolucci, *The Political Writings of St. Augustine* (Chicago: Henry Regnery, 1962), pp. 162-83.

11. Grotius, *The Law of War and Peace,* book 3, chapter 25, section 2, p. 861.

12. Ibid., Prolegomena 28, p. 20.

13. Ibid., Prolegomena 29, p. 20.

14. Ibid., book 1, chapter 1, section 2, subsection 1, p. 33.

15. Aristotle, *The Politics,* book 7, chapter 14 nos. 1333b-1334a.

16. Cicero, *On the Commonwealth,* book 3, chapter 23. Said Cicero:

Wars are unlawful which are undertaken without a reason. For no war can be justly waged except for the purpose of redressing an injury or of driving out an invader.

17. Paolucci, *The Political Writings of St. Augustine,* p. 163.

18. Ibid., p. 164. Because Augustine justified war "in obedience to God," he is frequently credited as being the advocate of a theory of "holy" war. He wrote:

A great deal depends on the causes for which men undertake wars, and on the authority they have for doing so. . . . When war is undertaken in obedience to God, who would rebuke, or humble, or crush the pride of man, it must be allowed to be a righteous war;

for even the wars which arise from human passion cannot harm the eternal well-being of God, nor even hurt His saints; for in the trial of their patience, and the chastening of their spirit, and in bearing fatherly correction, they are rather benefited than injured. No one can have any power against them but what is given him from above. For there is no power but of God, who either orders or permits. (p. 165)

19. Grotius, *The Law of War and Peace*, book 2, chapter 1, section 2, subsections 1 and 2, p. 171.

20. Ibid., book 3, chapter 1, sections 1, 2, 3, and 4, pp. 599-601.

21. Ibid., book 1, chapter 3, section 1, subsection 1, p. 91.

22. Ibid., book 2, chapter 23, section 13, subsection 2, p. 565.

23. Ibid., subsection 2, p. 565.

24. In ibid., book 1, chapter 3, section 4, subsection 1, p. 97, Grotius gave his explanation of a public formal war. By "formal," he said, he meant "legal." For a war to be formal, two conditions were required: first, on both sides it had to be waged by those who held the sovereign powers of the state; and secondly, certain formalities had to be observed. A less formal public war lacked such formalities. Cicero had argued, "No war is held to be lawful unless it is officially announced, unless it is declared, and unless a formal claim for satisfaction has been made." Cicero, *On the Commonwealth*, book 3, chapter 23.

25. Grotius, *The Law of War and Peace*, Prolegomena 41, p. 24.

26. Ibid., book 2, chapter 23, section 1, p. 557.

27. Ibid., book 2, chapter 23, section 2, subsection 2, p. 558.

28. Ibid., book 2, chapter 23, section 6, p. 560.

29. Ibid., book 2, chapter 23, section 8, subsections 3 and 4, p. 563.

30. Ibid., book 2, chapter 23, sections 9 and 10, pp. 563-64.

31. Ibid., book 3, chapter 20, section 46, subsection 2, pp. 823-24.

32. Ibid., book 2, chapter 23, section 8, subsections 3 and 4, p. 563.

33. Ibid., book 3, chapter 10, section 1, subsection 1, p. 716.

34. As one example, the heading of chapter 11 of book 3 is, "Moderation With Respect to the Right of Killings in a Lawful War." Ibid., book 3, chapter 11, p. 722.

35. Ibid., book 3, chapter 25, section 8, p. 862.

36. Resistance to monarchy had become a burning issue of the sixteenth and seventeenth centuries, especially in France. Those who wrote against absolutist power were primarily from the ranks of the French Calvinists (Huguenots), who became known as the Monarchomachs. Foremost among this group were men like Theodore Beza, Francis Hotman, and the author of the *Vindiciae contra Tyrannos* (this work was published under the pseudonym of Stephen Junius Brutus). In diverse arguments the Monarchomachs asserted the right of subjects to resist any monarch who became a tyrant by failing to fulfill his reponsibilities to God or to the people.

37. Scott discussed these topics in relation to the political thought of Suarez. See James Brown Scott, introduction to *Selections from Three Works.* Carnegie Endowment for International Peace (Oxford: Clarendon Press, 1944).

38. Grotius, *The Law of War and Peace,* book 1, chapter 4, section 1, subsection 2, p. 138.

39. Ibid.

40. The whole of book 1, chapter 4 was devoted to his argument on non-resistance.

41. Hersh Lauterpacht, "The Grotian Tradition in International Law," *British Yearbook of International Law,* 1946, p. 44.

42. Ibid.

43. Grotius, *The Law of War and Peace,* book 1, chapter 4, section 1, subsection 3, p. 138.

44. Ibid., book 1, chapter 4, section 7, subsection 2, p. 149.

45. Ibid., book 1, chapter 4, section 7, subsection 4, p. 150. The Barclay to whom Grotius referred was William Barclay, Scottish jurist (1540-1601). The specific citations which Grotius gave were from Barclay's work *De Regno et Regale Potestate . . . adversus Monarchomachas* (3, 6, 8, 23, 24).

46. Ibid., book 1, chapter 4, section 7, subsections 4-6, pp. 150-51.

47. Ibid., chapter 4, section 8, p. 156.

48. Ibid., section 9, p. 157.

49. Ibid., section 10, p. 157.

50. Ibid., section 11, p. 157.

51. Ibid., section 12, p. 158.

52. Ibid., section 13, p. 158.

53. Ibid., section 14, pp. 158-59.

54. Ibid., book 2, chapter 25, section 8, subsection 2, p. 584.

55. Ibid., book 2, chapter 20, section 40, subsection 1, pp. 504-5.

56. Ibid., section 8, subsections 1-3, pp. 583-84.

## Notes to Chapter 6

1. The indebtedness of Grotius to classical and late medieval predecessors on political and legal conceptualism is increasingly being acknowledged, and the contention which had gained acceptance for so long a time that he turned away from medieval thought to become the "father" of a "modern" theory of natural law, particularly a theory akin to that of Thomas Hobbes, is more and more being subjected to serious examination. E. H Kossman in the *International Encyclopedia of the Social Sciences,* edited by David L. Sills, 17 vols. (New York: Macmillan and the Free Press, 1968), vol. 6, pp. 256-58, clearly exemplifies the new evaluation. Says Kossman:

> Grotius' conception of natural law does not differ from scholastic conceptions, and it is somewhat misleading to claim, as has often been done, that Grotius made an original contribution by secularizing the medieval interpretation of natural law. For Grotius, just as for the medieval thinkers and the sixteenth-century Spanish lawyers whom he quoted, the law of nature is an objective datum, an absolute norm given for all eternity. It is only later in the century, with Hobbes and other theorists, that the law of nature identified with the instinct of self-preservation, developed into an essentially individualistic subjective and secular concept. Grotius . . . saw God, nature and heaven as only different names for the metaphysical foundation of life.

Richard Cox expresses a similar view. See his "Hugo Grotius," *History of Political Philosophy,* edited by Leo Strauss and Joseph Cropsey (Chicago: Rand McNally, 1963), pp. 346-47.

2. Thomas Aquinas, *Summa Theologica,* 3 vols., translated by Fathers of the English Domonican Province (New York: Benzinger Brothers, 1947), vol. 1, art. 2, qu. 97.

3. Francisco Suarez, *Selections from Three Works,* edited with an introduction by James Brown Scott, Carnegie Endowment for International Peace (Oxford: Clarendon Press, 1944), book 2, chapter 19, section 6, p. 345.

4. Hugo Grotius, *The Law of War and Peace,* translated by F. W. Kelsey with an introduction by J. B. Scott (New York: Bobbs-Merrill, 1925), Prolegomena 17, p. 15.

5. P. P. Remec, *The Position of the Individual in International Law According to Grotius and Vattel* (The Hague: Martin Nijhoff, 1960), pp. 59-60.

6. Roscoe Pound, "Philosophical Theory and International Law," *Bibliotheca Visseriana,* 20 vols. (Leyden: 1925), vol. 1, pp. 71-90.

7. See Richard Zouche, *An Exposition of Fecial Law and Procedure, or of Law Between Nations, and Questions Concerning the Same,* 2 vols., translated by James L. Brierly (Washington: The Carnegie Institute, 1916), vol. 2.

8. See Emerich Vattel, *Le Droit des Gens ou Principes de la Noi Naturelle,* translated by Charles G. Fenwick with introduction by Albert de Lapradelle (Washington: The Carnegie Institute, 1916).

9. See Jeremy Bentham, *An Introduction to the Principles of Morals and Legislation,* introduction by Laurence J. Lafleur (New York: Hafner, 1948).

10. See G. W. F. Hegel, *The Philosophy of Right* (Chicago: Encyclopaedia Britannica, 1952), sections 258 and 330-38.

11. This opinion of Grotius on Saurez is taken from Henry Wheaton's *History of the Law of Nations in Europe and America* (New York: Gould Banks and Co., 1845), p. 35. Other commentators have quoted the same opinion, but the exact citation has not been given.

12. See Grotius, *The Law of War and Peace,* book 1, chapter 4, section 15, subsection 1, p. 159; book 2, chapter 4, section 5, subsection 2, p. 223; book 2, chapter 14, section 5, p. 383; and book 2, chapter 23, section 13, subsection 2, p. 565.

13. Ibid., Prolegomena 59, p. 30.

14. A good illustration of Grotius' methodology on this can be found in ibid., book 1, chapter 1, section 10, subsection 7, p. 40. Wrote Grotius:

> Furthermore, some things belong to the law of nature not through a simple relation but as a result of a particular combination of circumstances. Thus, the use of things in common was in accordance with the law of nature so long as ownership by individuals was not introduced; and the right to use force in obtaining one's own existed before laws were promulgated.

This was a two-sentence confirmation of Aquinas' argument on "additions" to the natural law.

15. See Jan Kosters, "Les Fondements de Droit des Gens," *Bibliotheca Visseriana,* 20 vols. (Leyden: 1925), vol. 4, pp. 41-43.

16. Kosters said the handwriting in the summary was smaller and firmer, as, indeed, examination of the original manuscript by this writer at the University of Leiden has confirmed.

17. The original pagination of *De Jure Praedae* also provided evidence of change. The face pages were numbered 1, 2, 3, 4, 5, etc., while the back pages were numbered 1', 2', 3', 4', 5', etc. On page 5 Grotius jotted an asterisk about two-thirds of the way down and proceeded to draw ink lines through the sentences on the lower third of the page. Between pages 5' and 6 he then inserted his smaller sheet of paper (5'$^a$, 5'$^{a'}$) on which he had written his revised version of the law of nations. Of added interest, in the margin of page 6' Grotius made reference to "Ius Gentium Primarium," and, in the same manner, on page 12' he referred to "Ius Gentium Secundarium." In all likelihood these marginal notations were made after Grotius had inserted the smaller page into his manuscript.

18. James Brown Scott, introduction to Suarez, *Selections from Three Works* (Oxford: Clarendon Press, 1944), p. 18a, footnote 1.

19. Ibid., p. 19a.

20. Suarez, *Selections from Three Works,* book 3, chapter 4, p. 384.

21. Ibid., p. 386.

22. The treatise was entitled *A Defense of the Catholic and Apostolic Faith* (see Suarez, *Selections from Three Works*). In book 6, chapter 4, pp. 705-25, Suarez defined two types of illegitimate authority—the legitimate ruler who lapsed into tyranny and the usurper who never held legitimate power. Regarding the first, Suarez stated that a private person may not, on the ground of punishment, commit tyrannicide; punishment lay, rather, with a superior or with the whole political community. As to a claim for tyrannicide on the ground of self-defense, Suarez continued, a distinction had to be made between self-defense of person and of goods and defense of state. In defense of a person's life, both types of tyrants could be slain by private action. When tyranny was not in doubt and where there was no recourse to superior legitimate authority, an individual could resort to private action by the authority of a tacitly consenting

community and by the authority of God, who gave the right through natural law to defend one's self. In defense of one's own goods, however, tyrannicide was not permissible, because the prince's life was to be preferred above property and, further, disputes over property could be resolved by law rather than by violence. Slaying a ruler on the ground of defense of state was permissible if the ruler were actually attacking the state with the intention of destroying it and of slaughtering the citizens. Community action would be preferred here, but private action would be allowable if defense could not be achieved in any other way. Private action in any other situation was forbidden because it would result in undue social disruption.

23. J. B. Scott, introduction to Suarez, *Selections from Three Works,* p. 21a.

24. Grotius, *The Law of War and Peace,* section 2, subsection 1, p. 139.

25. Ibid., chapter 4, section 19, p. 161.

26. Suarez, *A Defense of the Catholic and Apostolic Faith,* book 6, chapter 4.

## Notes to Chapter 7

1. Hugo Grotius, *The Law of War and Peace,* translated by F. W. Kelsey with an introduction by J. B. Scott (New York: Bobbs-Merrill, 1925), book 2, chapter 23, section 8, subsections 3 and 4, p. 563. Walter Schiffer says that Grotius did not recommend any kind of formal organization for his natural community of mankind, but Schiffer adds that Grotius marked the beginning of a development which eventually led to the idea that a global organization like the League of Nations could be an institutional step in the direction of world peace. In *The Legal Community of Mankind* (New York: Columbia University Press, 1954), p. 46, Schiffer says:

> There obviously exists a certain similarity between Grotius' natural law doctrine, which stresses the solidarity of the peoples of the world, and the League of Nations concept of international collaboration in the interest of universal peace and welfare. In particular, the League concept of collective security can be compared with Grotius' idea of mutual assistance in a war waged

for just cause, that is, for the purpose of law enforcement in the legal community.

Schiffer believes it was logically consistent to appropriate the just war doctrine from the natural order of Grotius and to transpose it into the context of formal international organization.

2. C. van Vollenhoven, *The Three Stages in the Evolution of the Law of Nations* (The Hague: Martin Nijhoff, 1919), pp. 16 ff. P. P. Remec, *The Position of the Individual in International Law According to Grotius and Vattel* (The Hague: Martin Nijhoff, 1960), pp. 117-18, is of the same opinion:

> A conference of "Christian powers" may indeed take steps to improve relations between potential and actual belligerents and collectively enforce peace among nations through new rules. But from these few lines one cannot read into Grotius' work that he wholeheartedly advocated the procedures of international congresses and supra-national organizations in order to better the law of nations through international legislation, collective security, effective enforcement of international judicature, or anything similar to this.

3. Grotius, *The Law of War and Peace,* book 2, chapter 22, section 13, subsection 1, p. 552. It is interesting to note that Grotius made his comment in criticism of Dante, who in his *De Monarchia* had postulated that since all monarchs were equal, a single rulership over and above them in the form of imperial authority was essential to establish peace. Dante idealized Roman political universalism of old, but Grotius did not see this as an answer to the problem of war. He made no proposal for empire as a formal institutional counterpart for his natural human society. Grotius did make allowance for state alliances or state federations, however. In *The Law of War and Peace,* book 1, chapter 3, section 7, subsection 2, p. 105, he wrote:

> Again, it happens that several peoples may have the same head, while nevertheless each of them in itself forms a perfect association. While in the case of the natural body there cannot be one head belonging to several bodies, this does not hold in the case of a moral body. . . . It may also happen that several states are bound together by a confederation, and form a kind of "system" . . . while nevertheless the different members do not cease in each case to retain the status of a perfect state.

Such groupings, though they were an organizational form beyond the single state, did not, as Grotius made clear, alter the character of the state as "complete," and certainly he did not advocate in any way that they were a superior form of political association.

4. Henry David Thoreau, *Walden and Other Writings,* edited with an introduction by Brooks Atkinson (New York: Random House, 1950), p. 288.

5. Grotius, *The Law of War and Peace,* book 2, chapter 15, sections 8 and 9, p. 397.

6. A dedicated contemporary spokesman for improved international law and for global political change is Professor Richard A. Falk of the Woodrow Wilson School of Public and International Affairs at Princeton University. Professor Falk and other concerned academicians have created the Institute for World Order and have undertaken the World Order Models Project (WOMP) to give the elimination of war the status of a subject matter for an academic discipline and to provide peda-gogical assistance and instructional materials to achieve their purpose. The Institute has become a genuine transnational movement, essentially a worldwide educational reform effort, to realize the aims of peace, social justice, economic well-being, and ecological stability. Much progress has been made. Research groups have been set up to pursue national and regional studies for war prevention. Several books have already been published under the series title of *Preferred Worlds for the 1990s.* A transnational journal, *Alternatives,* is available, and an annual "State of the Globe Message" is issued. Annual conferences are held and seminars are sponsored for scholars, educators, public figures, and others. The overall goal is a mass public education movement on a global basis with the conviction that enlighten-ment must precede attitudinal change, and attitudinal change will lead to institutional transformation. The members of the Institute are not merely ivory-tower dilettantes. They are intensely serious in proposing alternative world order systems to the current "war system" and in recommending necessary transitional steps to achieve these alternatives.

7. Thomas Hobbes, *Leviathan* (Oxford:Clarendon Press, 1965), part 2, chapter 30, p. 273.

8. Nicholas J. Spykman, *America's Strategy in World Politics* (New York: Harcourt, Brace and Co., 1942), p. 7.

9. Ibid., pp. 11-12.

10. Ibid., p. 13.

11. Ibid., p. 18.

12. Ibid., pp. 21-22.

13. Ibid., p. 18.

14. Ibid., p. 32.

15. E. H. Carr, *The Twenty Years' Crisis, 1919-1939* (London: Macmillan, 1939).

16. Ibid., p. 39.

17. In opposition to Carr, one might argue that Wilsonian idealism was never really tried. It existed as a school of thought, and some token efforts were made to program it, but power politics as usual ground on. Whatever the merit of such a counter-argument, the fact remains that Carr's views, like those of Spykman, found a receptive readership.

18. "On First Looking into Chapman's Homer," from John Keats, *Poems*, selected, edited, and introduced by Aileen Ward (New York: Heritage Press, 1966), p. 16.

19. See Andrew Dickson White, *Hugo Grotius, Essays on His Life and Works,* selected by A. Leysen, with preface by Jacob ter Meulen (Leyden: A. W. Sythoff's Publishing Co., 1925), p. 31.

# Bibliography

Hugo Grotius was such a prolific scholar that any attempt to produce a complete bibliography of his works would necessitate a separate volume. Such an effort would be a duplication at best in view of the availability of the following bibliographies:

ter Meulen, Jacob and P. J. J. Diermanse. *Bibliographie des écrits imprimés de Hugo Grotius*. The Hague: Martinus Nijhoff, 1950. This work cites more than 1,300 items, which are divided into nine categories: (1) poetry; (2) philosophy and natural sciences; (3) philology; (4) international law; (5) history; (6) law; (7) church and state; (8) theology; and (9) correspondence.

ter Meulen, Jacob. *Concise Bibliography of Hugo Grotius*. The Hague: A. W. Sijthoff, 1925.

Rogge, Hendrik Cornelis. *Bibliotheca Grotiana*. The Hague: Martinus Nijhoff, 1883.

The following resource materials were utilized in preparation of *Hugo Grotius, the Miracle of Holland*:

## Books

Alexander, A. B. D. *A Short History of Philosophy*. Glasgow: James Maclehose and Sons, 1908.

Aquinas, Thomas. *Summa Theologica*. 3 vols. Translated by the Fathers of the English Dominican Province. New York: Benzinger Brothers, 1947.

Aristotle. *The Art of Rhetoric*. Translated by John Henry Freese. Cambridge: Harvard University Press, 1959.

Aristotle *Metaphysics.* Introduction and commentary by W. D. Ross. Oxford: The Clarendon Press, 1924.

Aristotle. *The Nichomachean Ethics.* Translated and introduced by David Ross. London: Oxford University Press, 1954.

Aristotle. *The Politics.* Translated with an introduction, notes, and appendixes by Ernest Barker. New York: Oxford University Press, 1958.

Augustine, Saint. *The Political Writings of St. Augustine.* Edited by Henry Paolucci. Chicago: The Henry Regnery Co., 1962.

Ayala, Balthazar. *On the Law of War and on the Duties Connected with War and on Military Discipline.* Edited by J. B. Scott. Translated by John Pawley Bate. Washington, D. C.: The Carnegie Institute, 1912.

Ballis, William. *The Legal Position of War: Changes in Its Practice and Theory from Plato to Vattel.* The Hague: Martinus Nijhoff, 1937.

Barbeyrac, Jean. *An Historical and Critical Account of the Science of Morality.* Translated by Mr. Carew. London: 1729. No publisher cited.

Barker, Ernest. *The Political Thought of Plato and Aristotle.* New York: Dover Publications, 1959.

Barker, Ernest. *The Politics of Aristotle.* London: Oxford University Press, 1946.

Barker, Ernest: *Traditions of Civility.* Cambridge: The University Press, 1948.

Barry, Nicholas. *An Introduction to Roman Law.* Oxford: The Clarendon Press, 1962.

Bentham, Jeremy. *An Introduction to the Principles of Morals and Legislation.* Introduction by Laurence J. Lafleur. New York: Hafner, 1948.

Bishop, William W., Jr. *International Law.* Boston: Little, Brown and Co., 1962.

Bodin, Jean. *The Six Books of a Commonweale.* Edited with an introduction by Kenneth Douglas McRae. Cambridge: Harvard University Press, 1962.

Boehmer, Heinrich. *Road to Reformation.* Philadelphia: Muhlenberg Press, 1946.

Breasted, James Henry. *Ancient Records of Egypt.* Chicago: The University of Chicago Press, 1906-1907.

Brierly, James L. *The Law of Nations.* Oxford: The Clarendon Press, 1955.

Briggs, Herbert W. *The Law of Nations.* New York: Appleton-Century-Crofts, 1952.

Bryce, James. *Studies in History and Jurisprudence.* 2 vols. New York: Oxford University Press, 1901. See vol. 2, essay 11, "The Law of Nature," pp. 556-606.

Calvin, John. *Institutes of the Christian Religion.* Translated by John Allen. Philadelphia: Presbyterian Board of Christian Education, 1936.

Carlyle, R. W. and A. J. *A History of Medieval Political Theory in the West.* 6 vols. London: W. Blackwood and Sons, 1903-1936.

Carr, Edward Hallett. *The Twenty Years' Crisis, 1919-1939.* London: Macmillan and Co., 1939.

Cassirer, Ernst. *The Myth of the State.* New Haven: Yale University Press, 1946.

Cicero. *De Officiis.* Translated by Walter Miller. Cambridge: Harvard University Press, 1938.

Cicero. *Moral Duties.* Translated with notes by Cyrus R. Edmonds. New York: Harper and Brothers, 1880.

Cicero. *On Moral Obligation.* Introduction and notes by John Higginbotham. Berkeley: University of California Press, 1967.

Cicero. *On the Commonwealth.* Translated by George H. Sabine and Stanley B. Smith. New York: Bobbs-Merrill, 1929.

Cicero. *Orationes. Selections.* Translated with an introduction by Michael Grant. Harmondsworth, Middlesex: Penguin Books, 1973.

Cicero. *Select Orations.* Chronologically arranged and edited by J. H. and W. F. Greenough. Boston: Ginn Brothers, 1873.

Cicero. *Tusculan Disputations.* Translated by J. E. King. Cambridge: Harvard University Press, 1950.

Cook, Thomas A. *History of Political Thought.* New York: Prentice Hall, 1936.

DeBurigny, M. *The Life of Hugo Grotius.* London: 1754. No publisher cited.

den Tex, Jan. *Oldenbarneveldt.* Translated from the Dutch by R. B. Powell. Cambridge: Cambridge University Press, 1973.

D'Entreves, A. P. *The Medieval Contribution to Political Thought.* London: Oxford University Press, 1939.

de Vattel, Emerich. *The Law of Nations or the Principles of Natural Law.* Translated by Charles G. Fenwick. Introduction by Albert de Lapradelle. Washington, D. C.: Carnegie Institute, 1916.

Dunning, William A. *A History of Political Theories: Ancient and Medieval*. New York: Macmillan, 1923.

Dunning, William A. *A History of Political Theories: From Luther to Montesquieu*. New York: Macmillan, 1905.

Fenwick, Charles G. *International Law*. New York: Appleton-Century-Crofts, 1948.

Figgis, John N. *Studies of Political Thought from Gerson to Grotius*. Cambridge: The University Press, 1931.

Friedrich, Carl. *Inevitable Peace*. Cambridge: Harvard University Press, 1948.

Gentili, Alberico. *De Iure Belli Libri Tres*. Oxford: Clarendon Press, 1933.

Gentili, Alberico. *Hispanicae Advocationis Libri Duo*. Translated by Frank Frost Abbot. New York: Oxford University Press, 1921.

Gettell, Raymond G. *History of Political Thought*. New York: Century, 1925.

Geyl, Peter. *The Netherlands in the Seventeenth Century. Part One, 1609-1648*. New York: Barnes and Noble, 1961.

Grotius, Hugo. *The Freedom of the Seas*. Translated by Ralph Magoffin. New York: Oxford University Press, 1916.

Grotius, Hugo. *De Jure Belli ac Pacis Libri Tres*. Selections, translated with an introduction by W. S. M. Knight. London: Sweet, 1922.

Grotius, Hugo. *De Jure Praedae Commentarius*. Translated by Gladys L. Williams. Oxford: Clarendon Press, 1950.

Grotius, Hugo. *The Law of War and Peace*. Translated by F. W. Kelsey with introduction by J. B. Scott. New York: Bobbs-Merrill, 1925.

Grotius, Hugo. *The Truth of the Christian Religion*. Translated by J. Clarke. London: 1800. No publisher cited.

Guthrie, W. K. C. *The Sophists*. London: Cambridge University Press, 1971.

Haley, H. D. *The Dutch in the Seventeenth Century*. New York: Harcourt Brace Jovanovich, 1972.

Hallowell, John H. *Main Currents in Modern Political Thought*. New York: Henry Holt, 1950.

Hammond, Mason. *City-State and World State*. Cambridge: Harvard University Press, 1951.

Hayes, Carlton J. H. *A Political and Cultural History of Modern Europe*. New York: Macmillan, 1948.

Hearnshaw, F. J. C. *The Social and Political Ideas of Some Great Medieval Thinkers*. London: George C. Harrap and Co., 1926.

Hegel, G. W. F. *The Philosophy of Right*. Chicago: Encyclopaedia Britannica, 1952.

Higgins, A. Pearce. *Studies in International Law and Relations*. Cambridge: The University Press, 1928.

Hill, David J. *A History of Diplomacy in the International Development of Europe*. 3 vols. New York: Longmans, Green, 1905-1914.

Hobbes, Thomas. *Leviathan*. Oxford: The Clarendon Press, 1965.

Holland, Thomas E. *The Elements of Jurisprudence*. Oxford: Clarendon Press, 1924.

Justinian. *Digest*. Translated by Charles Henry Monro. Cambridge: The University Press, 1909.

von Kaltenborn, C. *Die Vorlaufer des Hugo Grotius auf dem Gebiete des Ius Naturae et Gentium*. Leipzig: A. C. Liebeskind, 1848.

Knight, W. S. M. *The Life and Works of Hugo Grotius*. London: Sweet and Maxwell, 1925.

Konvitz, Milton R. and Murphy, Arthur E., editors. *Essays in Political Theory*. Ithaca: Cornell University Press, 1948.

Krieger, Leonard. *The Politics of Discretion*. Chicago: University of Chicago Press, 1965.

Lauterpacht, Hersh. *An International Bill of Rights of Man*. New York: Columbia University Press, 1945.

Lauterpacht, Hersh. *International Law: A Treatise*. New York: Longmans, Green, 1953.

Lauterpacht, Hersh. *International Law and Human Rights*. New York: Frederick A. Praeger, 1950.

Lawrence, T. J. *The Principles of International Law*. Sixth edition. New York: C. C. Heath and Co., 1910.

Lewis, Ewart. *Medieval Political Ideas*. New York: Knopf, 1954.

Littlejohn, J. Martin. *The Political Theory of the Schoolmen and Grotius*. New York, 1896. No publisher cited.

Luther, Martin. *Works of Martin Luther*. 6 vols. Philadelphia: Muhlenberg Press, 1930-1943.

Lysen, A. *Hugo Grotius*. Leyden: A. W. Sythoff's Publishing Co., 1925.

McGiffert, A. C. *Protestant Thought Before Kant*. New York: Charles Scribner's Sons, 1917.

Machiavelli, Niccolo. *The Prince and The Discourses*. Introduction by Max Lerner. New York: Modern Library, 1950.

McIlwain, C. H. *The Growth of Political Thought in the West*. New York: Macmillan, 1932.

McPherson, C. B. *The Political Theory of Possessive Individualism*. Oxford: Clarendon Press, 1962.

Maine, Sir Henry James Sumner. *Ancient Law*. London: J. Murray, 1861.

Mangone, Gerald J. *A Short History of International Organization*. New York: McGraw-Hill, 1954.

Maxey, Chester C. *Political Philosophies*. New York: Macmillan, 1938.

Mellone, Sydney Herbert. *Western Christian Thought in the Middle Ages*. London: W. Blackwood and Sons, 1935.

Morrall, John B. *Political Thought in Medieval Times*. New York: Harper and Row, 1962.

Munz, Peter. *The Place of Hooker in the History of Thought*. London: Routledge and Kegan Paul, 1952.

Nicholas, Barry. *An Introduction to Roman Law*. Oxford: The Clarendon Press, 1962.

Nussbaum, Arthur. *A Concise History of the Law of Nations*. New York: Macmillan, 1954.

Oppenheim, L. *The Future of International Law*. Oxford: Clarendon Press, 1921.

Oppenheim, L. *International Law*. London: Longmans, Green, 1928.

Palmer, R. R. *A History of the Modern World*. New York: Knopf, 1959.

Phillipson, Coleman. *The International Law and Custom of Ancient Greece and Rome*. 2 vols. London: Macmillan, 1911.

Pufendorf, Samuel. *De Jure Naturae et Gentium Libri Octo*. Translated by C. H. Oldfather and W. A. Oldfather. Oxford: Clarendon Press, 1934.

Pufendorf, Samuel. *De Officio Hominis et Civis Just Legem Naturalem Libri Duo*. Translated by Frank G. Moore. New York: Oxford University Press, 1927.

Pufendorf, Samuel. *Elementorum Jurisprudentiae Universalis Libri Duo*. Translated by W. A. Oldfather. Oxford: Clarendon Press, 1931.

Randall, John H., Jr. *The Making of the Modern Mind*. New York: Houghton Mifflin, 1940.

Remec, Peter P. *The Position of the Individual in International Law According to Grotius and Vattel.* The Hague: Martinus Nijhoff, 1960.

Ritchie, David G. *Natural Rights.* London: Sonnenschein and Co., 1903.

Robson, William A. *Civilisation and the Growth of Law.* New York: Macmillan, 1935.

Rommen, Heinrich A. *The Natural Law.* Translated by Thomas R. Hanley. St. Louis: B. Herder Book Co., 1946.

Rousseau, Jean Jacques. *The Social Contract.* Translated by G. D. H. Cole. New York: E. P. Dutton, 1950.

Sabine, George. *A History of Political Theory.* New York: Holt, Rinehart and Winston, 1961.

Sanders, Thomas C. *The Institutes of Justinian.* London: Longmans, Green, 1888.

Schiffer, Walter. *The Legal Community of Mankind.* New York: Columbia University Press, 1954.

Schultz, Fritz. *History of Roman Legal Science.* Oxford: Clarendon Press, 1946.

Scott, James Brown. *Law, the State and the International Community.* New York: Columbia University Press, 1939.

Scott, James Brown. *The Spanish Origin of International Law.* Lectures on Francisco de Vitoria and Francisco Suarez. Washington, D. C.: The School of Foreign Service, Georgetown University, 1928.

Scott, James Brown. *The Spanish Origin of International Law.* Oxford: Clarendon Press, 1934.

Sigmund, Paul E. *Natural Law in Political Thought.* Cambridge, Mass.: Winthrop Publishers, 1971.

Spykman, Nicholas J. *America's Strategy in World Politics.* New York: Harcourt, Brace, 1943.

Starke, J. G. *An Introduction to International Law.* London: Butterworth and Co., 1963.

Strauss, Leo. *Natural Right and History.* Chicago: University of Chicago Press, 1953.

Suarez, Francisco. *Selections from Three Works.* Edited by James Brown Scott. Carnegie Endowment for International Peace. Oxford: Clarendon Press, 1944.

Taylor, A. E. *Plato.* New York: World Publishing Co., 1964.

Thoreau, Henry David. *Walden and Other Writings.* Edited with an introduction by Brooks Atkinson. New York: Random

House, 1950.

van der Molen, G. H. J. *Alberico Gentili and the Development of International Law*. Amsterdam: H. J. Paris, 1937.

van Vollenhoven, Cornelis. *The Framework of Grotius' Book De Jure Bellli ac Pacis*. Amsterdam: Moord-Hollandsche Uitgeversmaatschappij, 1931.

van Vollenhoven, Cornelis. *The Three Stages in the Evolution of the Law of Nations*. The Hague: Martinus Nijhoff, 1919.

de Victoria, Franciscus. *De Indus et De Iure Belli Relectiones*. Edited by James Brown Scott. Introduction by Ernest Nys. Washington, D. C.: The Carnegie Institute, 1917.

Voigt, Moritz. *Romische Rechtsgeschichte*. Leipzig: A. C. Liebeskind, 1892-1902.

von Gierke, Otto F. *Political Theories of the Middle Ages*. Translated by F. W. Maitland. Boston: Beacon Press, 1958.

Vreeland, Hamilton. *Hugo Grotius*. New York: Oxford University Press, 1917.

Walker, Thomas A. *A History of the Law of Nations*. Cambridge: The University Press, 1899.

Walker, Thomas A. *The Science of International Law*. London: C. J. Clay and Sons, 1893.

Walker, Williston. *A History of the Christian Church*. New York: Charles Scribner's Sons, 1949.

Weber, Alfred. *History of Philosophy*. New York: Charles Scribner's Sons, 1925.

Wheaton, Henry. *Elements of International Law*. Sixth edition. Boston: Little, Brown, 1855.

Wheaton, Henry. *History of the Law of Nations*. New York: Gould, Banks and Co., 1845.

White, Andrew Dickson. *Hugo Grotius, Essays on His Life and Works*. Selected by A. Leysen, with preface by Jacob ter Meulen. Leyden: A. W. Sythoff's Publishing Co., 1925.

White, Andrew Dickson. *Seven Great Statesmen*. New York: Century, 1915.

Wolf, Erik. *Grotius, Pufendorf, Thomasius*. Tubingen: J. C. B. Mohr, 1927.

Wolff, Hans Julius. *Roman Law: An Historical Introduction*. Norman, Oklahoma: University of Oklahoma Press, 1951.

Wolfson, Harry A. *The Philosophy of the Church Fathers*. Cambridge: Harvard University Press, 1956.

Wright, Robert F. *Medieval Internationalism*. London: Williams and Norgate, 1930.

Young, Alexander. *A Short History of Belgium and Holland*. London: T. Fisher Unwin, 1915.

Zouche, Richard. *An Exposition of Fecial Law and Procedure, or Law Between Nations, and Questions Concerning the Same*. Translated by J. L. Brierly. Washington, D. C.: The Carnegie Institute, 1911.


## Articles

Chroust, Anton-Hermann. "Hugo Grotius and the Scholastic Natural Law Tradition." *The New Scholasticism* 17:2, April 1943, pp. 14-29.

Dumbauld, Edward. "Grotius' Introduction to the Jurisprudence of Holland." *Journal of Public Law* 2:1, Spring 1953, pp. 112-27.

Dumbauld, Edward. "Grotius on the Law of Prize." *Journal of Public Law* 1:2, Fall 1952, pp. 370-89.

Dumbauld, Edward. "Hugo Grotius: the Father of International Law." *Journal of Public Law* 1:1, Spring 1952, pp. 117-37.

Fruin, Robert. "An Unpublished Work of Hugo Grotius's." Bibliotheca Visseriana, vol. 5, 1925, pp. 1-74.

Kosters, Jan. "Les Fondements de Droit des Gens." *Bibliotheca Visseriana*, vol. 1, 1923, pp. 73-90.

Lauterpacht, Hersh. "The Grotian Tradition in International Law." *British Yearbook of International Law*, vol. 33, 1946, pp. 1-53.

Molhuysen, P. C. "The First Edition of Grotius' De Jure Belli ac Pacis." *Bibliotheca Visseriana*, vol. 5, 1925, pp. 103-49.

Pollock, Frederick. "The History of the Law of Nature: A Preliminary Study. I." *Columbia Law Review* 1:1, January 1901, pp. 11-32.

Pollock, Frederick. "The History of the Law of Nature: A Preliminary Study. II." *Columbia Law Review* 2:3, March 1902, pp. 131-43.

Pollock, Frederick. "The Sources of International Law." *Columbia Law Review* 2:8, December 1902, pp. 511-24.

Pound, Roscoe. "Grotius in the Science of Law." *American Journal of International Law* 19:4, October 1925, pp. 685-88.

Pound, Roscoe. "Philosophical Theory and International Law."

*Bibliotheca Visseriana*, vol. 1, 1923, pp. 73-90.

Reeves, Jesse. "The First Edition of Grotius' De Jure Belli ac Pacis, 1625." *American Journal of International Law* 19:1, January 1925, pp. 12-32.

Reeves, Jesse. "Grotius' De Jure Belli ac Pacis: A Bibliographical Account." *American Journal of International Law* 19:2, April 1925, pp. 251-62.

Sandifer, Durward V. "Rereading Grotius in the Year 1940." *American Journal of International Law* 34:3, July 1940, pp. 459-72.

van Vollenhoven, Cornelis. "Grotius and the Study of Law." *American Journal of International Law* 19:1, January 1925, pp. 1-11.

van Vollenhoven, Cornelis. "The Growth of Grotius' De Iure Belli ac Pacis as It Appears from Contemporary Correspondence." *Bibliotheca Visseriana*, vol. 6, 1926, pp. 131-77.

von Elbe, Joachim. "The Evolution of the Concept of Just War in International Law." *American Journal of International Law* 33:4, April 1939, pp. 665-88.

Wright, Herbert F. "Some Less Known Works of Hugo Grotius." *Bibliotheca Visseriana*, vol. 7, 1928, pp. 131-238.

# Index